Networking Basics
CCNA 1 Labs and Study Guide

Shawn McReynolds

Cisco Press

800 East 96th Street
Indianapolis, Indiana 46240 USA

Networking Basics
CCNA 1 Labs and Study Guide

Shawn McReynolds

Copyright © 2007 Cisco Systems, Inc.

Published by:

Cisco Press
800 East 96th Street
Indianapolis, IN 46240 USA

Printed in the United States of America 2 3 4 5 6 7 8 9 0

Second Printing September 2006

ISBN: 1-58713-165-X

Warning and Disclaimer

This book provides information about CCNA 1: Networking Basics of the Cisco Networking Academy Program CCNA curriculum. Every effort has been made to make this book as complete and as accurate as possible, but no warranty or fitness is implied.

The information is provided on an "as is" basis. The authors, Cisco Press, and Cisco Systems, Inc., shall have neither liability nor responsibility to any person or entity with respect to any loss or damages arising from the information contained in this book or from the use of the discs or programs that may accompany it.

The opinions expressed in this book belong to the author and are not necessarily those of Cisco Systems, Inc.

Feedback Information

At Cisco Press, our goal is to create in-depth technical books of the highest quality and value. Each book is crafted with care and precision, undergoing rigorous development that involves the unique expertise of members from the professional technical community.

Readers' feedback is a natural continuation of this process. If you have any comments regarding how we could improve the quality of this book, or otherwise alter it to better suit your needs, you can contact us through e-mail at feedback@ciscopress.com. Please make sure to include the book title and ISBN in your message.

We greatly appreciate your assistance.

Publisher
Paul Boger

Cisco Representative
Anthony Wolfenden

Cisco Press Program Manager
Jeff Brady

Executive Editor
Mary Beth Ray

Production Manager
Patrick Kanouse

Development Editor
Dayna Isley

Senior Project Editor
San Dee Phillips

Copy Editor
Sheri Cain

Technical Editor
William Chapman

Team Coordinator
Vanessa Evans

Book and Cover Designer and Compositor
Louisa Adair

Proofreader
Paul Wilson

CISCO SYSTEMS

Corporate Headquarters
Cisco Systems, Inc.
170 West Tasman Drive
San Jose, CA 95134-1706
USA
www.cisco.com
Tel: 408 526-4000
        800 553-NETS (6387)
Fax: 408 526-4100

European Headquarters
Cisco Systems International BV
Haarlerbergpark
Haarlerbergweg 13-19
1101 CH Amsterdam
The Netherlands
www-europe.cisco.com
Tel: 31 0 20 357 1000
Fax: 31 0 20 357 1100

Americas Headquarters
Cisco Systems, Inc.
170 West Tasman Drive
San Jose, CA 95134-1706
USA
www.cisco.com
Tel: 408 526-7660
Fax: 408 527-0883

Asia Pacific Headquarters
Cisco Systems, Inc.
Capital Tower
168 Robinson Road
#22-01 to #29-01
Singapore 068912
www.cisco.com
Tel: +65 6317 7777
Fax: +65 6317 7799

Cisco Systems has more than 200 offices in the following countries and regions. Addresses, phone numbers, and fax numbers are listed on the
Cisco.com Web site at www.cisco.com/go/offices.

Argentina • Australia • Austria • Belgium • Brazil • Bulgaria • Canada • Chile • China PRC • Colombia • Costa Rica • Croatia • Czech Republic
Denmark • Dubai, UAE • Finland • France • Germany • Greece • Hong Kong SAR • Hungary • India • Indonesia • Ireland • Israel • Italy
Japan • Korea • Luxembourg • Malaysia • Mexico • The Netherlands • New Zealand • Norway • Peru • Philippines • Poland • Portugal
Puerto Rico • Romania • Russia • Saudi Arabia • Scotland • Singapore • Slovakia • Slovenia • South Africa • Spain • Sweden
Switzerland • Taiwan • Thailand • Turkey • Ukraine • United Kingdom • United States • Venezuela • Vietnam • Zimbabwe

Trademark Acknowledgments

All terms mentioned in this book that are known to be trademarks or service marks have been appropriately capitalized. Cisco Press or Cisco Systems, Inc., cannot attest to the accuracy of this information. Use of a term in this book should not be regarded as affecting the validity of any trademark or service mark.

About the Author

Shawn McReynolds is the director of the Cisco Networking Academy Program at Southwest Virginia Community College. He has been a member of SwVCC's Cisco Area Training Center for Sponsored Curriculum (CATC-SC) since 1999, where he teaches CCNA, CCNP, FNS, and PNIE courses. Shawn is one of the original contributors to the IT Essentials 1 curriculum and served as a technical editor for *Cisco Networking Academy Program: IT Essentials 1 Companion Guide*, Second Edition. Shawn has a B.S. in business engineering from Bluefield College and a master's degree in information networking and telecommunications from Fort Hays State University. Shawn resides in Tazewell, VA, with his lovely wife Stephanie.

About the Technical Reviewer

William Chapman is a computer-science teacher at Arcadia High School where he teaches computer applications, C++, Java, CCNA, CompTIA A+, Robotics, and an occasional math class. He serves as a member of the Academic Mentor Planning Committee and the School Site Leadership Team, and he has served as a Leader in Integrating Technology in Education (LITE) Tech. William also taught part time for Pasadena City College in the Computer Information department, and he serves on the advisory committees for A+ and Cisco curricular issues for the Los Angeles County Regional Occupational Program. He is also a curriculum writer. He was the owner/operator of a computer-consulting company, which helped small companies integrate computer technology into their businesses. William graduated from California State University Los Angeles with a B.S. in Natural Science, Geoscience Option.

Jim Lorenz is a curriculum developer for the Cisco Networking Academy Program who co-authored the third editions of the *Lab Companions* for the CCNA courses. He has over 20 years experience in information systems and has held various IT positions in several Fortune 500 companies, including Allied-Signal, Honeywell, and Motorola. Jim has developed and taught computer and networking courses for both public and private institutions for more than 15 years.

Dedications

For Steph and my family.

Acknowledgments

I want to recognize Mrs. Peggy Barber and Dr. Charles King for their leadership and support of the Cisco Networking Academy Program at SwVCC. Also, thanks to professors Vaughn Lester and Dan Bowling for providing wonderful examples of what it takes to be a professional educator.

Thanks to Ed McCarty, Cheryl Schmidt, Ernie Friend, and Kevin Hampton for their mentoring within the Cisco Networking Academy Program. I am fortunate to have learned so much from the very best.

Finally, I want to thank the Cisco Press production team that supported and provided guidance for this project. Mary Beth Ray and Dayna Isley have been excellent editors to work with. Thank you for your patience.

Contents at a Glance

Contents

Icons Used in This Book

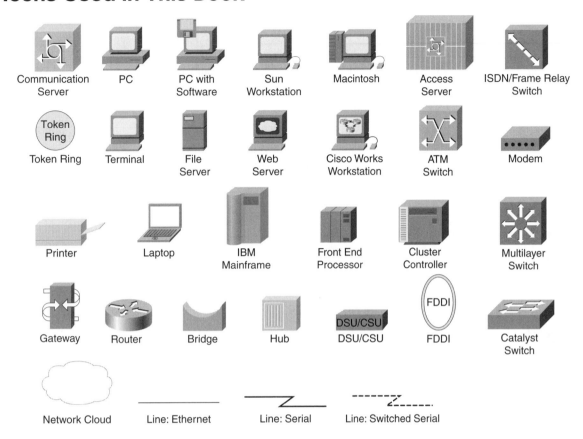

Command Syntax Conventions

The conventions that present command syntax in this book are the same conventions used in the IOS Command Reference. The Command Reference describes these conventions as follows:

- **Boldface** indicates commands and keywords that are entered literally as shown. In actual configuration examples and output (not general command syntax), boldface indicates commands that are manually input by the user (such as a **show** command).

- *Italics* indicate arguments for which you supply actual values.

- Vertical bars (|) separate alternative, mutually exclusive elements.

- Square brackets [ ] indicate optional elements.

- Braces { } indicate a required choice.

- Braces within brackets [{ }] indicate a required choice within an optional element.

Introduction

CCNA certification is globally accepted as a confirmation of information networking knowledge and skills. The Cisco Networking Academy Program provides a dynamic learning environment and a progressive course path that advances your understanding of internetworking and prepares you for CCNA certification. This learning environment includes multimedia-rich curriculum, electronic labs (e-labs), interactive study exercises, and online assessments that provide instant feedback. Four courses make up the Networking Academy CCNA curriculum.

Networking Basics CCNA 1 Labs and Study Guide is the official workbook for the first course in the CCNA program. This book contains exercises that help you learn the essential information presented in the CCNA 1 Networking Basics course through hands-on labs and other activities. Key learning objectives of CCNA 1 include the following:

- Understanding networks and network components

- Identifying number systems used in networking

- Defining conceptual models

- Creating network media

- Classifying network technologies and protocols

- Understanding network addressing and subnetting

- Configuring LANs

Networking Basics CCNA 1 Labs and Study Guide is a valuable learning tool that supplements version 3.1.1 of the CCNA 1 online course and the *Networking Basics CCNA 1 Companion Guide*. You are encouraged to take advantage of all these materials to gain the maximum amount of knowledge from CCNA 1.

Goals and Methods

This book's main goal is to provide a thorough introduction to information networking. A strong foundation of knowledge and skills is required for advanced learning and success in the networking field. You will be presented with opportunities to investigate important networking topics that must be understood before complex concepts are introduced in later courses. You will find that this knowledge base is also essential in preparing you for CCNA certification.

Each chapter in *Networking Basics CCNA 1 Labs and Study Guide* contains a Study Guide section and a Lab Exercises section. Each Study Guide section contains exercises that focus on crucial networking concepts presented in the corresponding portion of the CCNA 1 online course. These sections might include terminology identification, concept questions, Internet research activities, journal entries, and other exercises designed to help you learn the material.

The Lab Exercises sections focus on providing ample hands-on lab experiments that showcase technologies and concepts introduced in each module of the course. In these sections you will find three lab types:

- Curriculum Labs are step-by-step labs that introduce you to a new concept. These labs include detailed instructions for completing the lab and often reinforce steps through added explanations. Curriculum Labs are integrated into the CCNA 1 online course.

- Comprehensive Labs combine the concepts learned from the course and Curriculum Labs into new experiments and provide minimal guidance. You are encouraged to complete the Curriculum Labs before you move to a Comprehensive Lab.

- Challenge Labs are unique labs that require a thorough understanding of the previously learned network concepts. Complete all Curriculum and Comprehensive Labs before you attempt a Challenge Lab.

After completing all the exercises and hands-on labs in this book, you will be knowledgeable of a wide array of networking concepts and well-prepared to continue your networking education in the CCNA courses that follow.

Who Should Read This Book?

This book's primary audience is anyone taking the CCNA 1 course in the Cisco Networking Academy Program. This book contains printed versions of the CCNA 1 Curriculum Labs as well as other labs and exercises exclusive to this book. Therefore, *Networking Basics CCNA 1 Labs and Study Guide* is often a required course material for Networking Academies.

This book's secondary audience is anyone interested in learning more about networking basics through self-study or other networking courses.

How This Book Is Organized

This book contains 11 chapters and maps directly to the organization of the CCNA 1 online course. Most chapters build off of content presented in the previous chapters, so the content of the course and this book are meant to be read and worked through sequentially.

Chapters 1 through 11 cover the following topics:

- **Chapter 1, "Introduction to Networking"**—This introductory chapter opens with information and exercises that focus on the technologies and methods used to connect to the world's largest network: the Internet. Next, the importance of understanding number systems is emphasized through conversion and logic exercises. Eight Curriculum Labs walk you through network-configuration identification, a troubleshooting process, and converting number systems. The Challenge Lab tests your overall understanding of number systems.

- **Chapter 2, "Networking Fundamentals"**—This chapter introduces you to common networking terminology, the definition of bandwidth, and the concept of networking models. Chapter exercises include identifying network devices, calculating data-transfer rates, and working with network models. Two Curriculum Labs focus on industry-standard network models. The Comprehensive Lab brings these models and networking devices together.

- **Chapter 3, "Networking Media"**—Network communication requires a method of moving data between devices. Exercises in this chapter focus on the major types of network media and increase your understanding of signaling methods and media creation. Eleven Curriculum Labs walk you through the processes of measuring electrical characteristics of copper cabling, creating circuits, and cable creation. You learn an alternative method to test a cable with the Comprehensive Lab and learn to create a cable converter in the Challenge Lab.

- **Chapter 4, "Cable Testing"**—Exercises in this chapter increase your understanding of signaling properties and methods of testing network cables. Five Curriculum Labs introduce you to two pieces of cable-testing equipment and the tests they can perform.

- **Chapter 5, "Cabling LANs and WANs"**—This chapter presents exercises that focus on the cabling used to create LANs and WANs. These exercises challenge you to compare types of networks, identify network cables and components, and investigate server types. Ten Curriculum Labs focus on building LANs and WANs using the proper cabling and devices. In the Comprehensive Lab, you are asked to build a larger LAN.

- **Chapter 6, "Ethernet Fundamentals"**—Learning how Ethernet operates is required to completely understand how today's networks function. Chapter exercises include identifying technology fundamentals, understanding framing, and working with Ethernet addressing. A Challenge Lab tests your ability to gather MAC address information in your local network.

- **Chapter 7, "Ethernet Technologies"**—This chapter focuses on the family of Ethernet technologies, from 10-Mbps Legacy Ethernet to 10-Gbps Ethernet. Ethernet parameter identification exercises help you learn the similarities and differences in the Ethernet technologies. Three Curriculum Labs provide information on waveform decoding and using software to capture and analyze Ethernet frames.

- **Chapter 8, "Ethernet Switching"**—Exercises in this chapter help you understand the different modes of switching, identify collision and broadcast domains, and illustrate data flow. The Challenge Lab asks you to build a multiswitch network with redundant links and observe an antilooping mechanism.

- **Chapter 9, "TCP/IP Protocol Suite and IP Addressing"**—This chapter begins with exercises that pertain to the TCP/IP protocol suite before it focuses on IP addressing. You learn the multiple protocols that make up the protocol suite and the various methods used to obtain an IP address. Three Curriculum Labs cover the basics of addressing, setting up a DHCP client, and a method used to learn MAC addresses. The Comprehensive Lab prompts you to use tools and skills previously learned to identify internetworks. The Challenge Lab focuses on using software to monitor network processes.

- **Chapter 10, "Routing Fundamentals and Subnets"**—Early chapter exercises increase your understanding of routed and routing protocols. Later exercises focus on subnetting. Four of the five Curriculum Labs deal with subnetting, and one relates to purchasing a router. Two additional Comprehensive Labs also focus on subnetting and add address assignment components. Subnetting can be the most difficult concept to grasp in CCNA 1, so take your time with these exercises and labs.

- **Chapter 11, "TCP/IP Transport and Application Layers"**—This book's final chapter includes exercises that help you understand the functions of the transport and application layers of the TCP/IP model. A Curriculum Lab brings together multiple tools from other labs to investigate particular types of TCP traffic. A Challenge Lab focuses on client/server applications.

Introduction to Networking

The Study Guide portion of this chapter uses a combination of matching, fill in the blank, multiple choice, and open-ended question exercises to test your knowledge of connecting to the network and network math.

The Lab Exercises portion of this chapter includes all the online curriculum labs and a challenge lab to ensure that you have mastered the practical, hands-on skills needed to connect to the network and to understand network math.

As you work through this chapter, use Module 1 in the CCNA 1 online curriculum or use the corresponding Chapter 1 in the *Networking Basics CCNA 1 Companion Guide* for assistance.

Study Guide

Connecting to the Internet

In its most basic form, a network is a communication system. Computer networks are systems made up of devices, their connections to one another, and the technologies used for information transfer. Computer networks, also known as information networks, play an integral role in today's economy and society. A reliable connection to the Internet, the world's largest information network, is vital to governments, many businesses, organizations, and individuals. Learning how these connections occur and the requirements for connecting to the Internet is the first step to understand information networks.

In this section, you find exercises designed to help you identify terminology associated with information networking, compare and contrast Internet access technologies, and understand the basic components of personal computers (PC). These exercises help you build and test your knowledge in the fundamentals of networking.

Vocabulary Exercise: Matching

Match the definition on the left with a term on the right. This exercise does not necessarily use one-to-one matching. Some definitions might be used more than once and some terms might have multiple definitions.

It is important to understand key terms when learning about PCs and the Internet. Match the following definitions with the proper terms.

Definitions	Terms

Definitions

a. An interface that can be used for serial communication in which only one bit is transmitted at a time.

b. Electronically stored text that allows direct access to other texts by way of encoded links.

c. An expansion board that enables a computer to manipulate and output sounds. It is also known as a sound card.

d. A serial bus interface standard offering high-speed communications and isochronous real-time data services. Also known as IEEE 1394.

e. The network layer protocol in the TCP/IP stack that offers a connectionless internetwork service. It provides features for addressing, type-of-service specification, fragmentation and reassembly, and security.

f. The component that supplies power to a computer.

g. A board that plugs into a PC to give it display capabilities.

h. The main printed circuit board in a computer. It contains the bus, microprocessor, and integrated circuits used to control any built-in peripherals, such as the keyboard, text and graphics display, serial ports and parallel ports, joystick, and mouse interfaces.

i. Device made of semiconductor material that contains many transistors and performs a specific task.

j. A formal description of a set of rules and conventions that govern how devices on a network exchange information.

k. The main part of a PC, which includes the chassis, microprocessor, main memory, bus, and ports. The system unit does not include the keyboard, monitor, or any external devices connected to the computer.

l. A collection of wires on the motherboard through which data and timing signals are transmitted from one part of a computer to another.

m. A computer storage device that uses a set of rotating, magnetically coated disks called platters to store data or programs.

n. Electronic component that stores energy in the form of an electrostatic field that consists of two conducting metal plates separated by an insulating material.

o. The network layer Internet protocol that reports errors and provides other information relevant to IP packet processing.

p. A socket on the motherboard where a circuit board can be inserted to add new capabilities to the computer.

q. An interface capable of transferring more than one bit simultaneously that connects external devices, such as printers.

Terms

___ system unit

___ power supply

___ hypertext

___ Firewire

___ ICMP

___ capacitor

___ video card

___ parallel port

___ integrated circuit

___ expansion slot

___ bus

___ hard disk drive

___ audio card

___ motherboard

___ IP

___ serial port

___ protocol

Vocabulary Exercise: Completion

Complete the following statements by using the proper terms to fill in the blanks.

_____ devices are automatically recognized and configured by the computer operating system (OS).

_____ Internet access is an "always on" technology accessed across traditional cable television systems.

_____ is the process of configuring multiple devices to access the Internet through a single connection.

A _____ is a graphical user interface (GUI)–based hypertext client application, such as Internet Explorer, Netscape Navigator, and Firefox, that accesses hypertext documents and other services located on innumerable remote servers throughout the World Wide Web and Internet.

A _____ is an electronic circuit board containing circuitry and sockets into which additional electronic devices on other circuit boards or cards can be plugged. In a computer, it is generally synonymous with or part of the motherboard.

An _____ is a unique address the CPU uses to communicate with a device.

A _____ is a processor that consists of a purpose-designed silicon chip and is physically very small.

Primarily used to troubleshoot Internet connections, the _____ utility sends a packet to the specified address and waits for a reply.

A _____ is a device that amplifies a signal or opens and closes a circuit.

A _____ technology is a technology that was designed and developed and is owned privately.

A _____ is a small application used to enhance the capabilities of a web browser. They are commonly required to display special data types, such as movies or flash animations.

A _____ is a device that connects computers to telephone lines and passes data across voice circuits.

The _____ is the largest data network on earth.

A computer drive that reads and writes data to a 3.5-inch, circular piece of metal-coated plastic disk is known as a _____ .

A _____ connects workstations, peripherals, terminals, and other devices in a single building or other geographically limited area.

Vocabulary Exercise: Identifying Acronyms and Initialisms

An acronym is a word formed by the first letters in a multiword term. Initialisms are words made of initials pronounced separately. These are used extensively in the information technology (IT) field. Identify the terms associated with the following acronyms.

BBS   _____

CPU   _____

DSL   _____

FTP   _____

HTML   _____

IRQ _____

LED _____

NIC _____

PCB _____

PCMCIA _____

RAM _____

ROM _____

USB _____

Compare and Contrast Exercise: Internet Access Technologies

Although larger organizations have multiple methods for connecting to the Internet, home and small office users primarily use one of three access technologies for Internet connections. Complete the following table to compare and contrast dialup modem, DSL, and cable modem access technologies. You might need to consult other sources of information for advantages and disadvantages of these technologies.

	Dialup Modem	DSL	Cable Modem
What type of communication line does this technology use?			
Is it considered an "always on" technology?			
Does this technology provide a high-speed connection to the Internet?			
What is an advantage of this technology?			
What is a disadvantage of this technology?			

Concept Questions

Completely answer the following questions:

1. What are the three requirements for an Internet connection?

    _____

    - _____
    - _____
    - _____

2. What is the difference between a physical connection and a logical connection?

    _____

    _____

    _____

    _____

    _____

    _____

    _____

    _____

    _____

3. What factors must be considered when deciding on a NIC?

    _____

    _____

    _____

    _____

    _____

    _____

    _____

    _____

4. What logical protocols must be configured for Internet connectivity? Within the protocol components, what items must be configured?

    _____

    _____

    _____

    _____

    _____

    _____

    - _____
    - _____
    - _____
    - _____

    _____

5. A recently installed PC has problems connecting to the Internet. List the steps you use to troubleshoot the network connection.

_____

_____

_____

_____

_____

_____

Journal Entry

Many of today's PCs are designed for specific uses. Often, they are customized at the factory to target particular types of customers. The primary areas of customization include the processor, memory and storage, and expansion cards. Certain applications require powerful processors and plenty of memory. Other applications require generous amounts of storage and upgraded adapter cards. Almost all applications require some type of Internet access option.

You are starting up a small company that focuses on building customized PCs. You decide to design three unique PC types. These PCs will be designed for home, entertainment, and business use. The home PC will be marketed to users who use their home computer for basic word processing, balancing checkbooks, and accessing e-mail using a telephone line. The entertainment PC will be designed for customers who use their PC to play online games, listen to music, and watch movies. The business PC will need to be able to maintain large databases, work with complicated spreadsheets, and connect to the user's company network.

The first step in designing these PCs is to determine the components required to build each computer. List the key components of each type of PC. What are the processor, memory, storage, and expansion card requirements of each type? What Internet access option will be the most feasible for each user?

_____

_____

_____

_____

_____

_____

_____

_____

Note: Now would be a good time to complete the first five lab exercises for Chapter 1. The next section, and the remaining chapter labs, focuses on number systems, conversions, and binary logic.

Network Math

Math is often described as the "universal language," and it has a significant role in information networking. Specific number systems identify network devices and represent data. Network devices use numeric logic to make decisions on how data is handled. Internet connection speeds and information transfer rates are calculated using general math equations. It is important to learn the number systems and math used in networking to understand how networks function.

In this section, you find exercises designed to reinforce number system identification and conversion skills, apply binary logic, and identify different methods of addressing devices. These exercises reinforce the mathematical skills required in networking.

Vocabulary Exercise: Define

Define the following key technology terms:

ASCII _____

_____

_____

binary _____

bits _____

_____

_____

Boolean logic _____

_____

_____

byte _____

_____

decimal _____

dotted-decimal notation _____

_____

_____

hexadecimal _____

_____

_____

IP address _____

_____

subnetwork mask _____

_____

_____

Concept Questions

Answer the following questions completely:

1. Why is it important to understand binary?

_____

_____

_____

_____

_____

2. Most Internet connection speeds are expressed in bits per second (bps), and data transfer rates are expressed in kilobytes per second (1000 KBps) or megabytes per second (1,000,000 Bps). What is the maximum transfer rate (in KBps) using a 56 kbps dialup line? What is the transfer rate on a 1.5 Mbps DSL link? What is the transfer rate on a 3.0 Mbps cable modem link?

_____

_____

_____

3. How many 640 kb files can be stored on a 1.44 MB floppy disk?

_____

_____

_____

_____

4. A kilobit is defined as 1000 bits. How many bits are actually in a kilobit? Why is there a difference in a defined kilobit and an actual kilobit?

_____

_____

5. Explain the binary logic behind the AND process. How is it used in networking?

_____

_____

_____

_____

_____

6. Why is a subnet mask required when configuring TCP/IP settings?

_____

_____

_____

_____

Note: Now is a good time to complete Curriculum Lab 1-6, Lab 1-7, and Lab 1-8. The following conversion exercise expands on the lessons learned in these labs.

Number Systems Conversion Exercise

Developing the skills for converting between the number systems used in networking is extremely important. For additional practice, complete the following table by converting the given value to the other number systems.

	Decimal	Hexadecimal	Binary
1	23		
2	191		
3	278		
4	127.0.0.1		
5	10.50.148.91		
6		19	
7		3F	
8		0A-CE	
9		BE-AD	
10		87-C3-5E	
11			1011100
12			100111100
13			0010-1101
14			10101010-01010110-10101101
15			11000000.10101000.01100100.00011011

Note: Now would be a good time to test your understanding of number systems with Challenge Lab 1-9, which challenges you to create a unique number system.

Binary Logic ANDing Exercise

In binary logic, the AND operation compares two input values and provides a single output value. This process is used in networking to provide network and subnet addresses by ANDing an IP address with a subnet mask. Because ANDing is a binary operation, the possible inputs are combinations of 1s and 0s, and the resulting output is either a 1 or 0. If both input values are 1, the output is 1. If either input is 0 (or both inputs are 0), the output is 0. In the following example, an IP address of 192.168.10.17 is ANDed to a subnet mask of 255.255.255.0. Both numbers are converted to binary, and the ANDing process returns a result of 192.168.10.0 when converted back to dotted-decimal format. This is the address of the network to which the IP address belongs.

Example

IP Address	192.168.10.17	11000000.10101000.00001010.00010001
Subnet Mask	255.255.255.0	11111111.11111111.11111111.00000000
AND Result	192.168.10.0	11000000.10101000.00001010.00000000

Note: Subnet masks are 32-bit numbers written in dotted-decimal format. In a subnet mask, 1s represent network or subnet bits. 0s show the remaining host bits. Subnet masks always begin with 1s written from the left to the right.

Use the provided tables to AND the corresponding IP addresses with the subnet masks. Record the results as a dotted-decimal number.

IP Address 10.200.165.84

Subnet Mask   255.0.0.0

AND Result

128 64 32 16 8 4 2 1   128 64 32 16 8 4 2 1   128 64 32 16 8 4 2 1   128 64 32 16 8 4 2 1

IP Address 172.16.24.199

Subnet Mask 255.255.0.0

AND Result

128 64 32 16 8 4 2 1   128 64 32 16 8 4 2 1   128 64 32 16 8 4 2 1   128 64 32 16 8 4 2 1

IP Address 172.16.24.199

Subnet Mask 255.255.240.0

AND Result

128 64 32 16 8 4 2 1   128 64 32 16 8 4 2 1   128 64 32 16 8 4 2 1

IP Address 192.168.100.63

Subnet Mask 255.255.255.0

AND Result

| 128 | 64 | 32 | 16 | 8 | 4 | 2 | 1 | | 128 | 64 | 32 | 16 | 8 | 4 | 2 | 1 | | 128 | 64 | 32 | 16 | 8 | 4 | 2 | 1 | | 128 | 64 | 32 | 16 | 8 | 4 | 2 | 1 |

IP Address 192.168.100.63

Subnet Mask 255.255.255.224

AND Result

| 128 | 64 | 32 | 16 | 8 | 4 | 2 | 1 | | 128 | 64 | 32 | 16 | 8 | 4 | 2 | 1 | | 128 | 64 | 32 | 16 | 8 | 4 | 2 | 1 | | 128 | 64 | 32 | 16 | 8 | 4 | 2 | 1 |

Journal Entry

Because the Internet is a worldwide network, it requires a global-addressing scheme. IP addresses are unique addresses assigned to each host connected to the Internet. Network devices use these addresses to send data from the source to the destination. Without a global-addressing system in place, the Internet would be useless.

List other large-scale or global-addressing systems used in the world today. How are global "address books" maintained for each system? Who is responsible for updating the system?

_____

_____

_____

Lab Exercises

Curriculum Lab 1-1: PC Hardware (1.1.2)

Objectives

- Become familiar with the basic peripheral components of a PC system.

- Identify PC connections, including network attachments.

- Examine the internal PC configuration and identify major components.

- Observe the boot process for the Windows OS.

- Use the Control Panel to find out information about the PC.

Background/Preparation

Knowing the components of a PC is valuable when troubleshooting, and it is important to your success in the networking field. Before you begin, the instructor or lab assistant must have a typical desktop PC available with all peripherals, such as keyboard, monitor, mouse, speakers or headphones, a NIC, and network cable. The system unit cover should be removed, or you need to have tools to remove it. You can work individually or in teams. In addition, the instructor needs to identify the location of the A+ or PC hardware training materials.

Task 1: Examine the Computer and Peripheral Components Both Front and Back

Note: The components and configuration of the PC you are working with might vary.

Step 1.   What are the manufacturer and model number of this computer?

Manufacturer _____

Model Number _____

Step 2. What are the major external components of the PC, including the peripherals?

Component Name	Manufacturer/Description/Characteristics
_____	_____
_____	_____
_____	_____
_____	_____
_____	_____
_____	_____
_____	_____
_____	_____
_____	_____

Task 2: Remove the PC System Unit Cover and Examine the Internal Components

Step 1.   List at least eight major internal components inside the system unit. (Use the procedure in Task 4 to find CPU information and the amount of RAM.)

Component Name	Manufacturer/Description/Characteristics

Task 3: Assemble the PC Components and Observe the Boot Process

Step 1.   Assemble the PC components, attach all peripherals, and boot the PC. Observe the boot process. The computer should boot to the Windows OS. If the computer does not boot, contact the lab assistant.

Step 2.   Did the Windows OS boot okay?

Step 3.   Could you see the memory amount as the system booted?

Task 4: Gather Basic Information About the Computer's CPU and RAM

Step 1. Click **Start > Settings > Control Panel**. Click the **System** icon and then the **General** tab. You are viewing information about the computer using the OS. What is the CPU?

_____

Step 2. In MHz, what is the speed of the CPU?

_____
_____
_____

Step 3. How much RAM is installed?

_____

Curriculum Lab 1-2: PC Network TCP/IP Configuration (1.1.6)

Objectives

- Identify tools used for discovering a computer's network configuration with various OSs.

- Gather information, including the connection, hostname, MAC (Layer 2) address, and TCP/IP network (Layer 3) address information.

- Compare the network information to that of other PCs on the network.

Background/Preparation

This lab assumes that you are using any version of Windows. This is a nondestructive lab that you can perform on any machine without changing the system configuration.

Ideally, perform this lab in a LAN environment that connects to the Internet. You can use a single remote connection via a modem or DSL-type connection. You need the IP address information, which your instructor can provide.

The following instructions run the lab twice, reflecting the OS differences between Windows 95/98/Me systems and Windows NT/2000/XP systems. If possible, perform the lab on both types of systems.

Note: All users complete Task 1.

Task 1: Connect to the Internet

Establish and verify connectivity to the Internet. This task ensures that the computer has an IP address.

Note: Windows 95/98/Me users: Complete Tasks 2 through 6.

Task 2: Gather Basic TCP/IP Configuration Information

Step 1.   Using the taskbar, choose **Start > Run** to open the dialog box shown in Figure 1-1. Type **winipcfg** and press **Enter**. (The spelling of **winipcfg** is critical, but the case is not. It is short for Windows IP configuration.)

Figure 1-1   Run Dialog Box

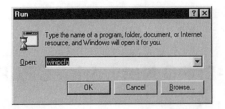

Step 2.   The first screen shows the adapter address (or MAC address), IP address, subnet mask, and default gateway. Figure 1-2 shows the basic IP configuration screen. Select the correct adapter if the list contains more than one.

Figure 1-2   Basic IP Configuration Screen

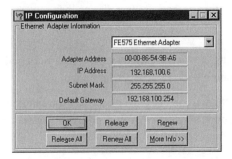

Step 3.   The IP address and default gateway should be in the same network or subnet; otherwise, this host would not be able to communicate outside the network. In Figure 1-2, the subnet mask reveals that the first three octets must be the same number in the same network.

If this computer is on a LAN, you might not see the default gateway if it is running behind a proxy server. Record the following information for this computer:

IP address: _____

Subnet mask: _____

Default gateway: _____

Task 3: Compare This Computer's TCP/IP Configuration to That of Others on the LAN

If this computer is on a LAN, compare the information on several machines. Answer the following questions:

1. Are there any similarities?

    _____

    _____

    _____

2. What is similar about the IP addresses?

    _____

    _____

    _____

3. What is similar about the default gateways?

    _____

    _____

    _____

4. What is similar about the adapter (MAC) addresses?

    _____

    _____

    _____

5. The IP addresses should share the same network portion. All machines in the LAN should share the same default gateway. Although it is not a requirement, most LAN administrators standardize components such as NICs, so it would not be surprising to find that all machines share the first three hexadecimal pairs in the adapter address. These three pairs identify the manufacturer of the adapter.

6. Record a couple of the IP addresses.

    _____

    _____

    _____

Task 4: Verify the Selection of a Network Adapter

Step 1.   The box at the top of the screen should display this computer's adapter model. Use the drop-down arrow in that box to see any other configurations for this adapter (such as PPP). If this computer connects to the Internet with a dialup account, you might see configurations for a modem. On a server, it is possible to find another NIC in this list, or a machine with both a NIC and a modem could include both configurations in this list. Figure 1-3 shows an AOL modem IP configuration screen. Notice that the figure shows no IP address. This configuration is what a home system could have if the user does not log on to the Internet.

Figure 1-3   AOL Modem IP Configuration Screen

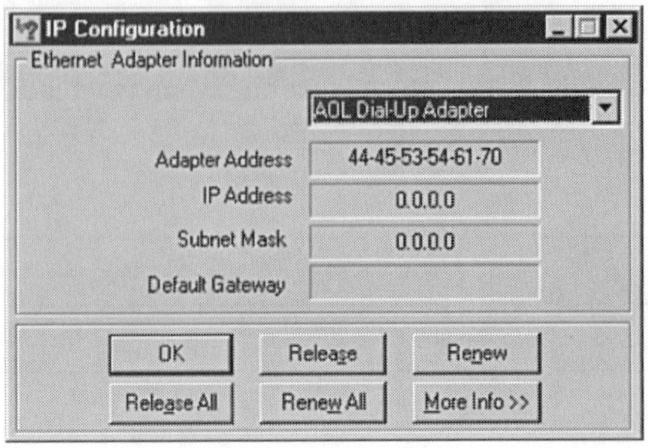

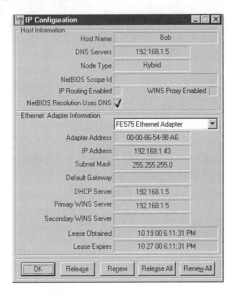

Step 2.   Return to the adapter that displays the NIC or modem data with an IP address.

Task 5: Check Additional TCP/IP Configuration Information

Step 1.   Click the **More Info** button. Figure 1-4 shows the detailed IP configuration screen.

Figure 1-4   Detailed IP Configuration Screen

Step 2.   You should see the following information: the hostname (computer name, NetBIOS name); the Dynamic Host Configuration Protocol (DHCP) server's address, if used; and the date the IP lease starts and ends. Review the remaining information. You might also see entries for DNS and Windows Internet Name Service (WINS) servers, which are used in name resolution.

Step 3.   Write the IP addresses of any servers listed.

_____

_____

_____

_____

Step 4.   Write the computer's hostname.

_____

Step 5.   Write the hostnames of a couple of other computers.

_____

Step 6.   Do all the servers and workstations share the same network portion of the IP address as your workstation?

_____

_____

_____

Task 6: Close the Screen When Finished Examining Network Settings

Repeat the preceding steps as necessary to ensure that you can return to and interpret this screen.

_____

Note: Windows NT/2000/XP users: Complete Tasks 7 through 11.

_____

Task 7: Gather TCP/IP Configuration Information

Step 1.   Use the Start menu to open the command prompt (MS-DOS–like) window (**Start > Programs > Accessories > Command Prompt** or **Start > Programs > Command Prompt**).

Step 2.   Figure 1-5 shows the command screen. Type **ipconfig** and press **Enter**. (The spelling of **ipconfig** is critical, but the case is not.)

Figure 1-5   Command Screen: ipconfig Results

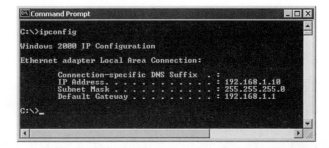

Step 3.   This screen shows the IP address, subnet mask, and default gateway. The IP address and the default gateway should be in the same network or subnet; otherwise, this host would not be able to communicate outside the network. In the figure, the subnet mask reveals that the first three octets must be the same number in the same network.

_____

Note: If this computer is on a LAN, you might not see the default gateway if it is running behind a proxy server. Record the following information for this computer.

_____

Task 8: Record the Following TCP/IP Information for This Computer

IP address: _____

Subnet mask: _____

Default gateway: _____

Task 9: Compare This Computer's TCP/IP Configuration to That of Others on the LAN

If this computer is on a LAN, compare the information of several machines.

1. Are there any similarities?

    _____

    _____

    _____

2. What is similar about the IP addresses?

    _____

    _____

    _____

3. What is similar about the default gateways?

    _____

    _____

    _____

4. Record a couple of the IP addresses.

    _____

    _____

    _____

Task 10: Check Additional TCP/IP Configuration Information

Step 1.   To see more information, type **ipconfig /all** and press **Enter**. Figure 1-6 shows the detailed IP configuration screen.

Figure 1-6   **Command Screen: ipconfig /all Results**

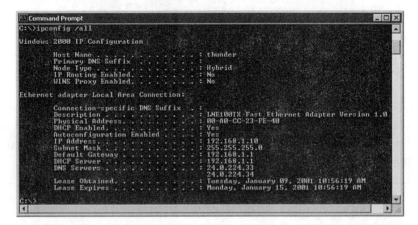

Step 2.   You should see the following information: the hostname (computer name, NetBIOS name); the DHCP server's address, if used; and the date the IP lease starts and ends. Review the information. You might also see entries for DNS servers, which are used in name resolution.

Step 3.   Figure 1-6 reveals that the router performs both DHCP and DNS services for this network. This network is likely a small office/home office (SOHO) or small branch office implementation.

Step 4.   You also see the physical (MAC) address and the NIC model (description). In the LAN, what similarities do you see in the physical (MAC) addresses?

_____

_____

_____

Step 5.   Although it is not a requirement, most LAN administrators standardize components such as NICs, so it would not be surprising to find that all machines share the first three hex pairs in the adapter address. These three pairs identify the manufacturer of the adapter.

Step 6.   Write the IP addresses of any servers listed:

_____

_____

Step 7.   Write the computer's hostname.

_____

Step 8.   Write the hostnames of a couple of other computers.

_____

Step 9.   Do all the servers and workstations share the same network portion of the IP address as your workstation?

_____

_____

Task 11: Close the Screen When Finished Examining Network Settings

Repeat the preceding steps as necessary to make sure that you can return to and interpret this screen.

Reflection

Based on your observations, what can you deduce about the following results from three computers connected to one switch?

Computer 1

    IP address: 192.168.12.113

    Subnet mask: 255.255.255.0

    Default gateway: 192.168.12.1

Computer 2

    IP address: 192.168.12.205

    Subnet mask: 255.255.255.0

    Default gateway: 192.168.12.1

Computer 3

    IP address: 192.168.112.97

    Subnet mask: 255.255.255.0

    Default gateway: 192.168.12.1

Should they be able to talk to each other? Are they all on the same network? Why or why not? If something is wrong, what is most likely the problem?

_____

_____

_____

_____

Curriculum Lab 1-3: Using ping and tracert from a Workstation (1.1.7)

Objective

- Learn to use the TCP/IP packet Internet groper (**ping**) command from a workstation.

- Learn to use the traceroute (**tracert**) command from a workstation.

- Observe name-resolution occurrences using WINS and DNS servers.

Background/Preparation

This lab assumes that you are using any version of Windows. This is a nondestructive lab that you can perform on any machine without changing the system configuration.

Ideally, perform this lab in a LAN environment that connects to the Internet. You can use a single remote connection via a modem or DSL-type connection. You need the IP addresses that were recorded in the previous lab. The instructor might also furnish additional IP addresses.

Note: Ping has been used in many denial of service (DoS) attacks, and many school network administrators have turned off ping and echo reply from the border routers. If the network administrator has turned off echo reply, it is possible for a remote host to appear to be offline when the network is operational.

Task 1: Establish and Verify Connectivity to the Internet

This task ensures that the computer has an IP address.

Task 2: Access the Command Prompt

Windows 95/98/Me users: Use the Start menu to open the MS-DOS prompt window (**Start > Programs > Accessories > MS-DOS Prompt** or **Start > Programs > MS-DOS**).

Windows NT/2000/XP users: Use the Start menu to open the Command Prompt window (**Start > Programs > Accessories > Command Prompt** or **Start > Programs > Command Prompt** or **Start > All Programs > Command Prompt**).

Task 3: Ping the IP Address of Another Computer

Step 1.   In the window, type **ping**, a space, and the IP address of a computer recorded in the previous lab. Figure 1-7 shows the successful results of pinging this IP address.

Figure 1-7   Successful Ping Results: IP Address

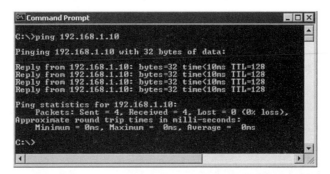

Ping uses the Internet Control Message Protocol (ICMP) echo-request and echo-reply feature to test physical connectivity. Because ping reports on four attempts, it gives an indication of the reliability of the connection. Review the results and verify that the ping is successful. Was the ping successful? If not, perform appropriate troubleshooting.

Step 2.   If a second networked computer is available, ping the IP address of the second machine. Note the results.

Task 4: Ping the IP Address of the Default Gateway

Ping the default gateway's IP address if you listed one in the previous exercise. A successful ping means there is physical connectivity to the router on the local network and probably the rest of the world.

Task 5: Ping the IP Address of a DHCP or DNS Server

Step 1.   Ping the IP address of any DHCP or DNS servers listed in the previous exercise. If the ping works for either server and it is not in the network, what do your results indicate?

Step 2.   Was the ping successful?

If not, perform appropriate troubleshooting.

Task 6: Ping This Computer's Loopback IP Address

Step 1.   Type the following command:

ping 127.0.0.1

The 127.0.0.0 network is reserved for loopback testing. If the ping is successful, TCP/IP is properly installed and functioning on this computer.

Step 2.   Was the ping successful?

If not, perform appropriate troubleshooting.

Task 7: Ping the Hostname of Another Computer

Step 1.   Ping the computer's hostname that you recorded in the previous lab. Figure 1-8 shows the successful result of pinging the hostname.

Figure 1-8   Successful Ping Results: Hostname

Step 2.   Review the results. Notice that the first line of output shows the hostname (**m450**, in the example) followed by the IP address. This output means that the computer was able to resolve the hostname to an IP address. Without name resolution, the ping would have failed because TCP/IP only understands valid IP addresses, not names.

Step 3.   A successful ping means that you can perform the connectivity and discovery of IP addresses with only a hostname. In fact, using hostnames is how many early networks communicated. Successfully pinging a hostname also shows that a WINS server is probably working on the network. WINS servers or a local **lmhosts** file resolves computer hostnames to IP addresses. If the ping fails, chances are the network is not running NetBIOS-name-to-IP-address resolution.

Note: It would not be uncommon for Windows 2000 or XP networks to not support this name-resolution feature. It is an old and often unnecessary technology.

Step 4.   If the last ping worked, ping the hostname of another computer on the local network. Figure 1-9 shows the possible results.

Note: You must type the name in quotes because the command language does not like the space in the name.

Figure 1-9   Successful Ping Results: Computer on the Local Network

Task 8: Ping the Cisco Website

Step 1.   Type the following command to ping the Cisco website (see Figure 1-10):

ping www.cisco.com

Figure 1-10   Successful Ping Results: Cisco Website

The first output line shows the Fully Qualified Domain Name (FQDN) followed by the IP address. A DNS server somewhere in the network was able to resolve the name to an IP address. DNS servers resolve domain names (not hostnames) to IP addresses.

Without name resolution, the ping would have failed because TCP/IP only understands valid IP addresses, not names. It would not be possible to use a web browser without name resolution.

With DNS, you can verify connectivity to computers on the Internet using a familiar web address (domain name) without needing the actual IP address. If the nearest DNS server does not know the IP address, it asks a DNS server higher in the Internet structure.

Task 9: Ping the Microsoft Website

Step 1.   Type the following command to ping the Microsoft website (see Figure 1-11):

ping www.microsoft.com

Figure 1-11   Unsuccessful Ping Results: Microsoft Website

Notice that the DNS server was able to resolve the name to an IP address, but there is no response. Some Microsoft routers are configured to ignore ping requests. Networks frequently implement this security measure.

Step 2.   Ping some other domain names and record the results. An example is **ping www.msn.de**.

_____

_____

_____

Task 10: Trace the Route to the Cisco Website.

Step 1.   Type **tracert www.cisco.com** and press **Enter** to generate the results shown in Figure 1-12.

Figure 1-12   Tracert Results for Cisco Website

Step 2.   **tracert** is TCP/IP's abbreviation for trace route. Figure 1-12 shows the successful result when you run **tracert** from Bavaria in Germany. The first output line shows the FQDN followed by the IP address. Therefore, a DNS server was able to resolve the name to an IP address. Then, you see a list of all the routers the tracert requests had to pass through to get to the destination.

Step 3.   **tracert** actually uses the same echo requests and replies as the **ping** command does but in a slightly different way. Observe that **tracert** actually contacted each router three times. Compare the results to determine the consistency of the route. In the preceding example, note the relatively long delays after routers 11 and 13, possibly because of congestion. The main thing to notice is the relatively consistent connectivity. Each router represents a point where one network connects to another network and the packet was forwarded through.

Task 11: Trace Other IP Addresses or Domain Names

Use **tracert** on other domain names or IP addresses and record the results. An example is **tracert www.msn.de**.

_____

_____

Task 12: Trace a Local Hostname or IP Address

Use the **tracert** command with a local hostname or IP address. It should not take long because the trace does not pass through any routers. Figure 1-13 offers a demonstration.

Figure 1-13   Tracert Results for a Local Hostname

Reflection

If the preceding tasks are successful and **ping** or **tracert** can verify connectivity with an Internet website, what does this indicate about the computer's configuration and about routers between the computer and the website? What, if anything, is the default gateway doing?

_____
_____
_____

Curriculum Lab 1-4: Web Browser Basics (1.1.8)

Objectives

- Learn how to use a web browser to access Internet sites.

- Become familiar with the concept of a URL.

- Use a search engine to locate information on the Internet.

- Access selected websites to learn the definitions of networking terms.

- Use hyperlinks to jump from the current website to other websites.

Background/Preparation

A web browser is a powerful tool that many people use every day to surf around different sites (cyber places) on the World Wide Web. With a web browser, you can find anything from airline flight information to the directions on how to get to a specific address. A browser is a client application program or software that is loaded on the PC to gain access to the Internet and local web pages.

The website name, such as **www.cisco.com,** is a uniform resource locator (URL). This URL points to the World Wide Web server (**www**) in the Cisco domain (**cisco**) under the commercial domain (**com**).

When you enter the URL, the browser makes a request of a DNS server to convert the URL to an IP address, which contacts the site.

You can use a browser to access search engines, such as http://www.yahoo.com, http://www.excite.com, http://www.lycos.com, and http://www.google.com, by typing the name in the address bar.

Several websites provide definitions of networking and computer terms and acronyms. You can use them to learn more about networking and to do research on the Internet. Two of these sites are http://www.whatis.com and http://www.webopedia.com. Most websites contain *hyperlinks*, which are underlined and highlighted words. By clicking a hyperlink, you "jump" to another page on the current site or to a page on another website.

To perform this lab, you must have a computer configured with an up-to-date browser and Internet access.

Task 1: Start the Web Browser

If you use a modem to make the connection, you must dial your service provider before you can start your web browser. What version of Netscape or Internet Explorer are you using?

_____

Task 2: Identify the Location or Address Field

After you start your browser, click and highlight the Location field (Netscape) or Address field (Internet Explorer) in the toolbar at the top of the page. Press the **Delete** key to delete the current address.

Task 3: Type in a Web URL

Type **http://www.cisco.com** and press **Enter**. This task is how you navigate from one site to another on the World Wide Web.

Task 4: Type in Another Web URL

To load a new page, type in a new URL, such as http://www.cnn.com. Notice the status on the bottom bar of your browser. What do you see?

_____

Task 5: Use the Browser Management Buttons

Step 1.   Each button on top of your browser has a function. If you position the mouse over a button, a box appears that identifies the button.

Step 2.   Click the **Back** button. What did it do?

_____

Step 3.   Click the **Forward** button. Does it return you to the CNN website?

_____

Step 4.   Click the **Reload** or **Refresh** button. What do you think it does?

_____

Step 5.   Type **http://www.microsoft.com** and press **Enter**. Click the **Stop** button as the window loads. What happens?

_____

Task 6. Use a Search Engine

Type the URL for a search engine, such as http://www.google.com. Search for the word **browser**. What is the result?

_____

Task 7: Access Networking Terms Definitions Websites

Step 1.   Enter the URL for **http://www.webopedia.com**. Enter the keyword **browser**. What is the result?

_____

Step 2.   What hyperlinks are available?

_____

_____

Step 3.   Enter the URL for **http://www.whatis.com**. Look up the keyword **domain name system**. Click the exact match for "domain name system" under whatis.com terms. What does it say about DNS?

_____

_____

_____

_____

_____

_____

_____

_____

Reflection

Identify a way in which you can navigate from one site to another.

If you see the same graphics or text at the NBA site, what should you do to ensure that you can see updated news?

_____

_____

Curriculum Lab 1-5: Basic PC/Network Troubleshooting Process (1.1.9)

Objectives

- Learn the proper sequence for troubleshooting computer and network problems.

- Become familiar with the more common hardware and software problems.

- Given a basic problem situation, be able to troubleshoot and resolve the problem.

Background/Preparation

The ability to effectively troubleshoot computer problems is an important skill. The process of identifying the problem and trying to solve it requires a systematic, step-by-step approach. This lab introduces some basic hardware and software problems to solve and helps you become more familiar with PC components and the software required to use the Cisco curriculum. The process of trying to solve a problem is fairly straightforward. Some of the suggestions here are more than you need to solve basic hardware and software problems, but they provide a framework and guidelines to use when more complex problems arise. The instructor's version of the lab provides a list of sample problems that the instructor can introduce.

Use the following seven basic tasks for PC and network troubleshooting.

Task 1: Define the Problem

Use the proper terminology to describe what is happening or not happening. For example, "the PC can't get to the Internet" or "the PC cannot print."

Task 2: Gather the Facts

Observe the symptoms and characterize or identify the source of the problem:

- Is it hardware (check for lights and noises) or software (errors on screen) related?

- Does it affect only this computer or user or are others also impacted?

- Does it affect only this software or more than one application?

- Is this the first time it has happened, or has it happened before?

- Did someone recently change anything on the PC?

- Get the opinions of others who might have more experience.

- Check websites and troubleshooting knowledge databases.

Task 3: Consider the Possibilities

Using the facts you gathered, identify one or more possible causes and potential solutions. Rank the solutions in order of the most likely to the least likely cause.

_____

_____

_____

Task 4: Create an Action Plan

Develop a plan that involves the single most likely solution. You can try the other options if the original solution fails. In developing your plan, consider the following:

- Check the simplest possible causes first. Is the power turned on or is the cable plugged in? Verify hardware first and then software. (Do any lights come on?)

- If it is a network problem, start at Layer 1 of the Open System Interconnection (OSI) model and work your way up. Studies show that the majority of problems occur at Layer 1.

- Can you use substitution to isolate the problem? If the monitor does not work, the problem could be the monitor, video adapter, or cables. Try another monitor to see whether that corrects the problem.

Task 5: Implement the Plan

Make changes from your plan to test the first possible solution.

Task 6: Observe the Results

Step 1.   If the problem is solved, document the solution. Double-check to make sure everything still works.

Step 2.   If the problem is not resolved, restore the changes and return to your plan to try the next solution. If you do not reverse this change, you will never know whether the solution was a later change or a combination of two changes.

Task 7: Document the Results

Always document your results to assist in solving similar problems as well as developing a documentation history for each device. If you are going to replace part of the devices, it might be nice to know if any are frequent sources of trouble or if they have recently been reconditioned.

Task 8: Introduce Problems and Troubleshoot

Step 1.   Work in teams of two. Team member A (or the instructor) selects two problems from a list of common hardware and software problems and introduces the problems into the computer. The desired goal is to run one of the videos or movies from the online curriculum or the CD.

Step 2.   Team member A (or the instructor) should create the hardware or software problems with the computer while the other team member is out of the room and then turn off the computer and monitor.

Step 3.   After team member B identifies the problems and corrects them, switch places, and let the other team member introduce some new problems.

Step 4.   Each team member solving a problem should fill in the following table based on the symptoms observed, problems identified, and solutions.

Team Member A

	Symptom Observed	Problem Identified	Solution
Problem 1			
Problem 2			

Team Member B

	Symptom Observed	Problem Identified	Solution
Problem 1			
Problem 2			

Curriculum Lab 1-6: Decimal to Binary Conversion (1.2.5)

Objectives

- Learn the process for converting decimal values to binary values.

- Practice converting decimal values to binary values.

Background/Preparation

Knowing how to covert decimal values to binary values is valuable when converting human readable IP addresses in dotted-decimal format to machine-readable binary format. This is normally done for calculation of subnet masks and other tasks. The following is an example of an IP address in 32-bit binary form and dotted-decimal form:

Binary IP address: 11000000.10101000.00101101.011110001

Decimal IP address: 192.168.45.121

Table 1-1 provides a simple tool to easily convert binary values to decimal values. You create the first row by counting right to left from one to eight for the basic eight bit positions (although it would work for any size binary value). The value row starts with one and doubles (Base 2) for each position to the left.

Table 1-1   Converting Binary to Decimal Values

Position	8	7	6	5	4	3	2	1
Value	128	64	32	16	8	4	2	1

You can use the same conversion table and simple division to convert decimal values to binary. To convert the decimal number 207 to binary, start with 128 (2^7) and divide by each lesser power of 2 until the remaining number is either a 0 or 1. Refer to the following division example and the steps list that follow.

```
128 ÷ 207

        128

      _____

64     79

        64

      _____

8      15

        8

      _____

4      7

        4

      _____

2      3

        2

      _____

        1
```

To convert 207 to binary, follow these steps:

Step 1.   Start with the leftmost value (largest) and see whether you can divide the decimal value by it. Because it will go once, put a 1 in the third row of Table 1-2 under the 128 value and calculate the remainder (79).

Step 2.   Because you can divide the remainder by the next value (64), put a 1 in the third row under the 64 value of Table 1-2.

Step 3.   Because you cannot divide the remainder by either 32 or 16, put 0s in the third row of Table 1-2 under the 32 and 16 values.

Step 4.   Continue until there is no remainder.

Step 5.   If necessary, use the fourth row in Table 1-2 to check your work.

Table 1-2   Converting 207 to Binary

Position	8	7	6	5	4	3	2	1	Result
Value	128	64	32	16	8	4	2	1	
	1	1	0	0	1	1	1	1	
	128	64			8	4	2	1	**207**

Step 6.   Convert the following decimal values to binary:

A. 123 _____

B. 02 _____

C. 67 _____

D. 7 _____

E. 252 _____

F. 91 _____

G. 116.127.71.3 _____

_____._____._____._____

H. 255.255.255.0 _____

_____._____._____._____

I. 192.143.255.255 _____

_____

_____._____._____._____

J. 12.101.9.16 _____

_____._____._____._____

Curriculum Lab 1-7: Binary to Decimal Conversion (1.2.6)

Objectives

- Learn the process for converting binary values to decimal values.

- Practice converting binary values to decimal values.

Background/Preparation

The following is an example of an IP address in 32-bit binary form and dotted-decimal form:

    Binary IP address: 11000000.10101000.00101101.01111001

    Decimal IP address: 192.168.45.121

Binary data consists of 1s and 0s (ON and OFF). Although you can group binary data in varying increments, such as 3 or 4 digits (110 or 1011), in TCP/IP, it is usually grouped in 8-digit groups called *bytes*.

A byte (8 bits) can range from 00000000 to 11111111, creating 256 combinations with decimal values ranging from 0 to 255. IP addressing uses 4 bytes (32 bits) to identify both the network and specific device (node or host). The example at the beginning of this lab is an example of an IP address in both binary decimal formats.

Table 1-3 provides a simple tool for easily converting binary to decimal values. You create the first row by counting right to left from one to eight for the basic eight bit positions (although it would work for any size binary value). The value row starts with 1 and doubles (Base 2) for each position to the left.

Table 1-3   Converting Binary to Decimal Values

Position	8	7	6	5	4	3	2	1
Value	128	64	32	16	8	4	2	1

Complete the following steps:

Step 1.   Enter the binary bits (for example, 10111001) in the third row of Table 1-4.

Step 2.   Put the decimal values in the fourth row only for the third row 1s. Technically, you are multiplying the second-row values by the third row.

Step 3.   Sum the fourth row (across).

Table 1-4   Converting 10111001 to Decimal

Position	8	7	6	5	4	3	2	1	Result
Value	128	64	32	16	8	4	2	1	
	1	0	1	1	1	0	0	1	
	128		32	16	8			1	**185**

Step 4.   Convert the following binary values to decimals:

A. 1110 _____

B. 100110 _____

C. 11111111 _____

D. 11010011 _____

E. 01000001 _____

F. 11001110 _____

G. 01110101 _____

H. 10001111 _____

I.   11101001.00011011.10000000.10100100 _____._____._____._____

J.   10101010.00110100.11100110.00010111 _____._____._____._____

Curriculum Lab 1-8: Hexadecimal Conversion (1.2.8)

Objectives

- Learn the process for converting hexadecimal values to decimal and binary values.

- Learn the process for converting decimal and binary values to hexadecimal values.

- Practice converting between decimal, binary, and hexadecimal values.

Background/Preparation

Table 1-5 provides a useful decimal-to-hexadecimal-to-binary conversion table.

Table 1-5   Decimal-to-Hexadecimal-to-Binary Conversion

Decimal	Hexadecimal	Binary
0	0	0000
1	1	0001
2	2	0010
3	3	0011
4	4	0100
5	5	0101
6	6	0110
7	7	0111
8	8	1000
9	9	1001
10	A	1010
11	B	1011
12	C	1100
13	D	1101
14	E	1110
15	F	1111

You use the hexadecimal number system to refer to the binary numbers in a NIC or Internet Protocol version 6 (IPv6) address. The word *hexadecimal* comes from the Greek word for 16 and is often abbreviated 0x (zero and lowercase x). Hexadecimal numbers use 16 unique digits to display any combination of 8 binary digits as only 2 hexadecimal digits.

A byte (8 bits) can range from 00000000 to 11111111, creating 256 combinations with decimal values ranging from 0 to 255 or hexadecimal values 0 to FF. Each hexadecimal value represents only 4 binary bits. The alpha (A–F) values are not case sensitive.

Table 1-6 provides a simple tool for easily converting hexadecimal to decimal values using the same techniques as covered in binary to decimal conversions in the previous lab. The first row is the two hexadecimal positions. The value row starts as 1 and 16 (Base 16) for each position to the left.

Table 1-6   Hexadecimal to Decimal Conversion

Position	2	1
Value	16	1

Note: At the end of this lab, you use the Windows scientific calculator to check your work.

Steps for Hexadecimal to Decimal Conversion

Step 1.   Break the hexadecimal value into pairs starting at the right edge, inserting a 0 if necessary to complete the first pair (for example, 77AE becomes 77 and AE), as done in Table 1-7.

Step 2.   Put each hexadecimal pair in the third row. The value in parentheses is the decimal value of hexadecimal values A–F.

Step 3.   To get the decimal values in the fourth row, multiply the second-row values by the third row.

Step 4.   Sum the fourth row (across).

Table 1-7   Converting Hexadecimal to Decimal

Position	2	1	Result	Position	2	1	Result
Value	16	1		Value	16	1	
	7	7			$A_{(10)}$	$E_{(14)}$	
	112	7	**119**		160	14	**174**

Add decimal 119 (hexadecimal 77) and decimal 174 (hexadecimal AE) for a total of decimal 293.

Steps for Decimal to Hexadecimal Conversion

Step 1.   To be valid for the purposes of this lab, the decimal value is between 0 and 256. You derive the first hexadecimal value by dividing the decimal value by 16. If the value is greater than 9, you need to put it in hexadecimal form (A–F).

Step 2.   The second value is the remainder from Step 1. If the value is greater than 9, you need to put it in hexadecimal form (A–F).

Step 3.   For example, 209 divided by 16 is 13 (D in hexadecimal) with a remainder of 1, equaling D1.

Steps for Hexadecimal to Binary Conversion

Step 1.   This is the easiest conversion, as long as you remember that each hexadecimal value converts to four binary bits, so work right to left. For example, convert 77AE to binary.

Step 2.   Starting with E, you can use Table 1-5 at the beginning of this lab to go directly to binary. The alternative is to convert the value to decimal (E = 14), and then use the last four binary positions of the table (see Table 1-8).

14 divided by 8 is 1 with a remainder of 6.

6 divided by 4 is 1 with a remainder of 2.

2 divided by 2 is 1 with no remainder.

If necessary, add 0s to end up with 4 bits.

Table 1-8   Hexadecimal to Decimal Conversion

Position	4	3	2	1	Result
Value	8	4	2	1	
	1	1	1	0	
	8	4	2		**14**

Step 3.   Using the same technique, A becomes 1010, and the total so far is 10101110 (see Table 1-9).

Table 1-9   Hexadecimal to Decimal Conversion

Position	4	3	2	1	Result
Value	8	4	2	1	
	1	0	1	0	
	8		2		**10**

Step 4.   Using the same technique, the two 7s each become 0111, and the total in binary is now is 01110111.10101110 (see Table 1-10).

Table 1-10   Hexadecimal to Decimal Conversion

Position	4	3	2	1	Result
Value	8	4	2	1	
	0	1	1	1	
		4	2	1	**7**

Steps for Binary to Hexadecimal Conversion

Step 1.   Each hexadecimal value equals 4 binary bits, so start by breaking the binary value into 4-bit units from right to left. Add any leading 0s required to end up with all 4-bit values. 01101110 11101100 would become 0110 1110 1110 1100.

Step 2.   You can use Table 1-5 to go directly to hexadecimal. The alternative is to convert each 4-bit binary value to decimal (0–15) and then convert the decimal to hexadecimal (0–F), as shown in Table 1-11.

Table 1-11   Converting Binary to Hexadecimal

Position	4	3	2	1	Result	Position	4	3	2	1	Result
Value	8	4	2	1		Value	8	4	2	1	
	1	1	0	0			1	1	1	0	
	8	4			**12 or C**		8	4	2		**14 or E**

Step 3.   In Table 1-12, binary 1100 is converted to decimal 12 or hexadecimal C. Binary 1110 is then converted to decimal 14 or hexadecimal E. Although not shown in the table, binary 1110 converts to hexadecimal E and 0110 converts to hexadecimal 6. The result is 6E–EC.

Practice

Convert the following values in Table 1-12 to the other two forms.

Table 1-12   Converting Decimal-to-Hexadecimal-to-Binary

	Decimal	Hexadecimal	Binary
1		A9	
2		FF	
3		BAD1	
4		E7-63-1C	
5	53		
6	115		
7	19		
8	212.65.119.45		
9			10101010
10			110
11			11111100.00111100
12			00001100.10000000.11110000.11111111

Checking Conversions with the Windows Calculator

It is important to be able to manually perform the preceding calculations. However, you can check your work using the Windows calculator applet. Access the calculator by choosing **Start > Programs > Accessories > Calculator**. Click the **View** menu and make sure that the calculator is in **Scientific** mode. Click the button for the type of number you will be entering (hexadecimal, decimal, or binary), and then enter the number in that form. To convert from one form to another, click one of the alternate options.

Challenge Lab 1-9: Understanding Number Systems

Objectives

- Learn the fundamental components of number systems.

- Create a unique number system.

- Test the newly created number system by converting new system values to the decimal format.

Background

Number systems are developed following a Base X notation. These systems use powers of the base value and a number of unique symbols. The Base 10, or decimal, number system uses the powers of 10 and 10 unique symbols (0, 1, 2, 3, 4, 5, 6, 7, 8, and 9). Binary is a Base 2 number system that uses 0 and 1 as its symbols. Hexadecimal is Base 16 and uses 0 through 9 and A through F for its 16 symbols.

Creating a unique number system is done by choosing a decimal number for the base value and identifying the symbols that will be used in the system. You can test the newly created system by converting the values to the decimal system.

Task 1: Create a Foundation for a Base 3 Numbering System

Draw a four-column, five-row table. Label the top row with Position, the next row with Power, and the third row from the top with Value.

Task 2: Label the Positions 1 Through 4 from Right to Left

Populate the Power row with the powers of 3. Begin with 3^0 in the right column followed by 3^1, 3^2, and 3^3. Reflect the corresponding decimal value of each power in the Value row.

Task 3: Define Symbols and Create a Symbol Table

Define the three symbols to be used in the numbering system, and create a table showing each symbol and its corresponding decimal value. Because it is a Base 3 system, the three values are 0, 1, and 2.

Task 4: Use Symbols to Fill in the Fourth Row

Write a four-character value using the newly defined symbols in the fourth row of the table.

Position	4	3	2	1
Power	3^3	3^2	3^1	3^0
Value	27	9	3	1
Symbol				
Value				

Task 5: Calculate Decimal Values to Fill in the Fifth Row

To get the decimal values for the fifth row, multiply the decimal value of each symbol in row four by the corresponding value in row three.

Position	4	3	2	1
Power	3^3	3^2	3^1	3^0
Value	27	9	3	1
Symbol	X	Y	X	Z
Value				

Task 6: Complete the Conversion

Add the values in the fifth row to complete the conversion process.

_____

Task 7: Convert Base 3 to Decimal

Convert the following Base 3 values to decimal format:

Base 3   Base 10

YXZY   _____

YZXX   _____

XZZZ   _____

Task 8: Determine the Largest Decimal Value

Determine the largest decimal value that can be expressed using four Base 3 characters. How would it be expressed in Base 3?

_____
_____

Task 9: Describe Converting Decimal to Base 3

Describe the process to convert decimal values into Base 3.

_____
_____
_____
_____
_____
_____
_____

Challenge

Create a Base 5 numbering system by following the tasks of this lab. Ensure the numbering system is unique by using five simple object drawings as the symbols of the system. Have the instructor or a friend test the system by converting the values into decimal format. (You need to provide them the symbol to decimal conversion chart you create.)

Networking Fundamentals

The Study Guide portion of this chapter uses a combination of matching, fill in the blank, multiple choice, and open-ended question exercises to test your knowledge of networking terminology, bandwidth, and networking models.

The Lab Exercises portion of this chapter includes all the online curriculum labs and a comprehensive lab to ensure that you have mastered the practical, hands-on skills needed to connect to the network and to understand network math.

As you work through this chapter, use Module 2 in the CCNA 1 online curriculum or use the corresponding Chapter 2 in the *Networking Basics CCNA 1 Companion Guide* for assistance.

Study Guide

Networking Terminology

Computer networks have existed for more than 35 years. Early on, computers were large, rather unreliable devices used for complex mathematical computations. As computer technology advanced, the advantages of connecting these devices became apparent. Computer networks were developed to allow for end-to-end communications and resource sharing. Business networks initially focused on creating local communication systems. Later on, the increased need to connect networks required the creation of standards to ensure network interoperability.

In this section, you find exercises designed to help you learn additional terminology associated with networking, compare and contrast types of networks, and understand multiple network physical topologies. These exercises focus on the key areas of the corresponding section of the curriculum.

Vocabulary Exercise: Matching

Match the definition on the left with a term on the right. This exercise does not necessarily use one-to-one matching. Some definitions might be used more than once and some terms might have multiple definitions.

Definitions

a. A device that connects end-user devices to allow them to communicate.

b. Defines how hosts access the network media to send data.

c. A collection of protocols that enable network communication between hosts.

d. A collection of computers, printers, routers, switches, and other devices that are able to communicate with each other over some transmission medium.

e. An end-user device that provides users with a connection to the network. These devices allow users to share, create, and obtain information.

f. A method of transferring data files by walking with a floppy disk from one computer to another.

g. In this type of topology, a host sends its data to all other hosts on the network medium.

h. A technology used to beam signals across public areas.

i. Actual layout of the wire or media in a network.

j. In this type of topology, an electronic token is passed sequentially to each host.

Terms

___ protocol suite

___ broadcast

___ wireless bridge

___ network

___ token passing

___ logical topology

___ host

___ network device

___ physical topology

___ sneakernet

Vocabulary Exercise: Define

Define the functions of the following network devices:

bridge _____

_____

hub _____

_____

_____

repeater _____

_____

router _____

_____

_____

workgroup switch _____

_____

_____

_____

Note: Knowledge of the functions of network devices is required for a complete understanding of computer networking. Now is a good time to look at Comprehensive Lab 2-3, "Networking Device Identification and Association." You can begin the lab by filling in the functions of each device. At this time, you might also want to sketch the symbol associated with each device. You are prompted to finish the lab in the section "Networking Models."

Compare and Contrast Exercise: Network Types

Networks are categorized by the characteristics they possess. Complete Table 2-1 to compare and contrast local-area networks (LAN), metropolitan-area networks (MAN), and wide-area networks (WAN).

Table 2-1   Compare and Contrast LANs, MANs, and WANs

	LAN	MAN	WAN
What is the typical geographic range of the network type?			
What is the typical use of the network type?			

continues

Table 2-1   Compare and Contrast LANs, MANs, and WANs   *continued*

	LAN	MAN	WAN
What are some common technologies used by the network type?			

Concept Questions

Completely answer the following questions:

1. Why were businesses the driving force behind computer network development?

_____

_____

_____

_____

_____

2. List three wide-area communications networks that existed prior to the Internet. What is an advantage of the system when compared to the systems that came before it? What is a disadvantage of each system when compared to the Internet?

_____

_____

_____

_____

_____

_____

_____

_____

_____

_____

_____

3. What motivated the U.S. Department of Defense (DoD) to develop large, reliable WANs?

_____

_____

_____

_____

_____

_____

_____

_____

4. Why are networking protocols necessary? Who develops these protocols?

_____

_____

_____

_____

_____

_____

_____

_____

_____

_____

_____

_____

5. What is a SAN? What are some of the factors contributing to the popularity of SANs?

_____

_____

_____

_____

_____

_____

- _____

- _____

- _____

6. What is a VPN? What are the main types of VPNs?

_____

_____

_____

_____

_____

_____

_____

- _____

- _____

- _____

Understanding Physical Network Topologies Exercise

A network topology identifies the structure of a network by defining its physical and logical design. The physical topology of a network illustrates the layout of the hosts, network devices, and media that make up the system. It is important to understand the various physical network topologies.

Sketch each type of topology by completing the following host diagrams (Figures 2-1 through 2-6). Add the appropriate media connections and network devices for each diagram.

Figure 2-1   Bus Topology

Figure 2-2   Ring Topology

Figure 2-3   Star Topology

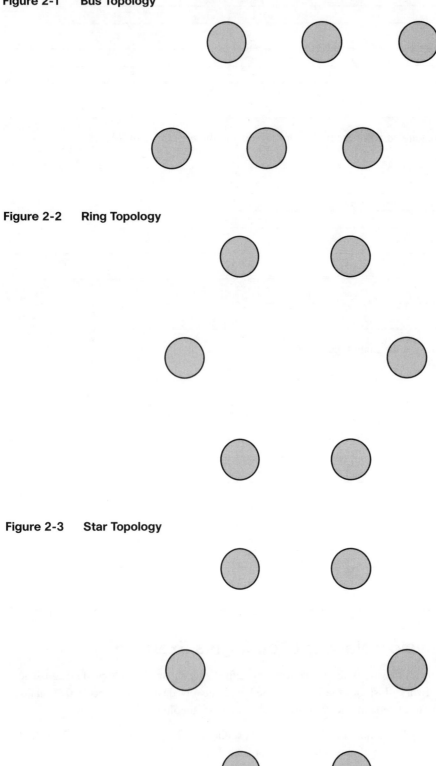

Figure 2-4   Mesh Topology

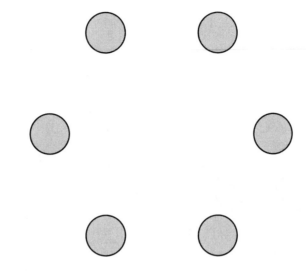

Figure 2-5   Hierarchical Topology

Figure 2-6   Extended Star Topology

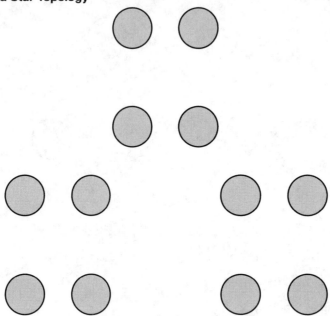

Journal Entry

Once an organization decides that it will benefit from the creation and use of a LAN, the organization must decide on what topology type it will use.

1. What factors do organizations evaluate when deciding on a network topology to deploy?

    _____

    ■ _____

    ■ _____

    ■ _____

    ■ _____

    ■ _____

    ■ _____

    ■ _____

2. Compare the physical topology types by listing the advantages and disadvantages of each.

    _____

    _____

    _____

    _____

3. What topology is being used in your classroom? Do you believe this topology to be the best choice for your environment? Explain.

    _____

    _____

    _____

    _____

_____

_____

_____

_____

_____

_____

Bandwidth

Bandwidth is a measurement of the rate of information that flows across a point or link within a given amount of time. It is important to have a thorough understanding of bandwidth because the concept is critical to networking. Bandwidth has both physical and technological limits, is not free, and analyzes network performance. Also, the demand for bandwidth is growing rapidly.

This section includes exercises that reinforce the concept of information flow and bandwidth. These exercises include identifying key terms, calculating data-transfer rates, and using Internet tools to measure bandwidth.

Vocabulary Exercise: Completion

Complete the following statements by using the proper terms to fill in the blanks.

_____ is the amount of information that can flow through a network connection in a given period of time.

Material, such as streaming video and audio, that requires tremendous amounts of network bandwidth is classified as_____.

_____ is the actual measured bandwidth, at a specific time of day, using specific Internet routes, and while a specific set of data is transmitted on the network.

On a network, _____ is calculated by dividing the size of a file by the bandwidth.

_____ is measured by how much of the electromagnetic spectrum is occupied by each signal. The basic unit is hertz (Hz), or cycles per second.

In _____, all information is sent as bits, regardless of the kind of information it is.

Concept Questions

Completely answer the following questions:

1. What factors contribute to the increased demand for bandwidth?

_____

- _____

- _____

- _____

- _____

- _____

- _____

- _____

2. Describe how the highway analogy is used to explain bandwidth.

_____

_____

_____

_____

_____

_____

_____

_____

_____

3. How is digital bandwidth measured?

_____

_____

_____

_____

_____

_____

_____

4. Throughput refers to the actual available bandwidth at a given moment. Name some factors that affect throughput.

_____

_____

■ _____

■ _____

■ _____

■ _____

■ _____

■ _____

■ _____

5. Why is calculating data-transfer times important when deciding on a WAN service?

_____

_____

_____

_____

_____

_____

6. List two types of analog communication devices. List two types of digital communication devices. What types of information can be communicated by each device?

_____

_____

_____

Calculating Data-Transfer Rates Exercise

Consider the following scenarios and calculate data-transfer rates to answer the following questions:

1. A user connects to the Internet from home using a 1.5-Mbps DSL line. How long will it take the user to download a 12-MB video file from a server connected to the Internet using a T3?

2. A branch office in Dallas needs to send a complicated database to a branch office in Arlington. The Dallas office connects to Atlanta using an OC-1 (51.840 Mbps) connection. Atlanta connects to Raleigh using an OC-3 (155.251 Mbps) connection. Raleigh connects to the Arlington office using an OC-1 connection. How long does it take for Dallas to send the 2.5 GB file to Arlington?

3. A videoconference needs to connect two offices on a campus. Office A uses a 10-Mbps link to connect to the 100-Mbps campus backbone. Office B uses a 54-Mbps wireless link to connect to the campus backbone. The videoconference software transfers data at a rate of 1100 KBps. Will Office A and Office B be able to participate in the videoconference?

4. A digital projection theater in San Jose is scheduled to show a new movie in four hours. The 2 terabyte (TB or 10^{12} bytes) movie file must be downloaded from a server in Orlando. The server is on a 10-Gbps LAN that connects to an OC-48 Internet backbone. The theater connects to the same Internet backbone using a 1-Gbps link. Can the movie be downloaded within four hours?

Measuring Bandwidth on the Internet Exercise

Many hardware and software tools can measure bandwidth and throughput. Some of these tools are available on the Internet and are free for anyone to use. To complete this exercise, use the Internet to search for bandwidth-measurement tools and use your results to answer the following questions:

1. What is the web-page address of the bandwidth-measurement tool you will use?

2. Does the website explain how the test calculates bandwidth? If so, how is the calculation performed?

_____

_____

_____

3. Does the website require you to specify connection information? If so, what information are you asked to provide?

_____

_____

4. Run the bandwidth-measurement tool. What are the test results?

_____

_____

5. Are the results what you expected to see? Explain.

_____

_____

_____

6. How can this information be useful? Explain.

_____

- _____

- _____

- _____

Note: Periodic bandwidth measurements might be run using the same tool to gauge throughput at different times of the day.

Journal Entry

Bandwidth can be a difficult concept to grasp initially. The pipe and highway analogies used in Module 2 of the online curriculum are useful aids for understanding bandwidth.

Create another analogy that can be used to help learn or teach the concept of information flow. Use illustrations as needed.

- _____

- _____

- _____

Networking Models

Computer networks are complicated communication systems. Each network is unique because of the various hardware and software used to communicate across the network. Networking models make it easier to understand these systems. Networking models are based on open standards and can be used for network design and troubleshooting. It is important to understand these models, their components, and how to apply the model concepts when learning how network devices communicate.

In this section, you find exercises that focus on the two major conceptual network models. These exercises include defining associated terms, comparing the Open Systems Interconnection (OSI) and Transmission Control Protocol/Internet Protocol (TCP/IP) models, identifying the functions of each layer in the models, and listing the encapsulation protocol data unit (PDU) used in information networking.

Vocabulary Exercise: Define

Define the following key technology terms related to networking models:

data communications protocol _____

_____

data field _____

destination _____

encapsulation _____

header _____

_____

IP _____

_____

_____

OSI _____

_____

_____

_____

packet _____

_____

PDU _____

_____

peer-to-peer communications _____

_____

source _____

TCP _____

_____

trailer _____

_____

Compare and Contrast Exercise: OSI and TCP/IP Models

The first step in understanding the OSI and TCP/IP conceptual models is to identify the layers that make up each model. Complete Figure 2-7 by labeling the layers of both models.

Figure 2-7   Label the OSI and TCP/IP Model Layers

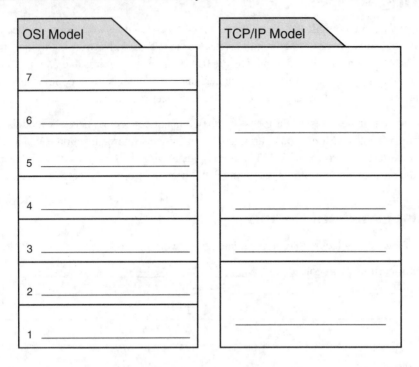

Each layer of the model performs functions vital to the communication process. Complete Figure 2-8 by listing the functions that each layer of the OSI model performs.

Figure 2-8   List the Functions of Each OSI Model Layer

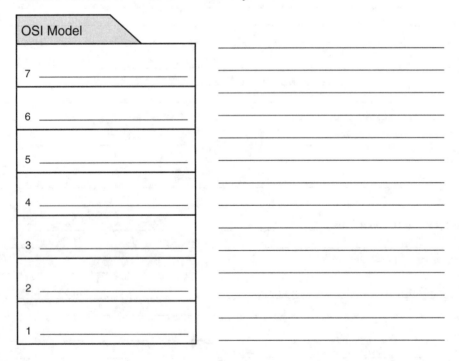

Complete Figure 2-9 by listing the functions performed by each layer of the TCP/IP model.

Figure 2-9   List the Functions of Each TCP/IP Model Layer

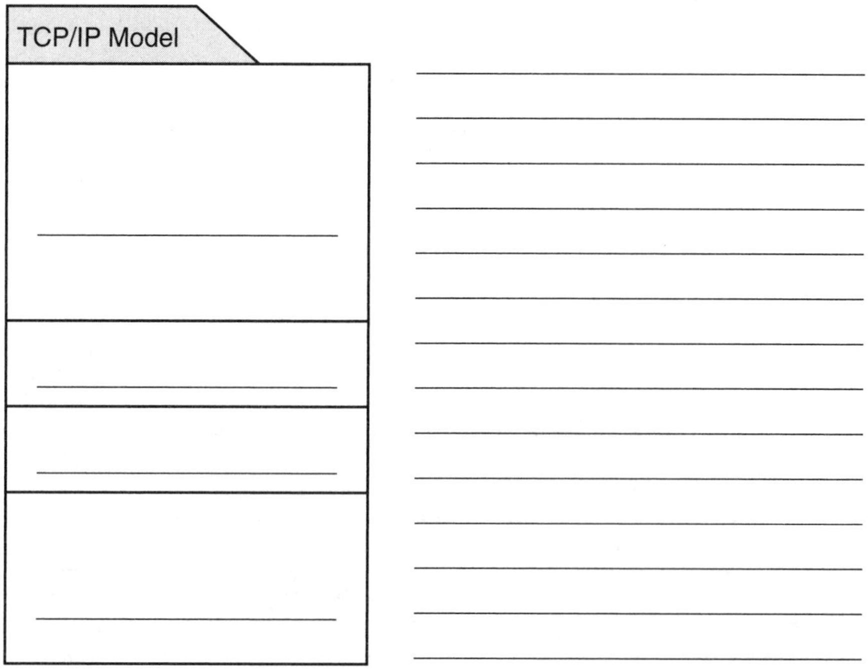

TCP/IP Model

_____   _____

_____   _____

                                                          _____

                                                          _____

_____   _____

                                                          _____

_____   _____

                                                          _____

_____   _____

                                                          _____

                                                          _____

_____   _____

                                                          _____

                                                          _____

Note: Now is a good time to complete Curriculum Lab 2-1, "OSI Model and TCP/IP Model." This lab reinforces your knowledge of the OSI and TCP/IP models.

Concept Questions

Completely answer the following questions:

1. Why use a layered communication model in networking?

   _____

   _____

   _____

   _____

2. What are the benefits of using the OSI model?

   _____

   _____

   ■ _____

   ■ _____

   ■ _____

   ■ _____

   ■ _____

   ■ _____

3. Explain how peer-to-peer communication works using the OSI model.

   _____

   _____

   _____

4. What are some of the commonly used TCP/IP application layer protocols?

_____

_____

- _____

- _____

- _____

- _____

- _____

5. What are the five conversion steps used to encapsulate data as it moves through a layered model?

_____

_____

1. _____

2. _____

3. _____

_____

4. _____

5. _____

Identifying Encapsulation PDUs Exercise

PDUs are used for peer-to-peer communications in networking. Encapsulation is the process of creating these PDUs as information passes through the networking model of one host to be delivered to another host. Complete Figure 2-10 by labeling the layers on each host and identifying the PDUs used at each layer.

Figure 2-10   List the Encapsulation PDUs Used at Each Layer of the OSI Model

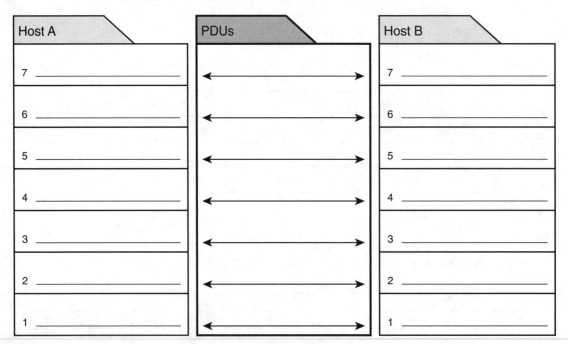

Note: Now is a good time to complete Lab 2-2 and Lab 2-3. Both labs focus on layered models and network devices.

Journal Entry

Mnemonics are commonly used to aid in the memorization of lists. A popular mnemonic used to identify the layers of the OSI model from the bottom up is "Please Do Not Throw Sausage Pizzas Away." The first letter of each word corresponds to the first letter of a layer in the OSI model. Create a unique mnemonic for each of the following:

- OSI model (from the application layer down to the physical layer)

- OSI model (from the physical layer up to the application layer)

- Encapsulation PDUs (from the top down)

- Encapsulation PDUs (from the bottom up)

Lab Exercises

Curriculum Lab 2-1: OSI Model and TCP/IP Model (Lab 2.3.6)

Objectives

- Describe the four layers of the TCP/IP model.

- Relate the seven layers of the OSI model to the four layers of the TCP/IP model.

- Name the primary TCP/IP protocols and uses that operate at each layer.

Background/Preparation

This lab helps you develop a better understanding of the seven layers of the OSI model as they relate to the most popular functioning networking model: the TCP/IP model. The Internet is based on TCP/IP, which has become the standard language of networking. Although the TCP/IP model is the most widely used, the seven layers of the OSI model describe and compare networking software and hardware from various vendors. It is important to know both the OSI and TCP/IP models and to relate (or map) the layers of one to the other. When troubleshooting a network, you must understand the TCP/IP model and the protocols and utilities that operate at each layer.

Compare the OSI Layers with the TCP/IP Protocol Stack

In column 2 of Table 2-2, indicate the proper name for each of the seven layers of the OSI model corresponding to the layer number. List the TCP/IP layer number and its correct name in the next two columns. Also, list the term for the encapsulation units, the related TCP/IP protocols, and the utilities that operate at each TCP/IP layer. More than one OSI layer relates to certain TCP/IP layers.

Table 2-2   OSI Comparison with TCP/IP Protocol Stack

OSI Layer No.	OSI Layer Name	TCP/IP Layer No.	TCP/IP Layer Name	Encapsulation Units	TCP/IP Protocols at Each TCP/IP Layer	TCP Utilities
7						
6						
5						
4						
3						
2						
1						

Curriculum Lab 2-2: OSI Model Characteristics and Devices (Lab 2.3.7)

Objectives

- Name the seven layers of the OSI model in order using a mnemonic.

- Describe the characteristics, functions, and keywords relating to each layer.

- Describe the packaging units used to encapsulate each layer.

- Name the physical devices or components that operate at each layer.

Background/Preparation

This lab helps you develop a better understanding of the seven layers of the OSI model—specifically as they relate to the most popular functioning networking model in existence: the TCP/IP model. The Internet is based on TCP/IP, so it has become the standard networking language. However, the seven layers of the OSI model are the ones most commonly used to describe and compare networking software and hardware from various vendors. It is important to know both models and to relate or map the layers of one to the other. When troubleshooting, an understanding of the TCP/IP model and the protocols and utilities that operate at each layer is essential.

Task 1: List the Seven Layers of the OSI Reference Model

In Table 2-3, list the seven layers of the OSI model from top to bottom. Give a mnemonic word (memory jogger) for each layer that can help you remember it and then list the keywords and phrases that describe the characteristics and function of each.

Table 2-3   OSI Reference Model Memorization Chart

Layer No.	Layer Name	Mnemonic	Keywords and Description of Function	Read from Bottom	Read from Top
7					
6					
5					
4					

continues

Table 2-3   OSI Reference Model Memorization Chart *continued*

Layer No.	Layer Name	Mnemonic	Keywords and Description of Function	Read from Bottom	Read from Top
3					
2					
1					

Task 2: List the OSI Model Layers, the Encapsulation Unit to Describe the Data Grouping at Each Layer, and the Network Devices That Operate at Each Layer

In Table 2-4, list the seven layers of the OSI model and the encapsulation unit used to describe the data grouping at each layer as well as the networking devices, if applicable, that operate at each layer.

Table 2-4   OSI Reference Model Encapsulation and Network Devices

Layer No.	Layer Name	Encapsulation Unit or Logical Grouping	Devices or Components That Operate at This Layer
7			
6			
5			
4			
3			
2			
1			

Comprehensive Lab 2-3: Networking Device Identification and Association

Objectives

- Learn the illustrative representations of networking devices.

- Understand the functions of networking devices.

- Identify the OSI model layers of operation for each networking device.

Background

This comprehensive lab helps reinforce many key concepts that are fundamental to understanding networking. As your networking education continues, you will design, build, configure, test, and troubleshoot networks by using networking devices and the OSI model. Use this opportunity to become more familiar with these items and their relationships.

Task 1: Provide Illustrations for Each Networking Device

Complete Table 2-5 by drawing the logical symbol for each networking device and providing a sketch of the physical device.

Table 2-5   Networking Devices: Symbols and Sketches

Networking Device	Logical Symbol	Physical Sketch
Repeater		
Hub		
Bridge		

Workgroup switch

Router

Task 2: Identify the Functions of Each Networking Device and Its OSI Layer

Complete Table 2-6 by defining the function of each networking device and listing the layers of the OSI model where the device functions.

Table 2-6   Networking Devices: Functions and Layers of Operation

Networking Device	Device Function	OSI Model Layers of Operation
Repeater		
Hub		
Bridge		
Workgroup switch		

Networking Device	Device Function	OSI Model Layers of Operation
Router		

Task 3: Draw a Network Topology That Contains Each Networking Device

Networking Media

The Study Guide portion of this chapter uses a combination of matching, fill in the blank, and open-ended question exercises to test your knowledge of networking media, including copper, optical, and wireless.

The Lab Exercises portion of this chapter includes all the online curriculum labs, a comprehensive lab, and a challenge lab to ensure that you have mastered the practical, hands-on skills needed to understand networking media.

As you work through this chapter, use Module 3 in the CCNA 1 online curriculum or use the corresponding Chapter 3 in the *Networking Basics CCNA 1 Companion Guide* for assistance.

Study Guide

Copper Media

Copper media has been used in information networking since the creation of networks, and it is still used extensively in LANs today. Copper's electrical properties make it an ideal medium for passing data communications using electrical current. Add this to the inexpensive cost of copper cable and the simplicity of its installation, and you can see that copper media is an effective, but not perfect, type of networking media.

In this section, you learn about copper media used for information networking through exercises that help you understand the associated terminology, compare and contrast copper cable types, identify network cable types, and learn common cable pinouts. Additional exercises challenge your knowledge of copper media and the basics of electricity.

Vocabulary Exercise: Matching

Match the definition on the left with a term on the right. This exercise does not necessarily use one-to-one matching. Some definitions might be used more than once and some terms might have multiple definitions.

Definitions

a. The opposition to the movement of electrons.

b. Communications path between two or more points.

c. Unwanted communication channel noise.

d. The undesirable communications channel signals.

e. The flow of charges created when electrons move.

f. A material that allows the amount of electricity it conducts to be precisely controlled.

g. The part of a network that acts as the primary path for traffic that is most often sourced from, and destined for, other networks.

h. Any material with a low resistance to electrical current.

i. An electrical force, or pressure, that occurs when electrons and protons are separated.

j. The reduction of signal energy during transmission.

k. Electrically neutral contact point.

l. An electronic device used to measure electrical signals relative to time.

m. An effect produced by the twisted wire pairs to limit signal degradation caused by electromagnetic interference (EMI) and radio frequency interference (RFI).

n. The number of charges per second that pass by a point along a path.

o. The total opposition to current flow in an alternating current (AC) circuit.

p. Any material with a high resistance to electrical current.

q. Indicates how much power a device consumes or produces.

Terms

___ ground

___ backbone

___ cancellation

___ oscilloscope

___ attenuation

___ circuit

___ interference

___ voltage

___ insulator

___ noise

___ current

___ resistance

___ conductor

___ impedance

___ wattage

___ ampere

___ semiconductor

Vocabulary Exercise: Identifying Acronyms and Initialisms

An acronym is a word formed by the first letters in a multiword term. Initialisms are words made of initials pronounced separately. These are used extensively in the information technology (IT) field. Identify the terms associated with the following acronyms:

AC _____

DC _____

EMF _____

EMI _____

ESD _____

STP _____

RFI _____

UTP _____

Compare and Contrast Exercise: Copper Cable Types

Coaxial, STP, and UTP are three types of copper cables used for networking. Although all three copper wires pass electrical current, each cable type has its advantages and disadvantages when compared to the other cable types. Complete Table 3-1 to compare and contrast these three copper cable types.

Table 3-1   Compare and Contrast Coaxial, STP, and UTP Cable Types

	Coaxial	STP	UTP
What is the typical speed and throughput?			
What is the relative cost?			
What is the media and connector size?			
What is the maximum cable length?			
What is the greatest advantage of this cable type when compared to the others in the table?			
What is the greatest disadvantage of this cable type when compared to the others in the table?			

Concept Questions

Completely answer the following questions:

1. What is ESD? Why should IT professionals be concerned with ESD? What can be done to minimize ESD?

   _____

   _____

   _____

   _____

   _____

   _____

   _____

   _____

   _____

   _____

   _____

2. What typical voltages can exist in networks and network equipment? Where can these voltages be found?

   _____

   ■ _____

   ■ _____

   ■ _____

   ■ _____

   ■ _____

   ■ _____

3. Power is expressed in wattage and calculated by multiplying voltage by the current (in amperes). What is the wattage if the voltage is 3.3 volts and the current is .05 amps? What is the wattage if the voltage is 12 volts and the current is 3 amps? What is the power rating for typical PC power supplies?

   _____

   _____

   _____

   _____

4. What is a series circuit?

   _____

   _____

5. Explain the x BASE y notation used for cable specifications. Provide examples and explanations.

   _____

   _____

   _____

   _____

   _____

   _____

   _____

6. What are the components of a coaxial cable?

_____

_____

_____

_____

_____

7. Why is UTP the most popular type of copper media for LANs?

_____

_____

_____

_____

_____

_____

_____

_____

_____

_____

_____

_____

Understanding Ohm's Law Exercise

When working with copper cable, it is important to understand certain electrical properties to ensure that cables and equipment are installed and functioning properly. A basic knowledge of Ohm's Law and its usage will benefit network professionals.

Ohm's Law defines the relationship between voltage (measured in volts), resistance (measured in ohms), and current (measured in amps). Using a water analogy, voltage is water pressure, resistance is the size of a water pipe, and current is the water's flow rate. Modifying one of the properties directly affects the other two properties.

Ohm's Law states that voltage (V) is equal to resistance (R) multiplied by current (I). If you know two of the variables, you can find the third rather easily. Resistance is equal to the voltage divided by the current. Current is equal to the voltage divided by the resistance. Figure 3-1 illustrates this relationship using a triangle model. Using this model, hide the value you are trying to find and use the remaining values to create the formula needed to solve for the hidden value.

Figure 3-1   Ohm's Law Triangle

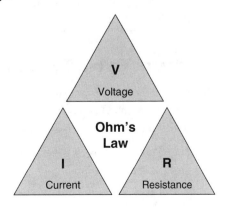

Answer the following questions using Ohm's Law. Be sure to show the formula used to find the unknown value:

1. If the current is 20 amps and the resistance is 2 ohms, what is the voltage?

_____

_____

_____

2. If the voltage is 120 volts and the current is 5 amps, what is the resistance?

_____

_____

_____

3. If the resistance is 3 ohms and the voltage is 12 volts, what is the current?

_____

_____

_____

4. If the current is 40 amps and the resistance is .6 ohms, what is the voltage?

_____

_____

_____

5. If the voltage is 54 volts and the current is 100 milliamps (mA or one thousandth of an amp), what is the resistance?

_____

_____

_____

6. If the resistance is .02 ohms and the voltage is 48 volts, what is the current?

_____

_____

_____

Note: Now is a good time to complete the first five curriculum labs in this chapter. These labs focus on tool usage, measuring electrical properties, and creating circuits.

Choosing the Correct Network Cable Type Exercise

The three most common copper-based LAN cable types are straight-through, crossover, and rollover cables. All three cables pass information, but each cable has its specific uses in a network environment. It is important to understand the role of each cable type and its proper usage.

Identify the network cable that needs to be used to properly connect the network devices and hosts shown in each of the following figures (Figures 3-2 through 3-7).

Figure 3-2   Identify the Proper Network Cable (a)

Figure 3-3   Identify the Proper Network Cable (b)

Figure 3-4   Identify the Proper Network Cable (c)

Figure 3-5   Identify the Proper Network Cable (d)

Figure 3-6   Identify the Proper Network Cable(e)

Figure 3-7   Identify the Proper Network Cable (f)

Note: Now is a good time to complete Lab 3-6, Lab 3-7, Lab 3-8, and Lab 3-9. Lab 3-6 focuses on using the Fluke 620 cable tester to verify cable types and functionality. Labs 3-7, 3-8, and 3-9 guide you through the network cable-creation process by illustrating the steps used to build straight-through, crossover, and rollover cables.

Identifying Network Cable Pinouts Exercise

Straight-through, crossover, and rollover cables are commonly created using four-pair (eight-wire) cabling and RJ-45 modular connectors. It is the specific pinout and termination of the eight wires on each cable end that creates the different cable types. Knowing the respective pinouts is necessary for cable creation and identification.

Complete Table 3-2, Table 3-3, and Table 3-4 by specifying the pinouts used to create straight-through, crossover, and rollover cables.

Table 3-2   Straight-Through Cable Pinout (TIA/EIA-568-B)

Near End			Opposite End		
Pin No.	Pair No.	Color	Pin No.	Pair No.	Color
1			1		
2			2		
3			3		
4			4		
5			5		
6			6		
7			7		
8			8		

Table 3-3   Crossover Cable Pinout

Near End (TIA/EIA-568-B)			Opposite End (TIA/EIA-568-A)		
Pin No.	Pair No.	Color	Pin No.	Pair No.	Color
1			1		
2			2		
3			3		
4			4		
5			5		
6			6		
7			7		
8			8		

Table 3-4   Rollover Cable Pinout (TIA/EIA-568-B)

Near End			Opposite End		
Pin No.	Pair No.	Color	Pin No.	Pair No.	Color
1			1		
2			2		
3			3		
4			4		
5			5		
6			6		
7			7		
8			8		

Journal Entry

Copper media is an inexpensive and effective type of network media, but it is not without its drawbacks. Because copper media uses electrical charges for data transmission, it is susceptible to noise generated by external sources. Network professionals must be aware of all potential sources of noise when installing and maintaining networks that use copper media.

You are a network administrator evaluating areas for network expansion. You are tasked with looking at existing computer labs and identifying potential sources of noise that could cause problems within the network. Using your classroom, perform the following steps:

Step 1.   Identify all potential sources of noise that could adversely affect network communications across copper media.

Step 2.   Prioritize the sources of noise. Place the most hazardous source near the top and list other sources accordingly.

Step 3.   Determine steps that can be taken to avoid or minimize the potential affect of the top three sources of noise.

Optical Media

Optical media use pulses of light to carry data across lines of fiber consisting of glass and plastic. This type of media has many advantages over copper media, including greater communication speeds and an immunity to external noise sources. But, this does not make it the perfect networking media. Optical media is expensive, difficult to install, and less forgiving than other media types. Optical media is commonly used for high-speed, long-distance links, but it can also be found in LANs.

In this section, you find exercises designed to build a better understanding of optical media and its use in information networking. Focused exercises include introducing optical media terminology, comparing and contrasting types of fiber-optic cables, understanding the electromagnetic (EM) spectrum, and identifying tools used to create and test fiber-optic cables.

Vocabulary Exercise: Matching

Understanding optical media requires familiarity with key terms associated with the media and light. Match the definition on the left with a term on the right. This exercise does not necessarily use one-to-one matching. Some definitions might be used more than once, and some terms might have multiple definitions.

Definitions

a. The process of data traveling over a network, from its source to its ultimate destination.

b. EM waves whose frequency range is above that of microwaves, but below that of the visible spectrum.

c. The boundary between two devices, systems, or materials.

d. Analog transmission device in which a suitable active material is excited by an external stimulus to produce a narrow beam of coherent light that can be modulated into pulses to carry data.

e. A desirable situation in which the entire incident light in the fiber is reflected back inside the fiber.

f. Cutting fiber in a way that results in a clean, properly angled edge on the core.

g. Semiconductor device that emits light produced by converting electrical energy.

h. How much a light ray slows down when it passes through a substance.

i. An area free of air and virtually any other matter.

j. The measure of how much a given material bends light.

k. A type of fiber noise caused by imperfections that exist within the fiber core.

l. A perpendicular line emanating from the point on a surface where a light ray contacts the surface.

m. The initial ray of light as it moves through a material before contacting another material.

Terms

____ normal

____ optical density

____ interface

____ cleaving

____ dispersion

____ LED

____ refraction

____ propagation

____ laser

____ total internal reflection

____ incident ray

____ vacuum

____ infrared

Compare and Contrast Exercise: Single-Mode and Multimode Fiber-Optic Cable

Single-mode and multimode are the two major types of fiber-optic cables used today. Each type has distinct qualities and is suited for specific uses. Complete Table 3-5 by identifying the characteristics of single-mode and multimode cables.

Table 3-5   Compare and Contrast Types of Fiber

	Single-Mode Fiber	Multimode Fiber
What is the common jacket color of the fiber?		
What is the typical light source for the fiber?		
What is the size of the core?		
What is the typical segment length of the fiber?		
How is this type of fiber used primarily?		

Concept Questions

Completely answer the following questions:

1. What is the index of refraction? How is it calculated for different materials?

2. What are the components of a typical fiber-optic cable? What is the function of each component?

3. Working with optical media requires knowledge of certain characteristics of light, including specific "angles." What is the angle of incidence? What is the angle of reflection? What is a critical angle?

    _____

    _____

    _____

    _____

    _____

    _____

4. Unlike copper media, fiber-optic cables are not susceptible to external noise sources, but optical signals are still prone to signal degradation. What factors can affect fiber-optic communication signals?

    _____

    _____

    ■ _____

       _____

    ■ _____

       _____

    ■ _____

       _____

5. What is an OTDR? How does it work?

    _____

    _____

    _____

    _____

6. Why is fiber more difficult to install than copper cable?

    _____

    _____

    _____

    _____

    _____

EM Spectrum Chart Exercise

An EM spectrum chart shows the relationship of all EM waves. The chart shows the wave types in order from the longest wavelength to the shortest. Although it might not be necessary to memorize the entire chart, it is beneficial to understand where each EM wave type falls on the chart in relation to the other wave types. Complete Figure 3-8 by identifying the EM wave types and their associated devices or uses. You might need to consult other sources of information to finish this exercise.

Figure 3-8   EM Spectrum Chart

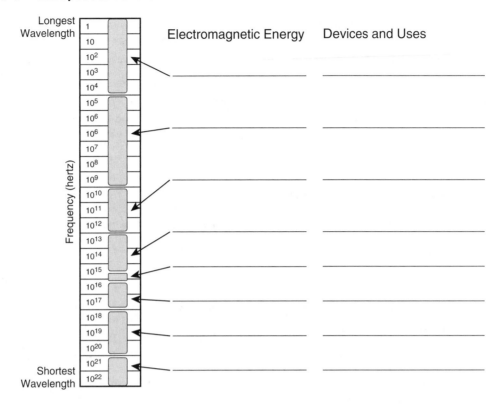

Note: Now is a good time to complete Curriculum Lab 3-11. The information you find when working on the lab will be beneficial in the following Journal Entry.

Journal Entry

You are the network administrator for an organization that is about to make a major investment in a fiber-optic infrastructure. Although the company plans to contract the majority of the fiber-optic cabling work to consultants, the organization must purchase the equipment necessary to terminate and test single-mode and multimode fiber-optic cables. You are tasked with building the fiber-optic toolkit.

Identify the items that make up a fiber-optic toolkit that can be used to prepare, terminate, and test fiber-optic cables. Find and document one specific example of each needed component. Be sure to include pricing information for each item. You will need access to the Internet or a fiber-optics supply catalog to complete this task.

_____
_____

- _____

- _____

- _____

- _____

- _____

_____
_____
_____
_____

Wireless Media

Wireless LANs (WLAN) can be found in homes, schools, businesses, and many public areas. Wireless network devices are inexpensive, easy to set up, and provide a convenience that cannot be found in wired networks. The key to understanding wireless networks is understanding the technologies used to communicate across an "invisible media."

Exercises in this section help you learn about wireless media and technologies. You are asked to define key wireless terms, compare and contrast three wireless technologies, and use the Internet to find local wireless networks available for public use. The final exercise of this section challenges you to determine the media types to be used in a campus network.

Vocabulary Exercise: Completion

Complete the following statements by using the proper terms to fill in the blanks.

A key technology contained within the _____ WLAN standard is Direct Sequence Spread Spectrum (DSSS).

802.11b might also be called _____ and refers to DSSS systems that operate at 1, 2, 5.5, and 11 Mbps.

In an _____ wireless network, both devices function as server and client in a fashion that is similar to those in a peer-to-peer wired environment.

_____ are commonly installed to act as central hubs for the WLAN infrastructure mode.

The process of altering the carrier signal that will enter the antenna of the transmitter is called _____.

_____ technologies hop across the entire 2.4 GHz spectrum many times per second and can cause significant interference on an 802.11b network.

_____ technology creates a tunnel on top of an existing protocol to increase the security of the connection.

_____ is the opposite of spread spectrum technology and does not affect the entire frequency spectrum of the wireless signal.

_____ is a simple type of client authentication, defined in 802.11, where a single authentication request and response is used to mutually authenticate the client and access point.

When the client and access point use the same passcode to authenticate with one another, _____ authentication is being used.

_____, performed after authentication, is the state that permits a client to use the services of the access point to transfer data.

Compare and Contrast Exercise: Wireless Networking Standards

The Federal Communications Commission (FCC) opened up several frequency bands in 1985 that would ultimately be used by many devices, including wireless networking devices. In 1990, the IEEE began working on the 802.11 standards for devices using these bands. Three popular variants of the standard include 802.11a, 802.11b, and 802.11g. Use Table 3-6 to compare and contrast these wireless networking standards.

Note: A great source of information of the IEEE 802.11 standards is the official IEEE 802.11 Working Group website: http://grouper.ieee.org/groups/802/11/.

Table 3-6   Compare and Contrast Wireless Networking Standards

	802.11a	802.11b	802.11g
What frequency range does the wireless standard use?			
What is the maximum bandwidth of the wireless standard?			
Is the wireless technology compatible with other standards?			

Concept Questions

Completely answer the following questions:

1. Why is the actual throughput on a wireless network usually a fraction of the potential bandwidth of the network?

   _____

   _____

   _____

   _____

   _____

   _____

2. Wireless clients can scan for suitable wireless networks. What is the difference between active scanning and passive scanning?

   _____

   _____

   _____

   _____

   _____

   _____

   _____

   _____

   _____

3. Like all other network media, wireless signals are vulnerable to attenuation and noise. What are some of the factors that can affect signals used for wireless networking?

_____

_____

_____

_____

_____

4. Wireless networking is an unbounded technology with an open-ended media. What are some methods that can be used to add security to wireless networks?

_____

_____

_____

_____

_____

_____

_____

Locating Wi-Fi Hotspots Using the Internet Exercise

Wi-Fi hotspots are 802.11b wireless networks that are open for public access. Many libraries, stores, restaurants, and other businesses provide free (or fee-based) Internet access services to patrons and customers. Hotspot providers can often be found through word of mouth, local advertisements, and on the Internet.

Use the Internet to locate a Wi-Fi search utility. What is the address of the site?

_____

Use the Wi-Fi search utility to locate hotspots in your home area. If you are unable to find a provider near your home, broaden your search radius or pick another city.

Select one of the search results. What is the name of the service provider?

_____

What types of wireless services are provided?

_____

_____

What are the access fees?

_____

Why are more and more businesses providing free Internet access to customers? How do the businesses benefit from this service?

_____

_____

_____

Journal Entry

Many of today's campus-area networks use a combination of copper, optic, and wireless media types to connect users and facilities. Figure 3-9 depicts a typical campus setting for a business with three separate buildings.

Figure 3-9   Typical Business Campus

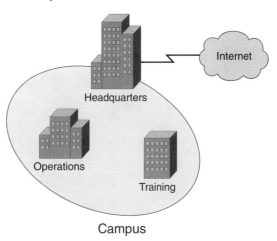

You are the new network administrator for Acme Technologies. Acme Technologies is planning to build a three-building campus similar to the one shown in Figure 3-9. Your job is to determine the media types that will be used within and between buildings on the campus. The following are overviews of each building's business functions:

Training—This facility is primarily used to educate new employees. It is a 10,000 square-foot single-story building housing multiple computer labs. New hires are trained on fixed-location PCs while instructors use mobile laptops and PDAs. The labs in this building require a high-speed connection to the servers located in Operations. Internet access is also needed, but it will only be used on a limited basis.

Operations—This building houses most of the company's servers and databases. It is a high-security, multistory building that contains personnel offices and server rooms. Reliable high-speed connectivity is required between server rooms. Operations also requires a high-speed Internet connection.

Headquarters—The largest building on campus houses the majority of employee offices. This large, multistory facility contains many conference rooms and auditoriums. The majority of users in this building has laptops and requires a great degree of mobile network access. This building has a high-speed Internet connection. All other campus facilities must connect to Headquarters for Internet access.

Record your thoughts on the media to be used on campus. What types of media should be used in each building? How should buildings be connected on campus? What is your reasoning behind the decisions?

_____

_____

_____

_____

_____

_____

_____

_____

_____

_____

_____

_____

_____

Lab Exercises

Curriculum Lab 3-1: Safe Handling and Use of a Multimeter (3.1.1)

Figure 3-10   Fluke 110 Series Multimeter

Objective

■ Learn how to use or handle a multimeter correctly.

Background/Preparation

A multimeter is a powerful electrical testing tool that can detect voltage levels, resistance levels, and open and closed circuits. It can check both alternating current (AC) and direct current (DC) voltage. Open and closed circuits are indicated by resistance measurements in ohms. Each computer and networking device consists of millions of circuits and small electrical components. You can use a multimeter to debug electrical problems within a computer or networking device or with the media between networking devices.

Prior to starting the lab, the teacher or lab assistant needs to have several multimeters available (one for each team of two students) and various batteries for testing. Work in teams of two. You need the following resources:

■ Digital multimeter (Fluke 110 Series, 12B or similar) for each team

■ Manual for the multimeter

■ Battery (for example, a 9 V, 1.5 V, or lantern—it doesn't matter) for each team to test

---

Caution: The multimeter is a sensitive piece of electronic testing equipment. Be sure that you do not drop it or handle it carelessly. Be careful not to accidentally nick or cut the red or black wire leads (probes). Because it is possible to check high voltages, take extra care when doing so to avoid electrical shock.

Perform the following steps to become familiar with the handling of the multimeter.

Task 1: Insert the Red and Black Leads (Probes) into the Proper Jacks on the Meter

The black probe should go in the COM jack, and the red probe should go in the + (plus or positive) jack.

Task 2: Turn On the Multimeter (Click or Turn the On Button)

1. What model of multimeter are you working with?

    _____

2. What action must you take to turn on the meter?

    _____

Task 3: Switch or Turn to Different Measurements (For Example, Voltage, Ohms, and So On)

1. How many different switch positions does the multimeter have?

    _____
    _____
    _____

2. What are they?

    _____
    _____
    _____
    _____

Task 4: Switch or Turn the Multimeter to the Voltage Measurement

What is the symbol for this?

_____

Task 5: Put the Tip of the Red (Positive) Lead on One End of a Battery (the + Side), and Put the Tip of the Black (Negative) Lead on the Other End of a Battery

Is any number showing on the multimeter?

_____

If not, make sure you switch to the correct type of measurement (Vol, voltage, or V). If the voltage is negative, reverse your leads.

Reflection

1. Name one thing that you should not do to a multimeter.

    _____
    _____

2. Name one important function of a multimeter.

    _____
    _____

3. Why would you get a negative voltage when measuring a battery?

_____

_____

Curriculum Lab 3-2 Voltage Measurement (3.1.2)

Figure 3-11   Fluke 110 Series Multimeter-AC Voltage Scale

Objective

- Demonstrate the ability to safely measure voltage with the multimeter.

Background/Preparation

The digital multimeter is a versatile testing and troubleshooting device. This lab covers both DC and AC voltage measurements. Voltage is measured in either AC or DC volts (indicated by a V). _Voltage_ is the pressure that moves electrons through a circuit from one place to another. Voltage differential is essential to the flow of electricity. The voltage differential between a cloud in the sky and the earth is what causes lightning to strike.

Warning: Be careful when taking voltage measurements because it is possible to receive an electrical shock.

DC—DC voltage rises to a set level and then stays at that level and flows in one direction (positive or negative). Batteries produce DC voltage and are commonly rated at 1.5 V or 9 V (flashlight batteries) and 6 V (lantern and vehicle batteries). Typically, the battery in your car or truck is a 12 V battery. When you place an electrical "load," such as a light bulb or motor between the positive (+) and negative (-) terminals of a battery, electricity flows.

AC—AC voltage rises above zero (positive) and then falls below zero (negative) and actually rapidly changes direction. The most common example of AC voltage is the wall outlet in your home or business. In North America, these outlets provide approximately 120 volts of AC directly to any electrical appliance that is plugged in, such as a computer, toaster, or television. Some devices, such as small printers and laptop computers, have a transformer (small black box) that plugs in to a 120 V AC wall outlet and then converts the AC voltage to DC voltage for use by the device. Some AC outlets can provide a higher voltage of 220 V for use by devices and equipment with heavier requirements, such as clothes dryers and arc welders.

Prior to starting the lab, the teacher or lab assistant should have several multimeters available (one for each team of students) and various items for testing voltage. Work in teams of two. You need the following resources:

- Fluke 110 or 12B multimeter (or equivalent)

- An assortment of batteries: A cell, C cell, D cell, 9 volts, 6 V lantern

- Duplex wall outlet (typically 120 V)

- Power supply (for laptop or other networking electrical device). The following resources are optional:

  - A lemon with a galvanized nail stuck in one side and a piece of uninsulated copper wire stuck in the opposite side

  - Solar cell with leads attached

  - Homemade generator (wire wound around a pencil 50 times and a magnet)

Task 1: Select the Proper Voltage Scale

Step 1. The method of selecting the voltage scale will vary, depending on the type of meter. The Fluke 110 has two separate positions for voltage: a letter V with a wave over it for AC and a V with a solid and a dashed line above it for DC. With the Fluke 12B, move the rotary selector to the V symbol for voltage (black V) to be able to measure voltage. Press the button that has the VDC and VAC symbol to select between DC and AC measurements.

> **DC measurements**—The screen will show a V (voltage) with a series of dots and a line over the top. The available scales depend on the voltage to be measured. They start from millivolts (abbreviated mV, 1000th of a volt) to voltages up to hundreds of volts. Use the Range button to change the range of DC voltage to be measured based on what voltage you expect to measure. You can typically measure batteries (less than 15 V) accurately with the VDC scale and 0.0 range. You can use DC voltage measurements to determine whether batteries are good or whether there is voltage coming out of an AC adapter (transformer or converter). AC adapters are common; you use them with hubs, modems, laptops, printers, and other peripherals. These adapters can take wall-outlet AC voltage and step it down to lower AC voltages for the device, or they can convert the AC voltage to DC and step it down. Check the back of the adapter to see what the input (AC) and output voltages (AC or DC) should be.

> **AC measurements**—The screen will show a V (voltage) with a tilde (~) after it. This symbol represents AC. The available scales depend on the voltage to be measured. They start from millivolts (abbreviated mV, 1000th of a volt) to voltage up to hundreds of volts. Use the Range button to change the range of AC voltage to be measured based on what voltage you expect to measure. You can typically measure voltage from power outlets (120 V or greater) accurately with the VAC scale and 0.0 range. AC voltage measurements are useful in determining whether there is adequate voltage coming from an AC outlet to power equipment.

Step 2. Use a Fluke 110 or 12B multimeter (or equivalent) to measure the voltage of the items in Task 2.

Task 2: Check the Voltages of the Items in Table 3-7. Be Sure to Turn Off the Meter When Finished

Table 3-7   Taking Voltage Measurements

Item to Measure the Voltage Of	Set Selector and Voltage Range Scale To	Reading
Batteries: A cell (AA, AAA), C cell, D cell, 9 V, 6 V lantern.		
Duplex wall outlet (typically 120 V).		
Power supply (converts AC to lower AC or DC) for laptop, mobile phone, or other networking electrical device.		
(Optional) A lemon with a galvanized nail stuck in one side and a piece of uninsulated copper wire stuck in the opposite side.		

Reflection

Why might you want to measure voltage when troubleshooting a network?

_____

_____

Curriculum Lab 3-3: Resistance Measurement (3.1.3)

Figure 3-12   Fluke 110 Series Multimeter-Resistance Scale

Objective

- Demonstrate the ability to measure resistance and continuity with the multimeter.

Background/Preparation

The digital multimeter is a versatile testing and troubleshooting device. This lab covers resistance measurements and related measurements called *continuity*. Resistance is measured in ohms (indicated by the Greek letter Omega or Ω). Copper wires (conductors), such as those commonly used in network cabling (unshielded twisted-pair [UTP] and coaxial), normally have low resistance or "good" continuity (the wire is continuous) if you check them from end to end. If the wire has a break, it is called "open," which creates high resistance. (Air has nearly infinite resistance, indicated by the infinity symbol, ∞, a sideways 8.)

The multimeter has a battery in it, which it uses to test the resistance of a conductor (wire) or insulator (wire sheathing). When you apply the probes to the ends of a conductor, the battery current flows and the meter measures the resistance it encounters. If the battery in the multimeter is low or dead, you must replace it or you will not be able to take resistance measurements. With this lab, you test common networking materials so that you can become familiar with them and their resistance characteristics. You first learn to use the resistance setting on the multimeter. As you measure small resistances, also note the continuity feature. The instructions apply to the Fluke 110 and 12B. Other meters function in a similar way.

Prior to starting the lab, the teacher or lab assistant should have several multimeters available (one for each team of two students) and various networking items for testing resistance. Work in teams of two. You need the following resources:

- Fluke 110 Series or 12B multimeter (or equivalent)
- 1000 ohm resistor
- 10,000 ohm resistor
- Pencil for creating graphite paths on paper
- Category 5 jack
- Small section (0.2 m or approximately 6 to 8 inches) of Category 5 UTP solid cable
- BNC terminated coaxial cable
- Unconnected DB9 to RJ-45 adapter
- Terminated Category 5 UTP patch cable

Task 1: Select the Resistance Scale on the Multimeter

Fluke 110

Resistance measurements—Move the rotary selector to the omega symbol for ohms (Ω) to measure resistance. Use the Range button to change the range of resistance to be measured based on what resistance you expect to get. The screen will show Ω (ohms), KΩ (kilohms, thousands of ohms), or MΩ (megohms, millions of ohms).

Continuity measurements—Move the rotary selector to the Beeper Sound symbol to the left of the ohms symbol to measure continuity. When there is good continuity (less than 20 ohms), the beep sounds. You use the continuity setting when you just want to know whether there is a good path for electricity, and you don't care about the exact amount of resistance.

Fluke 12B

Resistance measurements—Move the rotary selector to the omega symbol for ohms Ω to measure resistance. Press the button with the ohms symbol on it to select resistance mode instead of continuity. The screen should not show a diode symbol, which is a small black triangle pointing to a vertical bar. Use the Range button to change the range of resistance to be measured based on what resistance you expect to get.

Continuity measurements—Move the rotary selector to the omega symbol for ohms Ω to measure resistance. Press the button that has the ohms symbol on it to select continuity mode. The screen will show a diode symbol, which is a small black triangle pointing to a vertical bar. A *diode* is an electronic device that either passes or blocks electrical current. When there is good continuity (low resistance), the beep sounds. You use the continuity setting when you just want to know whether there is a good path for electricity and you don't care about the exact amount of resistance.

Task 2: Check the Resistances in Table 3-8. Turn Off the Meter When Finished or the Battery Will Drain

Table 3-8   Taking Resistance Measurements

Item to Measure the Resistance Of	Set Selector and Range Scale To	Resistance Reading
1000Ω resistor.		
10kΩ resistor.		
Graphite marking from a pencil on a piece of paper.		

continues

Table 3-8   Taking Resistance Measurements   *continued*

Item to Measure the Resistance Of	Set Selector and Range Scale To	Resistance Reading
Category 5 jack.		
0.2 m section of Category 5 UTP solid cable.		
Touch red and black probe contacts together.		
Your own body. (Touch the tips of the probes with your fingers.)		
BNC terminated coaxial cable.		
Unconnected DB9 to RJ-45 adapter.		
Terminated Category 5 UTP patch cable.		

Reflection

What purpose might the multimeter serve in maintaining and troubleshooting a computer network?

Curriculum Lab 3-4: Series Circuits (3.1.5)

Figure 3-13   Series Circuit

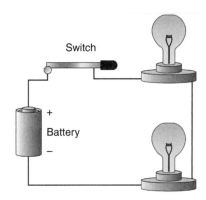

Objective

- Build series circuits and explore their basic properties.

Background/Preparation

One of the most basic concepts in electronics is that of a continuous loop through which electrons flow, called a *circuit*. Throughout networking materials are references to ground loop circuit, circuit versus packet switching, and virtual circuits, in addition to all the real circuits formed by networking media and networking devices. One of the fundamental electrical circuits is the *series circuit*. Although most networking devices and networks are built from complex circuits that are beyond the scope of the lessons in this course, the process of building some series circuits helps you with some of the terminology and networking concepts. This lab also helps increase your overall understanding of some of the most basic electrical-circuit building blocks.

Prior to starting the lab, the teacher or lab assistant should have several multimeters available (one for each team of students) and various items to create circuits. Work in teams of two. You need the following resources:

- Fluke 110 Series or 12B multimeter (or equivalent)
- Light switch
- Wire cutters and stripper
- Copper wire
- Two light bulbs (6 V) with bulb bases
- 6 V lantern battery

Task 1: Measure the Resistance of All Devices

Step 1.   Measure the resistances of all devices and components except the battery. All resistances should be less than 1Ω (ohm), except the light bulbs. All the devices except the battery should register continuity (with the tone), which indicates a short circuit or a conducting path.

Step 2.   Check the resistance of the items in Table 3-9. Turn off the meter when finished or it will drain the battery.

Table 3-9   Measuring Device Resistance

Item to Measure the Resistance Of	Set Selector and Range Scale To	Resistance Reading
Pieces of wire to connect components.		
Light switch.		
Light bulbs.		

Task 2: Measure the Voltage of the Battery and Unloaded (With Nothing Attached to It)

Fill in the information in Table 3-10.

Table 3-10   Measuring Battery Voltage

Item to Measure the Voltage Of	Set Selector and Range Scale To	Voltage Reading
Lantern battery (6 V) with no load		

Task 3: Build a Series Circuit One Device at a Time

Step 1.   Use one battery, one switch, one bulb, and connecting wires.

Step 2.   Connect the battery's positive lead to the end of one wire, and connect the negative lead to the other wire. If you turn on the switch, the bulb should light.

Step 3.   Disconnect one item, and see that the circuit is broken. Did the bulb go out?

Task 4: Measure the Battery Voltage While the Circuit Runs

Step 1.   The switch should be turned on and the light bulb should be lit.

Step 2.   What is the voltage of the battery with the light bulb on?

Task 5: Add the Second Bulb to the Series and Measure the Battery Voltage Again

What is the voltage of the battery with the light bulbs on?

_____

Reflection

How do series circuits apply to networking?

_____
_____
_____

Curriculum Lab 3-5: Communications Circuits (3.1.9a)

Objective

- Design, build, and test a simple, complete, fast, and reliable communications system using common materials.

Background/Preparation

For reliable communications to take place on a network, you must define many things ahead of time, including the physical method of signaling and the meaning of each signal or series of signals. With this lab, you create a simple physical network and agree on some basic rules for communication to send and receive data. You will base this digital network on the American Standard Code for Information Interchange (ASCII). It will be somewhat similar to the old telegraph Morse-code systems, where the only means of communicating over long distances was by sending a series of dots and dashes as electrical signals over wires between locations. Although the technology is simpler than that of real systems, you learn many of the key concepts of data communications between computers. This lab also helps clarify the functions of the layers of the OSI model.

Prior to starting the lab, the teacher or lab assistant should have several multimeters available (one for each team of students) and various items for the construction of a simple communication network. Work in teams of two to four.

Table 3-11 lists the required resources. Review the purpose of each of the required items because it will help in designing your network.

Table 3-11 Required Network Construction Items

Network Construction Item Required	Purpose
Fluke 110 or 12B multimeter (or equivalent)	For testing communications connections
20' Category 5 UTP cable cabling medium) ASCII chart (If you do not have a hard copy of the 7-bit ASCII code chart, search the Internet for the words "ACSII chart," and you will find several.)	For the physical communications lines (the To help with coding and interpretation of signals
Light switch	To activate the signaling device to create the digital on/off (binary) signals

continues

Table 3-11   Required Network Construction Items *continued*

Network Construction Item Required	Purpose
Light bulbs (6 V) with bulb bases	To act as the signaling device
6 V lantern battery	To power the signaling device
Wire cutters and stripper	To adjust the length and prepare the ends of the communication lines

Lab Goals

Your group must design, build, and test a communications circuit with another team. You must communicate as much data as possible, as quickly and as error-free as possible. Spoken, written, or miscellaneous nonverbal communication of any kind is forbidden; you communicate only over the wire. You will agree as a team on the physical connections and on the coding you will use. One of the main goals is to send a message to the other team and have it interpret what you intended without it knowing the message ahead of time. Keep the OSI model in mind as you design your system.

- **Layer 1 issues**—You must connect two pairs of wire to have communication in both directions (half or full duplex).

- **Layer 2 issues**—You must communicate some sort of frame start and stop sequence. This sequence of bits is different from the character and number bits you will be transmitting.

- **Layer 3 issues**—You must invent an addressing scheme (for hosts and networks) if it is more than point-to-point communication.

- **Layer 4 issues**—You must include some form of control to regulate quality of service (QoS) (such as error correction, acknowledgment, windowing, flow controls, and so on).

- **Layer 5 issues**—You must implement some way of synchronizing or pausing long conversations.

- **Layer 6 issues**—You must use some means of data representation (for example, ASCII encoded as optical bits).

- **Layer 7 issues**—You must be able to communicate an idea supplied by your instructor or come up with a message on your own.

Reflection

1. What issues arose as you built your communications system that you think apply to data communications between computers?

    _____

    _____

    _____

    _____

    _____

    _____

2. Analyze your communications system in terms of the OSI layers.

    _____

    _____

    _____

    _____

    _____

    _____

_____
_____
_____
_____

Curriculum Lab 3-6: Fluke 620 Basic Cable Testing (3.1.9b)

Figure 3-14   Fluke 620 LAN CableMeter

Objectives

- Use a simple cable tester to verify whether a straight-through or crossover cable is good or bad.

- Use the Fluke 620 advanced cable tester to test cables for length and connectivity.

Background/Preparation

In this lab, you work with several prepared cables and test them for basic continuity (breaks in wires) and shorts (two or more wires touching) using a basic cable tester. You will create similar cables in the future labs.

Simple cable testers—A number of simple and inexpensive basic cable testers are available (less than $100). They usually consist of one or two small boxes with RJ-45 jacks to plug the cables into. Many models test only Ethernet UTP cable. Plug both ends of the cable into the proper jacks; the tester will test all eight wires and indicate whether the cable is good or bad. Simple testers might just have a single light to indicate the cable is good or bad; others might have eight lights to tell you which wire is bad. These testers, which have internal batteries, are performing continuity checks on the wires.

Advanced cable testers—Advanced cable testers, such as the Fluke 620 LAN CableMeter, perform basic cable-testing functions and more. The Fluke 620 advanced cable testers can cost from hundreds to thousands of dollars. You will use an advanced cable tester in future labs to do wire maps and so on. The 620 LAN CableMeter verifies connectivity for all LAN cable types. This rugged tester can measure cable length; test for faults such as opens, shorts, reversed, crossed, or split pairs; and show the distance to the defect. Each 620 LAN CableMeter comes with one cable identifier.

The Fluke 620 has the following characteristics:

- Requires only single-person verification

- Tests all LAN cable types: UTP, STP, FTP, and coaxial

- Detects a multitude of wiring problems: open, short, crossed, reversed, and split pair

- Locates wiring and connection errors (distance to the open or short)

- Measures cable length

Prior to starting the lab, the teacher or lab assistant should have several basic cable testers or several Fluke CableMeters and various lengths of wire with induced problems. Work in teams of two. You need the following resources:

- Basic cable tester

- Advanced cable tester (Fluke 620 or equivalent)

- Two good Category 5 or higher cables—one crossover and one straight-through

- Two bad Category 5 or higher cables—one with a break and one with a short (use different colors or labels)

Task 1: Test the Cables

Simple cable tester—Refer to the instructions from the manufacturer and insert the ends of the cable to be tested into the jacks accordingly.

Fluke 620—Insert the RJ-45 from one end of the cable into the UTP/FTP jack on the tester and turn the dial to test. Test all conductors to verify they are not broken or shorted. (Note: This test does not verify that the pins are connected correctly from one end to the other.)

For each test, insert the cable into the RJ-45 jacks of the cable tester and record your results in Table 3-12.

Table 3-12   Cable Test Results

Color or Cable Number	Category Type	Straight-Through or Crossover?	Length of Cable	Test Results Pass/Fail
Cable 1				
Cable 2				
Cable 3				
Cable 4				

Curriculum Lab 3-7: Straight-Through Cable Construction (3.1.9c)

Figure 3-15   Straight-Through Cable

Objectives

- Build a Category 5 or Category 5e (CAT 5 or 5e) UTP Ethernet network patch cable (or patch cord).

- Test the cable for good connections (continuity) and correct pinouts (correct color of wire on the right pin).

Background/Preparation

The cable constructed will be a four-pair (eight-wire) straight-through cable, which means that the color of wire on pin 1 on one end of the cable will be the same as that of pin 1 on the other end. Pin 2 will be the same as pin 2, and so on. You will wire the cable to either TIA/EIA-568-B or A standards for 10BASE-T Ethernet, which determines what color wire is on each pin. T-568-B (also called AT&T specification) is more common in the U.S., but many installations are also wired to T-568-A (also called ISDN).

Prior to starting the lab, the teacher or lab assistant should have a spool of Category 5 UTP cable, RJ-45 (8-pin) connectors, an RJ-45 crimping tool, and an Ethernet/RJ-45 continuity tester available. Work individually or in teams. You need the following resources:

- Two- to three-foot length of Category 5 cabling (one per person or one per team)

- Four RJ-45 connectors (two extra for spares)

- RJ-45 crimping tools to attach the RJ-45 connectors to the cable ends

- Ethernet cabling continuity tester that can test straight-through or crossover cables (T-568-A or T-568-B)

- Wire cutters

Figure 3-16 shows the wire color scheme for both the T-568-A and T-568-B wiring standards. Table 3-13 provides the cabling pinout information for the T-568-B wiring standard.

Figure 3-16   T-568-A and T-568-B Wire Colors

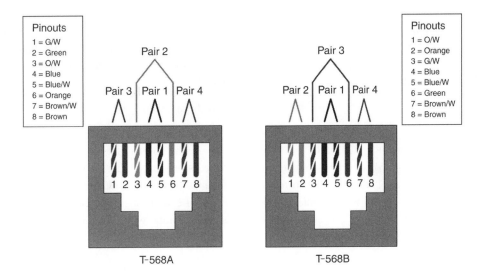

Table 3-13   T-568-B Cabling Pinout

Pin No.	Pair No.	Function	Color	Used with 10/100BASE-T Ethernet?	Used with 100BASE-T4 and 1000BASE-T4 Ethernet?
1	2	Transmit	White/orange	Yes	Yes
2	2	Transmit	Orange	Yes	Yes
3	3	Receive	White/green	Yes	Yes
4	1	Not used	Blue	No	Yes
5	1	Not used	White/blue	No	Yes
6	3	Receive	Green	Yes	Yes
7	4	Not used	White/brown	No	Yes
8	4	Not used	Brown	No	Yes

Steps

Use Figure 3-16 and Table 3-13 to create a T-568-B patch panel cable. You should wire both cable ends the same when looking at the conductors.

Step 1.   Determine the distance between devices, or device and plug, and then add at least 12" to it. According to TIA/EIA structured wiring standards, the maximum length for this cable is 3 meters, although it can vary somewhat. Standard lengths are 6' and 10'.

Step 2.   Cut a piece of stranded Category 5 UTP cable to the desired length. Use stranded cable for patch cables because it is more durable when bent repeatedly. Solid wire is fine for cable runs that are punched down into jacks.

Step 3.   Strip 2" of the jacket off of one end of the cable.

Step 4.   Hold the four pairs of twisted cables tightly where the jacket was cut away and then reorganize the cable pairs into the order of the T-568-B wiring standard. Take care to maintain as much of the twist as possible because it provides noise cancellation.

Step 5.   Holding the jacket and cable in one hand, untwist a short length of the green and blue pairs and reorder them to reflect the T-568-B wiring color scheme. Untwist and order the rest of the wire pairs according to the color scheme.

Step 6.   Flatten, straighten, and line up the wires and then trim them in a straight line to within 1/2" to 3/4" from the edge of the jacket. Be sure not to let go of the jacket and the wires, which are now in the proper order! Minimize the length of untwisted wires because overly long sections near connectors are a primary source of electrical noise.

Step 7.   Place an RJ-45 plug on the end of the cable, with the prong (clip) on the underside and the orange pair to the left side of the connector.

Step 8.   Gently push the plug on to wires until you can see the copper ends of the wires through the end of the plug. Make sure that the end of the jacket is inside the plug (to provide for stress relief) and that all wires are in the correct order. If the jacket is not inside the plug, it will not be properly gripped and will eventually cause problems. If everything is correct, crimp the plug hard enough to force the contacts through the insulation on the wires, as shown in Figure 3-17, thus completing the conducting path.

Figure 3-17 Crimping the Wires

Step 9. Repeat Steps 3 through 8 to terminate the other end of the cable using the same scheme to finish the straight-through cable.

Step 10. Test the finished cable and have the instructor check it. How can you tell whether your cable is functioning properly?

_____

_____

_____

_____

_____

_____

_____

_____

_____

_____

_____

_____

_____

_____

Curriculum Lab 3-8: Rollover Cable Construction (3.1.9d)

Objectives

- Build a Category 5 or Category 5e (CAT 5 or 5e) UTP console rollover cable.

- Test the cable for good connections (continuity) and correct pinouts (correct wire on the right pin).

Background/Preparation

This cable will be a four-pair (eight-wire) _rollover_ cable. This type of cable is typically 10 feet long, but it can be as long as 25 feet. You can use it to connect a workstation or dumb terminal to the console port on the back of a Cisco router or switch. Both ends of the cable you build will have RJ-45 connectors on them. One end plugs directly in to the RJ-45 console-management port on the back of the router or switch, and the other end plugs in to an RJ-45-to-DB9 terminal adapter. This adapter converts the RJ-45 to a 9-pin female D connector for attachment to the PC or dumb-terminal serial (COM) port. A DB25 terminal adapter is also available to connect with a PC or dumb terminal, which uses a 25-pin connector. Figure 3-18 shows a (rollover) console cable kit that ships with most Cisco devices.

Figure 3-18   Rollover Console Cable Kit

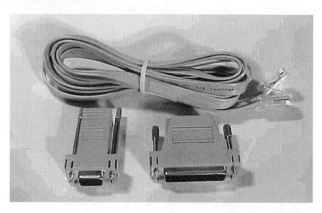

For all practical purposes, if you put the second RJ-45 on upside-down when you build a straight-through jumper, you have a rollover cable. It's called a rollover cable because the pins on one end are all reversed on the other end, as if you rotated or rolled over one end of the cable.

Prior to starting the lab, the teacher or lab assistant should have a spool of Category 5 or 5e UTP cable, RJ-45 (8-pin) connectors, an RJ-45 crimping tool, and a continuity tester. Work individually or in teams. You need the following resources:

- Ten- to 20-foot length of Category 5 cabling (one per person or one per team)

- Four RJ-45 connectors (two extra for spares)

- RJ-45 crimping tools to attach the RJ-45 connectors to the cable ends

- An RJ-45 to DB9 female terminal adapter (available from Cisco)

- Cabling continuity tester

- Wire cutters

Steps

Step 1.   Use Table 3-14 as a reference to help you create a rollover console cable.

Table 3-14   Rollover Console Cable Information

Router or Switch Console Port (DTE)	RJ-45 to RJ-45 Rollover Cable (Left End)	RJ-45 to RJ-45 Rollover Cable (Right End)	RJ-45 to DB9 Adapter	Console Device (PC Workstation Serial Port)
Signal	From RJ-45 Pin Number	To RJ-45 Pin Number	DB9 Pin Number	Signal
RTS	1	8	8	CTS
DTR	2	7	6	DSR
TxD	3	6	2	RxD
GND	4	5	5	GND
GND	5	4	5	GND
RxD	6	3	3	TxD
DSR	7	2	4	DTR
CTS	8	1	7	RTS

Signal legend—RTS = Request to Send, DTR = Data Terminal Ready, TxD = Transmit Data, GND = Ground (one for TxD and one for RxD), RxD = Receive Data, DSR = Data Set Ready, CTS = Clear to Send

Step 2. Determine the distance between devices and then add at least 12" to it. Make your cable about 10" unless you are connecting to a router or switch from a greater distance. The maximum length for this cable is about 8 m (approximately 25").

Step 3. Strip 2" of the jacket off of one end of the cable.

Step 4. Hold the four pairs of twisted cables tightly where jacket was cut away and then reorganize the cable pairs and wires into the order of the T-568-B wiring standard. You can order them in any sequence, but use the T-568-B sequence to become more familiar with it.

Step 5. Flatten, straighten, and line up the wires and then trim them in a straight line to within 1/2" to 3/4" from the edge of the jacket. Be sure not to let go of the jacket and the wires, which are now in order!

Step 6. Place an RJ-45 plug on the end of the cable, with the prong on the underside and the orange pair to the left side of the connector.

Step 7. Gently push the plug on to wires until you can see the copper ends of the wires through the end of the plug. Make sure that the end of the jacket is inside the plug and that all the wires are in the correct order. If the jacket is not inside the plug, it will not be properly protected from stress and will eventually cause problems.

Step 8. If everything is correct, crimp the plug hard enough to force the contacts through the insulation on the wires, thus completing the conducting path.

Step 9. Repeat Steps 2 through 6 to terminate the other end of the cable but reverse every wire as indicated in Table 3-14 (pin 1 to pin 8, pin 2 to pin 7, pin 3 to pin 6, and so on).

Alternate method: Arrange the wires into the order of the T-568-B wiring standard. Place a RJ-45 plug on the end with the prong on the top side of the connector. This method achieves the proper reversing of every pair of wires.

Step 10. Test the finished cable and have the instructor check it. How can you tell whether your cable is functioning properly?

_____
_____
_____
_____
_____
_____
_____
_____
_____
_____
_____

Curriculum Lab 3-9: Crossover Cable Construction (3.1.9e)

Objectives

- Build a Category 5 or Category 5e (CAT 5 or 5e) UTP Ethernet crossover cable to T-568-B and T-568-A standards.

- Test the cable for good connections (continuity) and correct pinouts (correct wire on the right pin).

Background/Preparation

This cable will be a four-pair (eight-wire) crossover cable, which means that pairs 2 and 3 on one end of the cable are reversed on the other end. The pinouts will be T-568-A on one end and T-568-B on the other end. Terminate all eight conductors (wires) with RJ-45 modular connectors.

This patch cable will conform to the structured cabling standards. If you use it between hubs or switches, it is part of the "vertical" cabling, also known as a backbone cable. You can use a crossover cable as a backbone cable to connect two or more hubs or switches in a LAN or to connect two isolated workstations to create a mini-LAN. This setup allows you to connect two workstations or a server and a workstation without the need for a hub between them. Such a connection can be helpful for training and testing. If you want to connect more than two workstations, you need a hub or a switch.

Prior to starting the lab, the teacher or lab assistant should have a spool of Category 5 or 5e UTP cable, RJ-45 (8-pin) connectors, an RJ-45 crimping tool, and an Ethernet/RJ-45 continuity tester. Work individually or in teams. You need the following resources:

- Two- to three-foot length of Category 5 cabling (one per person or one per team)
- Four RJ-45 connectors (two extra for spares)
- RJ-45 crimping tools to attach the RJ-45 connectors to the cable ends
- Ethernet cabling continuity tester that can test crossover cables (T-568-A to T-568-B)
- Wire cutters

Steps

Step 1.   Refer to Table 3-15 and Table 3-16 as well as Figure 3-19 and follow the steps to create a crossover cable. You should wire one end of the cable to the T-568-A standard and the other end to the T-568-B standard. This setup crosses the transmit and receive pairs (2 and 3) to allow communication to take place.

You use only four wires with 10BASE-T or 100BASE-TX Ethernet.

Table 3-15   T-568-A Cabling Pinout

Pin No.	Pair No.	Function	Color	Used with 10/100BASE-T Ethernet?	Used with 100BASE-T4 and 1000BASE-T4 Ethernet?
1	3	Transmit	White/green	Yes	Yes
2	3	Transmit	Green	Yes	Yes
3	2	Receive	White/orange	Yes	Yes
4	1	Not used	Blue	No	Yes
5	1	Not used	White/blue	No	Yes
6	2	Receive	Orange	Yes	Yes
7	4	Not used	White/brown	No	Yes
8	4	Not used	Brown	No	Yes

Table 3-16   T-568-B Cabling Pinout

Pin No.	Pair No.	Function	Color	Used with 10/100BASE-T Ethernet?	Used with 100BASE-T4 and 1000BASE-T4 Ethernet?
1	2	Transmit	White/orange	Yes	Yes
2	2	Transmit	Orange	Yes	Yes
3	3	Receive	White/green	Yes	Yes
4	1	Not used	Blue	No	Yes
5	1	Not used	White/blue	No	Yes
6	3	Receive	Green	Yes	Yes
7	4	Not used	White/brown	No	Yes
8	4	Not used	Brown	No	Yes

Figure 3-19   T-568-A and T-568-B Wire Colors

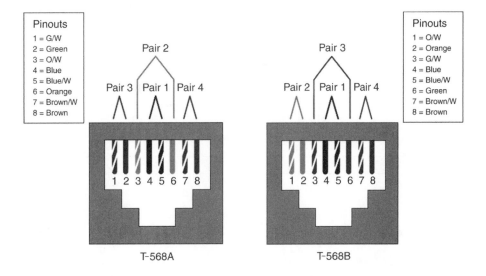

Step 2.   Determine the distance between devices, or between device and plug, and then add at least 12" to it. Standard lengths for this cable are 6' and 10'.

Step 3.   Cut a piece of stranded UTP cable to the desired length. You use stranded cable for patch cables because it is more durable when bent repeatedly. Solid wire is fine for cable runs that are punched down into jacks.

Step 4.   Strip 2" of the jacket off one end of the cable.

Step 5.   Hold the four pairs of twisted cables tightly where the jacket was cut away and then reorganize the cable pairs into the order of the T-568-B wiring standard. Take care to maintain the twist because it provides noise cancellation.

Step 6.   Hold the jacket and cable in one hand, untwist a short length of the green and blue pairs, and reorder them to reflect the T-568-B wiring color scheme. Untwist and order the rest of the wire pairs according to the color scheme.

Step 7.   Flatten, straighten, and line up the wires and then trim them in a straight line to within 1/2" to 3/4" from the edge of the jacket. Be sure not to let go of the jacket and the wires, which are now in order! Minimize the length of untwisted wires because overly long sections near connectors are a primary source of electrical noise.

Step 8.   Place an RJ-45 plug, prong down, on the end of the cable with the green pair on the left side of the T-568-A end and the orange pair on the left side of the T-568-B end.

Step 9.   Gently push the plug on to wires until you can see the copper ends of the wires through the end of the plug. Make sure that the end of the jacket is inside the plug and that all wires are in the correct order. If the jacket is not inside the plug, it will not be protected from stress and will eventually cause problems.

Step 10.   If everything is correct, crimp the plug hard enough to force the contacts through the insulation on the wires, thus completing the conducting path.

Step 11.   Repeat Steps 4 through 8 to terminate the other end of the cable using the T-568-A scheme to finish the crossover cable.

Step 12.   Test the finished cable and have the instructor check it. How can you tell whether your cable is functioning properly?

_____
_____
_____
_____
_____
_____
_____
_____
_____
_____
_____
_____
_____

Curriculum Lab 3-10: UTP Cable Purchase (3.1.9f)

Objectives

- Introduce the variety and prices of network cabling and components in the market.

- Gather pricing information for UTP patch cables and bulk cable.

Background/Preparation

You must put together a price list for an upcoming cabling project. You need to gather pricing information for the horizontal (UTP) cabling. If your area does not use UTP, substitute shielded products. The items include the following:

- Twenty-four 1 m (3 feet) Category 5 or higher UTP patch cables

- Twenty-four 3 m (10 feet) Category 5 or higher UTP patch cables

- Two 15 m (50 feet) Category 5 or higher UTP patch cables

- Five-hundred feet of UTP (compare the price to STP)

- Five-hundred feet of UTP plenum

Task 1: Research Cable Pricing

Use at least three sources for pricing. If you do web searches, try **http://www.cdw.com** and **http://www.google.com**, plus any others you prefer. Perform searches from those sites looking for **CAT 5 jumpers**, **CAT 5 patch**, and **CAT 5 bulk**. Although the CDW site quickly gives you prices, the Google search turns up many interesting sites, from custom cable-building firms to instructions for building your own cables. You might also refer to networking equipment and supplies catalogs.

Task 2: Compile Your Results in Table 3-17

Table 3-17   UTP Cable Pricing Results

Site, Catalog, or Store
Twenty-four 1 m (3 feet) **Category 5 or higher**
Twenty-four 3 m (10 feet) **Category 5 or higher**
Two 15 m (50 feet) **Category 5 or higher**
500 feet of UTP
500 feet of STP
500 feet of UTP plenum

Curriculum Lab 3-11: Fiber-Optic Cable Purchase (3.2.8)

Objectives

- Introduce the variety and prices of network cabling and components in the market.

- Gather pricing information for fiber patch cables and fiber bulk cable.

Background/Preparation

You must put together a price list for an upcoming cabling project. You need to gather pricing information for the vertical or fiber cabling. You will be using multimode (MM) fiber. The items include the following:

- Twenty-four 2 m (6 feet) MM patch cables

- Twenty-four 5 m (15 feet) MM patch cables

- Two 15 m (50 feet) MM patch cables

- One-thousand feet of MM fiber-optic bulk cable

Task 1: Research Cable Pricing

Use at least three sources for pricing. If you do web searches, try **http://www.cdw.com** and **http://www.google.com**, plus any others you prefer. Perform searches from those sites looking for **fiber-optic jumpers**, **fiber-optic patch**, and **fiber-optic bulk**. Although the CDW site quickly gives you prices, a Google search turns up many interesting sites, from custom cable-building firms to instructions for building your own cables. You can also refer to networking equipment and supplies catalogs.

Task 2: Compile Your Results in Table 3-18

Table 3-18   Fiber-Optic Cable Pricing Results

Site, catalog, or store
Twenty-four 2 m (6 feet) MM patch cables
Twenty-four 5 m (15 feet) MM patch cables
Two 15 m (50 feet) MM patch cables
One-thousand feet of MM fiber-optic cable

Comprehensive Lab 3-12: Testing a Crossover Cable

Objectives

- Identify TCP/IP settings of networked PCs.

- Test a crossover cable by connecting two PCs and passing ping traffic between the hosts.

Background

Commonly, crossover cables directly connect two computers and create a peer-to-peer network. Computers on a peer-to-peer network share similar TCP/IP configurations and can reliably communicate with one another. Crossover cables allow this to happen by reversing transmit and receive pairs on each computer.

Creating a two-computer, direct-connection network can also be used to test the functionality of a crossover cable. Successfully passing data from one computer across the cable to another computer confirms that the crossover cable works properly.

Note: It is recommended that you use the crossover cable you created in Lab 3-9 to complete this lab.

Task 1: Verify Functionality of Two Computers

Choose two computers to be connected to one another using a crossover cable. Ensure that each computer is functioning correctly and is able to connect to the Internet. Be sure that the computers are close enough to one another to be connected with a crossover cable.

Task 2: Gather TCP/IP Configuration Information

You must identify the TCP/IP settings on each computer before continuing with the lab. Determine the operating system (OS) used on each computer. If the computer is using Windows 95/98/Me, choose **Start > Run** to open the Run dialog box. Type **winipcfg** and press **Enter**. You see an IP Configuration screen similar to Figure 3-20. Choose the correct adapter from the available list.

Figure 3-20   Windows 95/98/Me IP Configuration Screen

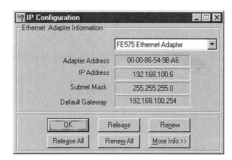

If the computer is using Windows NT/2000/XP, choose **Start > Programs > Accessories > Command Prompt** or **Start > Programs > Command Prompt**. Type **ipconfig** and press **Enter** on the Command Prompt screen. Figure 3-21 shows the Command Prompt screen.

Figure 3-21   Windows NT/2000/XP ipconfig Results

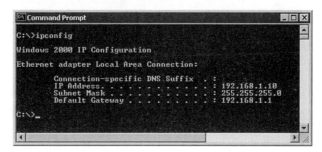

Record the TCP/IP settings for each computer:

Host A

IP address: _____

Subnet mask: _____

Default gateway: _____

Host B

IP address: _____

Subnet mask: _____

Default gateway: _____

Confirm that the IP addresses are similar and that each computer is using the same subnet mask and default gateway.

Note: If the subnet mask is 255.255.255.0, the IP addresses of the two computers should have the same numbers in the first three octets. If the subnet mask is 255.0.0.0 or 255.255.0.0, the IP addresses should have the same numbers in the first or first two octets. If this is not the case, ask your instructor for assistance.

Task 3: Connect the Computers

Carefully disconnect the cable from the network interface card (NIC) of each computer. Mark the cable end to ensure that the proper cable is reconnected at the end of the lab.

Connect the computers using the crossover cable.

Task 4: Verify Connectivity Using the Crossover Cable

Access the command prompt on Host A. If it is using Windows 95/98/Me, choose **Start > Programs > Accessories > MS-DOS Prompt** or **Start > Programs > MS-DOS**. If it is using Windows NT/2000/XP, choose **Start > Programs > Accessories > Command Prompt** or **Start > Programs > Command Prompt**.

From the command prompt, type **ping** followed by the IP address of host B. Figure 3-22 shows the successful results of pinging this IP address.

Figure 3-22   Successful Ping Results

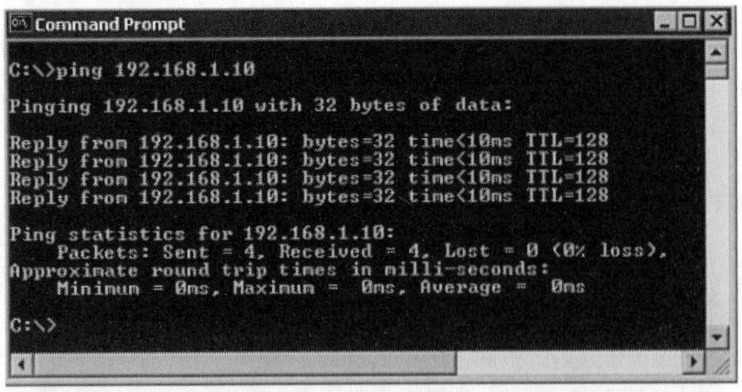

A successful ping verifies Layer 3 connectivity between the computers and a functional crossover cable. If the ping attempt is unsuccessful, the crossover cable might not be functional. Troubleshoot the cable and TCP/IP settings.

Task 5: Reconnect the Computers to the Network

Remove the crossover cable and reconnect the proper cable ends to the computer NICs. Ensure that each computer can connect to the Internet.

Challenge Lab 3-13: Creating a Cable Converter

Objective

■ Create an adapter to convert a straight-through cable to a crossover cable.

Background

Straight-through cables are the most common type of four-pair copper cables used today. Straight-through cables are used extensively in LANs to connect computers to network devices and interconnect network devices. Crossover cables are not as common in LANs. Crossover cables connect similar devices and create two computer peer-to-peer networks. Crossover cables can also serve as useful troubleshooting and testing tools. Because most networking professionals have a generous amount of straight-through cables at their disposal at any given time, having an adapter that can be used to temporarily convert one of these cables to a crossover cable can be beneficial.

Task 1: Gather Resources

You need the following items to create and test the cable converter:

- Single one-foot length of CAT 5 cabling

- One RJ-45 connector

- RJ-45 preparation tools (wire cutter, stripper, and so on)

- RJ-45 crimping tools

- One RJ-45 modular jack

- One complete straight-through cable

- Ethernet cabling continuity tester that can test crossover cables (T-568-A to T-568-B)

Task 2: Terminate the RJ-45 Connector

Use cabling best practices to terminate one end of the Category 5 cable with the RJ-45 connector using the T-568-A standard.

Task 3: Terminate the RJ-45 Modular Jack

Following the manufacturer's instructions, terminate the opposite end of the Category 5 cable with the modular jack using the TIA/EIA-568-B standard.

Note: Modular jacks are commonly used in telecommunications rooms and at network wall outlets.

Task 4: Test the Cable Converter

Connect the converter to the straight-through cable by plugging one end of the straight-through cable in to the modular jack of the converter. Use the continuity tester to test from the free end of the straight-through cable to the RJ-45 plug end of the converter. The test should show a functional crossover cable. If the test is not successful, troubleshoot the cable converter. Verify that the modular jack is configured and installed according to the manufacturer's instructions.

Reflection

What other type of copper cable converters would be useful for networking professionals?

CHAPTER 4

Cable Testing

The Study Guide portion of this chapter uses a combination of matching, fill in the blank, and open-ended question exercises to test your knowledge of frequency-based cable testing, signals, and noise.

The Lab Exercises portion of this chapter includes all the online curriculum labs to ensure that you have mastered the practical, hands-on skills needed to test cables.

As you work through this chapter, use Module 4 in the CCNA 1 online curriculum or use the corresponding Chapter 4 in the *Networking Basics CCNA 1 Companion Guide* for assistance.

Study Guide

Frequency-Based Cable Testing

Frequency-based cable testing evaluates the properties of waves to determine the effectiveness of the communication media. Understanding this type of testing procedure requires an understanding of different wave types, their common and unique properties, and the tools and methods used to measure these properties. Frequency-based cable analysis is key to evaluate the strength of analog and digital signals, determine the influence of noise on a cable, and determine potential bandwidth.

This section includes exercises that help you identify signal attributes, determine the types of waves used in information networking, and calculate power gain or loss across a communication circuit.

Vocabulary Exercise: Completion

Complete the following statements by using the proper terms to fill in the blanks.

The _____ of the waves is the amount of time between each wave, measured in seconds.

An electronic device called a _____ creates graphs for frequency-domain analysis.

Noise that equally affects all transmission frequencies is called _____.

The maximum value of an analog or a digital waveform is known as _____.

_____, measured in hertz (Hz), is the number of waves per second or cycles per second.

_____, or sinusoids, are graphs of mathematical functions that vary continuously.

_____ are periodic waves that represent digital signals by maintaining one value and suddenly changing to a different value.

The loss or gain of power in a wave is measured in _____.

Time-domain analysis is performed with an _____ that visually traces fluctuations in voltage and current over time.

If a disturbance is deliberately caused and involves a fixed, predictable duration, it is called a _____.

The location of a position on an alternating waveform is known as the _____.

Concept Questions

Completely answer the following questions:

1. Understanding network communications requires an understanding of waves and the methods used to measure them. What common terms describe waves?

   _____

   ■ _____

   _____

   ■ _____

   ■ _____

2. How are number systems created? What are the most common number systems used in information networking?

    _____

    _____

    _____

    _____

3. Changes in power from source to destination are measured in decibels (dB). What is a reference power level, and why is it necessary to calculate gain or loss?

    _____

    _____

    _____

    _____

4. Amplitude, frequency, and phase modulation are used in many modern telecommunications technologies. Explain each type of modulation and list a telecommunication technology that is based on the modulation.

    _____

    _____

    _____

    _____

    _____

    _____

    _____

5. What is the difference between white noise and narrowband noise? What is a potential cause of each type of noise?

    _____

    _____

    _____

    _____

6. What are the differences between analog bandwidth and digital bandwidth?

    _____

    _____

    _____

    _____

    _____

Signal Types Exercise

Analog and digital signals are used extensively in information networking. Both transmission types can carry data and share similar properties. A major difference between analog and digital signals is the wave type used to carry the information. Analog signals use a sine wave that varies continuously over time. Digital signals follow a more uniform square wave model.

Complete Figure 4-1 by drawing a sine wave and labeling the amplitude and period of the wave. Complete Figure 4-2 by drawing a comparable square wave and labeling the same components of the wave.

Figure 4-1   Sketch and Label a Sine Wave

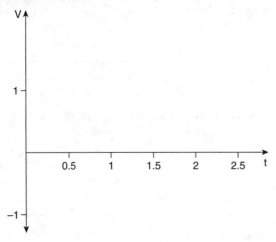

Figure 4-2   Sketch and Label a Square Wave

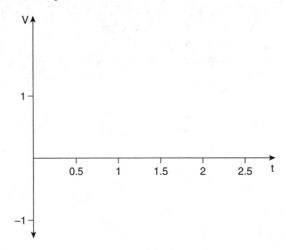

Calculating Power Loss or Gain Exercise

The decibel (dB) is perhaps most familiar as a measure of sound intensity. It is also used to describe all networking signals, whether voltage waves on copper, optical pulses in fiber, or microwaves in a wireless system. The following formulas use beginning (ref) and ending (final) power (P) and voltage (V) measurements to calculate the loss or gain of power and voltage as a wave travels from its source to destination.

$dB = 10 \log_{10} (P_{final} / P_{ref})$ calculates power loss or gain.

$dB = 20 \log_{10} (V_{final} / V_{ref})$ calculates voltage loss or gain.

In these formulas, dB represents the loss or gain of the power of a wave. Decibels can be negative values, which represent a loss in power as the wave travels, or a positive value, which represents a gain in power if the signal is amplified.

Use the formulas to calculate the power loss or gain in the following problems:

1. One volt was measured at the end of a cable. The source voltage was 5 volts. What is the gain or loss in decibels?

_____

_____

2. A cable with a source voltage of 100 millivolts has a voltage of 112 millivolts at the end. What is the gain or loss in decibels?

_____

_____

_____

3. Eighty-eight milliwatts were measured at the end of a cable. The source power was 107 milliwatts. What is the gain or loss in decibels?

_____

_____

_____

4. If the maximum amount of loss can be no more than 3 dB, what voltage must be sent to ensure that 5 volts can be measured at the end of a cable?

_____

_____

_____

_____

5. A source LED provides 5 microwatts of power. If the maximum loss is .001 dB, what is the minimum power reading at the end of the multimode cable?

_____

_____

_____

_____

6. One watt was injected into a line and 135 milliwatts were measured at the end. What is the gain or loss in decibels?

_____

_____

_____

7. If 500 milliwatts of power are sourced onto a line with a maximum loss rating of .2 dB, what is the minimum amount of power at the end of the line?

_____

_____

_____

8. A source laser provides 20 microwatts of power. What is the dB loss if 9 microwatts are measured at the end of the single-mode fiber-optic line?

_____

_____

Journal Entry

Bandwidth is defined as the maximum data-carrying capacity of a given network medium. *Throughput* is the rate at which information arrives, and possibly passes through, a particular point in a network system. Bandwidth is limited by the physical characteristics of the medium and the technologies used for data encoding and transmission. Theoretically, the maximum amount of throughput is limited to the maximum bandwidth of the link. Why is throughput always less than the bandwidth in an information network? Explain.

_____

_____

_____

_____

_____

_____

_____

_____

Signals and Noise

In order for a LAN to function properly, the physical layer medium should meet the industry-standard specifications. Following industry-defined cable-testing procedures, network professionals can verify the effectiveness of a cable by comparing test results to the defined standards. Cables that do not meet or exceed these standards do not perform as expected in a LAN environment. Factors that can cause poor test results include wire map faults, improper connector attachments, and cable manufacturing deficiencies. Testing and verifying cable quality is essential to the functionality of an information network.

The exercises in this section increase your knowledge of the cable testing and verification process. These exercises include identifying terms associated with signals and noise, understanding common wire map faults, listing industry-standard testing procedures, and learning the effects of and the methods to combat crosstalk.

Vocabulary Exercise: Matching

Match the definition on the left with a term on the right. This exercise does not necessarily use one-to-one matching. Some definitions might be used more than once and some terms might have multiple definitions.

Definitions

a. A reference point used by computing devices to measure and compare incoming digital signals to.

b. Analog communication line distortion caused by the variation of a signal from its reference timing positions.

c. This type of wiring fault occurs when one wire from one pair is switched with one wire from a different pair at both ends.

d. The delay difference between pairs is a critical parameter for high-speed networks in which data is simultaneously transmitted over multiple wire pairs.

e. This problem occurs if two wires are connected to each other.

f. A device that has the capability to send signals through a network medium to check cable continuity, length, and other attributes.

g. This is computed as the ratio of voltage amplitude between the test signal and the crosstalk signal when measured from the same end of the link.

h. The combination of the effects of signal attenuation and impedance discontinuities on a communications link.

i. A broken path along a transmission medium.

j. This fault occurs when a wire pair is correctly installed on one connector, but reversed on the other connector.

k. A measure (in dB) of reflections that are caused by the impedance discontinuities at all locations along the link.

l. Interfering energy transferred from one circuit to another.

m. Crosstalk occurring further away from the transmitter that creates less noise on a cable than NEXT because of attenuation.

n. A simple measurement of how long it takes for a signal to travel along the cable being tested.

Terms

___ crosstalk

___ split-pair fault

___ return loss

___ propagation delay

___ near-end crosstalk (NEXT)

___ jitter

___ short circuit

___ delay skew

___ signal reference ground

___ far-end crosstalk (FEXT)

___ reversed-pair fault

___ insertion loss

___ time domain reflectometer (TDR)

___ open circuit

Concept Questions

Completely answer the following questions:

1. Signal attenuation can significantly contribute to insertion loss. What are some of the factors that cause attenuation?

    _____

    _____

    _____

    _____

2. Crosstalk involves the transmission of signals from one wire to a nearby wire. How can network professionals keep crosstalk to a minimum when installing network cable?

    _____

    _____

    _____

    _____

    _____

    _____

    _____

    _____

3. What is a wire map test? What types of cabling problems can this test identify? What tools can be used to perform wire mapping?

    _____

    _____

    _____

    _____

    _____

    _____

4. A time domain reflectometer (TDR), sometimes called a cable radar, can perform multiple types of tests on copper and optical cables. How does a TDR work?

    _____

    _____

    _____

    _____

    _____

    _____

    _____

5. The most common problem encountered when testing fiber-optic cables stems from improperly attached connectors. Why are these connectors difficult to install correctly?

_____

_____

_____

_____

_____

_____

6. The standard for Category 6 cable was published in 2002. What tests must be passed to certify a Category 6 cable?

_____

_____

■ _____

■ _____

■ _____

■ _____

■ _____

■ _____

■ _____

■ _____

■ _____

■ _____

■ _____

_____

_____

_____

Wiring Fault Identification Exercise

A wire map test is one of the ten primary tests used to verify cables according to TIA/EIA standards. Wire maps confirm that all eight wires are connected to the correct pins at each end of the cable link. Although multiple tools can perform this type of test, networking professionals should be able to identify different types of faults through a visual inspection of each end of the cable.

Identify and label the TIA/EIA-568-B straight-through cable wiring faults in Figure 4-3. Circle the problem area and label the type of wiring fault underneath each example.

Figure 4-3   Identify the TIA/EIA-568-B Wiring Faults

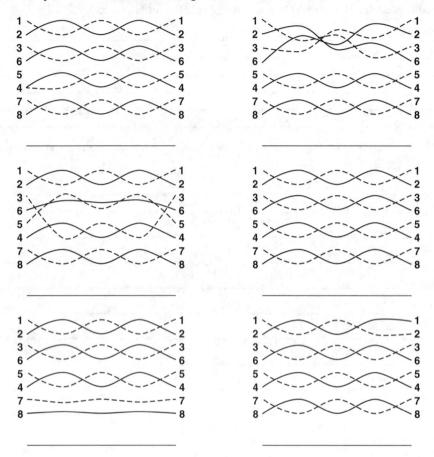

Note: Now is a good time to begin the Chapter 4 labs. Lab 4-1, Lab 4-2, and Lab 4-3 focus on using the Fluke 620 Cable Tester (or equivalent) to verify wire maps, test for faults, and measure wire length in a cable. Lab 4-4 and Lab 4-5 use the Fluke LinkRunner to test cable and network properties.

Journal Entry

Cable manufacturers certify their products through testing based on industry standards. For a cable to certify as a Category 5, 5e, or 6 cable, the physical medium must pass ten tests with scores falling in acceptable ranges.

List and briefly explain each test. Why is it necessary for every network professional to have a basic knowledge of these tests?

- _____
  _____
- _____
  _____
  _____
  _____
- _____
  _____
  _____

- _____
  _____
- _____
  _____
  _____
- _____
  _____
- _____
  _____
- _____
  _____
- _____
  _____
- _____
  _____
  _____

_____
_____
_____
_____

Lab Exercises

Curriculum Lab 4-1: Fluke 620 Cable Tester—Wire Map (4.2.9a)

Figure 4-4   Fluke 620 LAN CableMeter

Objectives

- Learn the wire-mapping features of the Fluke 620 LAN CableMeter (or its equivalent).

- Learn how to use a cable tester to check for the proper installation of unshielded twisted-pair (UTP) Category 5 cable according to Telecommunications Industry Association/Electronic Industries Association (TIA/EIA)-568 cabling standards in an Ethernet network.

Background/Preparation

Wire maps can help troubleshoot cabling problems with UTP cable. A wire map allows the network technician to verify which pins on one end of the cable are connected to which pins on the other end.

Before starting the lab, the teacher or lab assistant should have several correctly wired Category 5 cables (both straight-through and crossover) to test. Several Category 5 cables should have problems to test, such as poor connections and split pairs. The teacher or lab assistant should number the cables to simplify the testing process and to maintain consistency. You should have access to a cable tester that can test at least continuity, cable length, and wire maps. Work individually or in teams.

You need the following resources:

- Category 5 straight-wired cables of different colors

- Category 5 crossover-wired cable (T-568-A on one end and T-568-B on the other)

- Category 5 straight-wired cables of different colors and different lengths with open-wire connections in the middle or one or more conductors shorted at one end

- Category 5 straight-wired cable with a split-pair miswire

- Fluke 620 LAN CableMeter or similar to test cable length, continuity, and wire maps

Steps

Step 1.   Turn the rotary switch selector on the tester to the **Wire Map** position. Press the **Setup** button to enter setup mode, and observe the LCD screen on the tester. The first option should be Cable: Press the **Up/Down** arrows until you select the cable type **UTP**. Press **Enter** to accept that setting and go to the next one. Continue pressing the **Up/Down** arrows and pressing **Enter** until the tester is set to the cabling characteristics shown in Table 4-1. After you complete setting up the meter, press the **Setup** button to exit setup mode.

Table 4-1   Fluke 620 Cabling Characteristic Settings

Tester Option	Desired Setting—UTP
Cable	UTP
Wiring	10BASE-T or EIA/TIA 4PR
Category	CAT 5
Wire Size	American wire gauge (AWG) 24
Cal to Cable	No
Beeping	On or Off
LCD Contrast	From 1 through 10 (brightest)

Step 2.   For each cable, use the procedure that follows, placing the near end of the cable into the RJ-45 jack labeled UTP/FTP on the tester. Place the RJ-45-to-RJ-45 female coupler on the far end of the cable and then insert the cable identifier into the other side of the coupler. The coupler and the cable identifier, shown in Figure 4-5, are accessories that come with the Fluke 620 LAN CableMeter.

Figure 4-5   Coupler and Cable Identifier Tools

Step 3.   Using the tester Wire Map function and a cable ID unit, you can determine the wiring of both the near and far ends of the cable. The top set of numbers on the LCD screen is the near end, and the bottom set is the far end. Perform a wire-map test on each of the cables and fill in the following table based on the result for each Category 5 cable. Write down the number and color, whether the cable is straight-through or crossover, the tester screen test results, and what you think the problem is. Record your results in Table 4-2.

Table 4-2   Cable Test Results

Cable Number	Cable Color	How Cable Is Wired (Straight-Through or Crossover)	Tester Displayed Test
Results*	Description		
1			Top: Bot:
2			Top: Bot:
3			Top: Bot:
4			Top: Bot:
5			Top: Bot:

* Refer to the Fluke manual for a detailed description of test results for wire maps.

Curriculum Lab 4-2: Fluke 620 Cable Tester—Faults (4.2.9b)

Figure 4-6   Fluke 620 LAN CableMeter

Objectives

- Learn the cable test pass/fail features of the Fluke 620 LAN CableMeter (or its equivalent).

- Learn how to use a cable tester to check for the proper installation of UTP for an Ethernet network.

- Test different cables to determine some problems that can occur from incorrect cabling installation and termination.

Background/Preparation

Basic cable tests can be helpful in troubleshooting cabling problems with UTP. The cabling infrastructure (or cable plant) in a building is expected to last at least ten years. Cabling-related problems are one of the most common causes of network failure. The quality of cabling components, the routing and installation of the cable, and the quality of the connector terminations are the main factors in determining how trouble-free the cabling will be.

Before starting the lab, the teacher or lab assistant should have several correctly wired Category 5 cables (both straight-through and crossover) to test. Several Category 5 cables should have problems to test. The teacher or lab assistant should number the cables to simplify the testing process and to maintain consistency. You need the following resources:

- Category 5 straight-through and crossover wired cables of different colors (some good and some bad)

- Category 5 straight-through and crossover wired cables of different colors and different lengths with open-wire connections in the middle or one or more conductors shorted at one end

- Cable tester (Fluke 620 LAN CableMeter or similar) to test cable length

Steps

Step 1. Turn the rotary switch selector on the tester to the Test position. Press the **Setup** button to enter setup mode and observe the LCD screen on the tester. The first option should be Cable. Press the **Up/Down** arrows until you select the cable type **UTP**. Press **Enter** to accept that setting and go to the next one. Continue pressing the **Up/Down** arrows and pressing **Enter** until the tester is set to the cabling characteristics shown in Table 4-3. After the options are properly selected, press the **Setup** button to exit setup mode.

Table 4-3   Fluke 620 Cabling Characteristic Settings

Tester Option	Desired Setting—UTP
Cable	UTP
Wiring	10BASE-T or EIA/TIA 4PR
Category	Category 5
Wire Size	AWG 24
Cal to Cable	No
Beeping	On or Off
LCD Contrast	From 1 through 10 (brightest)

Step 2. For each cable, use the procedure that follows, placing the near end of the cable into the RJ-45 jack labeled UTP/FTP on the tester. Place the RJ-45-to-RJ-45 female coupler on the far end of the cable, and then insert the cable identifier into the other side of the coupler. The coupler and the cable identifier are accessories that come with the Fluke 620 LAN CableMeter (see Figure 4-7).

Step 3.   Using the tester Test function and a cable ID unit (for UTP), you can determine the functionality of the cable. Perform a basic cable test on each cable, and fill in Table 4-4 based on the result for each Category 5 cable. Write down the number and color, whether the cable is straight-through, crossover, or coaxial, the tester screen test results, and what you think the problem is. For UTP cables, press the **Up/Down** arrows to see all pairs.

Figure 4-7   Coupler and Cable Identifier Tools

Table 4-4   Cable Test Results

Cable Number	Cable Color	Tester Test Results	Problem
1			
2			
3			
4			

Curriculum Lab 4-3: Fluke 620 Cable Tester—Length (4.2.9c)

Figure 4-8   Fluke 620 LAN CableMeter

Objectives

- Learn the cable-length feature of the Fluke 620 LAN CableMeter (or its equivalent).

- Learn how to use a cable tester to check the length of Ethernet cabling to verify that it is within the standards specified and that the wires inside are the same length.

Background/Preparation

Cable-length tests can be helpful to troubleshoot cabling problems with UTP. The cabling infrastructure (or cable plant) in a building is expected to last at least ten years. Cabling-related problems are one of the most common causes of network failure. The quality of cabling components, the routing and installation of the cable, and the quality of the connector terminations are the main factors in determining how trouble-free the cabling will be.

Before starting the lab, the teacher or lab assistant should have several correctly wired Category 5 cables (both straight-through and crossover) to test. The teacher or lab assistant should number the cables to simplify the testing process and to maintain consistency. You should have access to a cable tester that can do cable-length tests for UTP. Work individually or in teams. You need the following resources:

- Category 5 straight or crossover cables of different colors (some good and some bad)

- Cable tester (Fluke 620 LAN CableMeter or similar) to test cable length

Steps

Step 1.   Turn the rotary switch selector on the tester to the Length position. Press the **Setup** button to enter setup mode, and observe the LCD screen on the tester. The first option should be Cable: Press the **Up/Down** arrows until you select the cable type **UTP**. Press Enter to accept that setting and go to the next one. Continue pressing the **Up/Down** arrows and pressing **Enter** until the tester is set to the cabling characteristics shown in Table 4-5. After the options are properly selected, press the **Setup** button to exit setup mode.

Table 4-5   Fluke 620 Cabling Characteristic Settings

Tester Option	Desired Setting—UTP
Cable	UTP
Wiring	10BASE-T or EIA/TIA 4PR
Category	Category 5
Wire Size	AWG 24
Cal to Cable	No
Beeping	On or Off
LCD Contrast	From 1 through 10 (brightest)

Step 2.   For each cable, use the procedure that follows, placing the near end of the cable into the RJ-45 jack labeled UTP/FTP on the tester. Place the RJ-45-to-RJ-45 female coupler on the far end of the cable and then insert the cable identifier into the other side of the coupler. The coupler and the cable identifier are accessories that come with the Fluke 620 LAN CableMeter (see Figure 4-9).

Figure 4-9   Coupler and Cable Identifier Tools

Step 3.   Using the tester Length function and a UTP cable ID unit, you can determine the length of the cable. Perform a basic cable test on each of the cables, and fill in Table 4-6 based on the result for each cable. Write down the number and color, the cable length, the tester screen test results, and what you think the problem is (if a problem exists). For UTP cables, press the **Up/Down** arrows to see all pairs.

Table 4-6   Cable Test Results

Cable No.	Cable Color	Cable Length	Tester Test Results	Problem
1				
2				
3				
4				

Curriculum Lab 4-4: Fluke LinkRunner—LAN Tests (4.2.9d)

Figure 4-10   Fluke LinkRunner

Objectives

- Become familiar with the capabilities of the Fluke LinkRunner.

- Determine whether a cable drop is active.

- Identify the cable drop speed, duplex capabilities, and service type.

- Verify network layer connectivity with ping.

Background/Preparation

In this lab, you work with Ethernet cable drops that are attached to networking devices, such as hubs and switches, to determine the characteristics and cabling of the devices and identify potential networking problems. You will use some of the key capabilities of the Fluke LinkRunner, such as drop activity and ping, to perform the analysis.

As networks run faster and become more complex, infrastructure cabling and devices must operate to precise levels in a tighter performance window. As a result, nearly 80 percent of network problems stem from simple wiring and connection problems. You need the following resources:

- Ethernet hub and switch

- Several Ethernet straight-through patch cables

- Cable run from a wall plate to a switch through a patch panel

The following URLs provide information on the Fluke LinkRunner. The first one is a virtual demo of LinkRunner capabilities, and the second is a link to the downloadable *LinkRunner Quick Reference Guide* in various languages:

- http://www.flukenetworks.com/us/LAN/Handheld+Testers/LinkRunner/_see+it+live.htm#

- http://www.flukenetworks.com/us/LAN/Handheld+Testers/LinkRunner/_manuals.htm

Task 1: Become Familiar with the Capabilities of the Fluke LinkRunner

Access the virtual demo of the LinkRunner using the first URL. You can try different tests to become familiar with its capabilities.

Task 2: Obtain Access to the LinkRunner Quick Reference Guide

You can directly access the *Quick Reference Guide* online or download it to your PC using the link provided. Your instructor might also have a copy of the *Quick Reference Guide*. This lab reproduces selected pages of the *Quick Reference Guide*. Figure 4-11 shows the connectors and buttons on the LinkRunner.

Figure 4-11   LinkRunner Connectors and Buttons

1. RJ-45 LAN port
2. RJ-45 MAP port
   (cable testing)
3. Selection buttons
   Left – Highlight
   Right – Action
4. Power Button

Power off - press and hold
Backlight – press once briefly

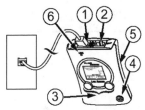

5. Batteries (2) AA
6. Link indicator light

Task 3: Configure the LinkRunner

Step 1.   From any screen, you can access the main configuration by simultaneously pressing both buttons. You have the option to configure LinkRunner or go into the ping configuration.

Step 2.   Press the left button to get to the LinkRunner configuration, where you can find the MAC address of the LinkRunner and toggle between feet and meters.

What is the Layer 2 MAC address?

_____

_____

_____

Pressing the right button takes you to the ping configuration, which is covered later.

Task 4: Test Active Workstation Links to a Switch

Step 1.   LinkRunner allows you to determine to what type of service users are connected (for example, Ethernet, Token Ring, or telco). On Ethernet segments, determine whether the drop is active and identify its speed, duplex capabilities, and autonegotiation settings.

This test determines whether the cable drop is active while identifying its speed, duplex, and service type. (10 or 10/100 indicates Ethernet.)

Step 2.   Turn on the LinkRunner by pressing the small button in the lower-right corner.

Step 3.   Disconnect a functioning LAN patch cable from a workstation and plug it into the RJ-45 LAN port on the LinkRunner. You can perform this nondestructive test on a live network. The cable should be attached to a wall plate, which then attaches to a switch through a patch panel in a wiring closet. Cabling should be in accordance with current structured-cabling standards.

Step 4.   Observe the display on the LinkRunner and record the information for Drop #1 in Table 4-7. Figure 4-12 provides a sample display from the *Quick Reference Guide*.

Step 5.   Obtain another patch cable of any length and plug one end directly into the switch. Plug the other end into the LinkRunner LAN port. Record the information for Drop #2 in Table 4-7.

Table 4-7   LinkRunner Cable Test Results

Link Active?	Cable Type/ Link Status	Advertised Speed/Duplex	Actual Link Speed/Duplex	Network Utilization
Drop #1				
Drop #2				

Figure 4-12   LinkRunner Sample Display

Is this an active Ethernet port?

1. Activity indicator
2. Cable/Link Status:
   ═══ Straight patch
   ⊃⊂ Crossover patch

   ∷x∷ Unknown patch (Auto-MDIX port on hub or switch)
   ⌐⌐! Link Level (displays when low)
3. Advertised speed/duplex
4. Actual link speed/duplex

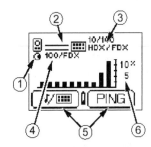

5. Softkeys (correspond to L/R selection buttons).
   ▯ Battery Low Indicator: displays when low.
6. Network utilization

Step 6.   Disconnect the end of the cable from the switch and observe the display. What is the result?

_____

_____

Task 5: Test a Direct Link to a Hub

Step 1.   Obtain another patch cable of any length and plug one end directly into an active regular hub port. Plug the other end into the LinkRunner LAN port. Describe the results.

_____

How does this display differ from that of a cable drop attached to a switch?

_____

_____

Step 2.   Disconnect the power from the hub and describe the display now.

_____

Step 3.   Plug the hub back in.

Step 4.   Move the cable from one of the regular ports on the hub to the uplink port on the hub. Make sure that the uplink is not active. (The button is not pushed in.) Describe the results.

_____

Step 5.   Activate the uplink port. (Push in the button.) What happens to the wires in the display?

_____

Why did this occur?

_____

_____

Task 6: Use the Dynamic Host Configuration Protocol (DHCP) Ping Function to Verify Network Layer Connectivity

If you connect the LAN port in a DHCP network environment, LinkRunner acts as a DHCP client. It acquires an IP address and verifies basic connectivity to key devices by pinging the default gateway (router) and Domain Name System (DNS) server. See Figure 4-13 for a sample of the screen display.

Figure 4-13   LinkRunner Ping Capabilities

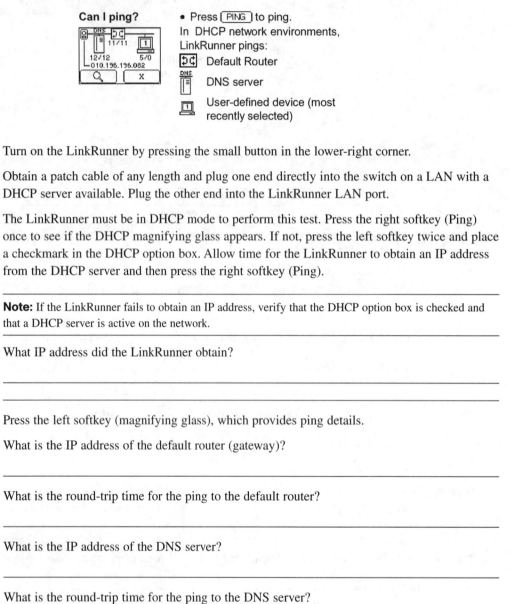

Step 1.   Turn on the LinkRunner by pressing the small button in the lower-right corner.

Step 2.   Obtain a patch cable of any length and plug one end directly into the switch on a LAN with a DHCP server available. Plug the other end into the LinkRunner LAN port.

Step 3.   The LinkRunner must be in DHCP mode to perform this test. Press the right softkey (Ping) once to see if the DHCP magnifying glass appears. If not, press the left softkey twice and place a checkmark in the DHCP option box. Allow time for the LinkRunner to obtain an IP address from the DHCP server and then press the right softkey (Ping).

Note: If the LinkRunner fails to obtain an IP address, verify that the DHCP option box is checked and that a DHCP server is active on the network.

What IP address did the LinkRunner obtain?

_____

_____

Step 4.   Press the left softkey (magnifying glass), which provides ping details.

What is the IP address of the default router (gateway)?

_____

What is the round-trip time for the ping to the default router?

_____

What is the IP address of the DNS server?

_____

What is the round-trip time for the ping to the DNS server?

_____

If one response time is slower than the other, why do you think that it is?

_____

_____

Task 7: Ping a User-Defined IP Address

You can use the LinkRunner to ping user-defined IP addresses (up to four common IP address ping targets). See Figure 4-14 for a sample of the screen display used to edit the IP address for computer target 1.

Figure 4-14   LinkRunner Pings Target

Step 1.   Turn on the LinkRunner by pressing the small button in the lower-right corner.

Step 2.   Disconnect any cables from the LinkRunner.

Step 3.   Press the right softkey (wrench) to access configuration options.

Step 4.   Press the right softkey again (ping and wrench). If you will be working on a network with a DHCP server, turn off the LinkRunner DHCP client by removing the checkmark from the DHCP checkbox. Press the right softkey (checkmark) to uncheck it.

Step 5.   Press the left softkey (down arrow) to get to the computer icon and then press the right softkey (computer, IP, and wrench) to access the IP address configuration function.

Step 6.   Press the right softkey (down arrow and computer) to cycle through the four IP targets. Zero indicates no ping for the computer target. Select IP Target 1.

Step 7.   Press the left softkey (down arrow) to access the IP address, and press the right softkey (IP x.x.x.x) to begin configuring the IP address for target computer 1 (refer to Figure 4-14).

Step 8.   Identify the IP address of a lab server or a partner's workstation and record it here.

_____

Step 9.   Press the left softkey (right arrow) to advance the cursor from one number to the next in the IP address. Press the right softkey (IP and up arrow) to change the value of the number. You must account for all 12 decimal digits, including 0s. While working with the first digit of any of the four octets, press the up arrow four or five times. What is the maximum number that the LinkRunner lets you set for the first number of an octet?

_____

_____

Step 10.   After you finish with the last digit, the left softkey becomes a down arrow. Press the left softkey until you get to the X (exit) and then press the right softkey (X). Press the left softkey (down arrow) again until you get to the X, and press the right softkey again to exit the configuration function.

Step 11.   After you set the IP address to be pinged and exit the configuration function, connect a patch cable from the LAN port on the LinkRunner to a wall-plate jack, hub, or switch on the network you will be pinging. What does the cable display look like?

_____

Step 12.   Press the right softkey (Ping) to start the ping function. You should see a workstation icon with a target number 1 on the screen. Does the workstation have solid lines or dashed lines?

_____

What do you think this means?

_____

_____

_____

_____

Step 13. Press the left softkey (magnifying glass) to see the IP addresses of all the devices being pinged and the round-trip time for each in milliseconds.

Which devices did you ping, and what were the round-trip times for each?

_____

Step 14. Press the right softkey (X) twice to exit the detailed view and ping function.

Task 8: Disconnect the Equipment and Store the Cabling and Devices

Curriculum Lab 4-5: Fluke LinkRunner—Cable and NIC Tests (4.2.9e)

Figure 4-15   Fluke LinkRunner

Objectives

- Become familiar with the capabilities of the Fluke LinkRunner.
- Verify cable length and integrity.
- Determine where a cable terminates.
- Verify PC NIC functionality.

Background/Preparation

In this lab, you work with Ethernet cables to determine their characteristics and identify potential problems. You will use some of the key capabilities of the Fluke LinkRunner, such as cable mapping and NIC testing.

As networks run faster and become more complex, infrastructure cabling and devices must operate to precise levels in a tighter performance window. As a result, nearly 80 percent of network problems stem from simple wiring and connection problems. You need the following resources:

- Ethernet straight-through patch cables (good and bad)

- Ethernet crossover cables

- An Ethernet cable from a wall-plate RJ-45 jack through a patch panel

- A hub or switch

- A computer with a NIC

The following URLs provide information on the Fluke LinkRunner. The first one is a virtual demo of LinkRunner capabilities, and the second is a link to the downloadable *LinkRunner Quick Reference Guide* in various languages:

- http://www.flukenetworks.com/us/LAN/Handheld+Testers/LinkRunner/_see+it+live.htm#

- http://www.flukenetworks.com/us/LAN/Handheld+Testers/LinkRunner/_manuals.htm

Task 1: Become Familiar with the Capabilities of the Fluke LinkRunner

Access the virtual demo of the LinkRunner using the first URL. You can try different tests to become familiar with its capabilities.

Task 2: Obtain Access to the LinkRunner Quick Reference Guide

You can directly access the *Quick Reference Guide* online or download it to your PC using the link provided. Your instructor might also have a copy of the *Quick Reference Guide*. This lab reproduces selected pages of the *Quick Reference Guide*. Figure 4-16 shows the connectors and buttons on the LinkRunner.

Figure 4-16   LinkRunner Connectors and Buttons

1. RJ-45 LAN port
2. RJ-45 MAP port (cable testing)
3. Selection buttons
   Left – Highlight
   Right – Action
4. Power Button

Power off - press and hold
Backlight – press once briefly

5. Batteries (2) AA
6. Link indicator light

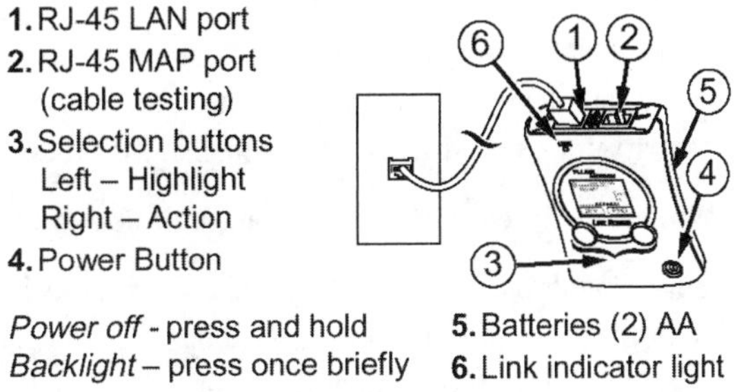

Task 3: Configure the LinkRunner

From any screen, you can access the main configuration by simultaneously pressing both buttons. You have the option to configure LinkRunner or go into the ping configuration.

Pressing the left button takes you to the LinkRunner configuration, where you can find the MAC address of the LinkRunner and toggle between feet and meters.

What is the Layer 2 MAC address?

_____

_____

Pressing the right button takes you to the ping configuration, which is covered in the preceding lab.

Task 4: Test the Length and Continuity for a Long Cable Run

LinkRunner's cable-test function helps you determine whether the cable length is within specification. This basic test determines that all four pairs of wires are intact and have the same length. Figure 4-17 shows a good cable test.

Figure 4-17   LinkRunner Cable Test Display

Step 1.   Turn on LinkRunner by pressing the small button in the lower-right corner. What does the display look like now?

_____

Step 2.   Use a long straight-through cable drop that is not connected to a patch panel, hub, or switch at the other end. Plug one end of the cable into the RJ-45 LAN port on the LinkRunner. What does the display look like now?

_____

What is the length of the cable being tested?

_____

Task 5: Test the Length and Wire Map for Good and Bad Patch Cables

The cable-test function helps you determine whether the cable length is within specification, whether it is a straight or crossover cable, and whether it has any faults. These tests work for both structured and patch cables. You will test cable integrity for excessive length, opens, shorts, crossed wires, and split pairs.

Step 1.   Turn on the LinkRunner by pressing the small button in the lower-right corner.

Step 2.   Use a good straight-through patch cable. Plug one end of the cable into the RJ-45 LAN port on the LinkRunner and the other end into the LinkRunner RJ-45 MAP port. Figure 4-18 shows the result of testing a good straight-through cable. What is the length of the cable?

_____

How can you tell whether this is a straight-through or crossover cable?

_____

Step 3.   Use a good crossover cable. Plug one end of the cable into the RJ-45 LAN port on the LinkRunner and the other end into the LinkRunner RJ-45 MAP port. What is the length of the cable?

_____

How can you tell whether this is a straight-through or crossover cable?

Figure 4-18   LinkRunner Straight-Through Cable Test Results

Step 4.   Use a bad straight-through patch cable that is improperly wired or has some faults in the wires. Plug one end of the cable in to the RJ-45 LAN port on the LinkRunner and the other end in to the RJ-45 MAP port. Figure 4-19 shows a problem cable with symbols indicating the type of problems. What problem did you encounter?

_____

_____

Figure 4-19   LinkRunner Cable Test Problem Results

⚠ indicates a problem cable and details display below.

‖ Good   Ⴤ Short
⚠ Unknown   ◊ Split
⥮ Open (wiremap or cable ID)

Task 6: Test the Length and Wire Map for Long Cable Runs

Step 1.   Turn on LinkRunner by pressing the small button in the lower-right corner.

Step 2.   Use a good workstation patch cable drop to a wall plate that is connected to a patch panel at the other end (but not to a hub or switch). Plug the cable into the RJ-45 LAN port on the LinkRunner. Plug the wire-map adapter into the associated patch panel port on the opposite end. You will test the cable run from the patch cable in the work area through all horizontal cabling to the patch panel in the wiring closet.

What is the length of the cable?

_____

Does the cable test okay?

_____

If not, indicate problems you encountered.

_____

Task 7: Use Link Pulse to Test the Connection to a Hub or Switch and Identify the Cable Location

Link pulse blinks the hub or switch port-link light while simultaneously sending a tone on the wire to aid in cable location. You can use the optional Microprobe Tone Receiver to pick up the tone and audibly locate cables. You can use the optional cable ID kit to identify unmarked segments.

Step 1.   Obtain a good patch cable of any length. Plug one end directly into an active regular hub or switch port. Plug the other end into the LinkRunner LAN port.

Step 2.   Press the left softkey (musical note and hub symbol). What does this cause the link light on the hub or switch port to do?

_____

What does this test do and how could it be useful in locating or identifying where cables terminate?

_____

_____

_____

_____

_____

_____

_____

Task 8: Test PC NIC Functionality

Step 1.   Turn on the LinkRunner by pressing the small button in the lower-right corner.

Step 2.   Plug one end of a patch cable into the RJ-45 LAN port on the LinkRunner and the other end into the PC NIC. If the PC NIC link light comes on, the NIC is good. Did the NIC test okay?

_____

Task 9: Disconnect the Equipment and Store the Cabling and Devices

Cabling LANs and WANs

The Study Guide portion of this chapter uses a combination of fill in the blank, compare and contrast, and open-ended question exercises to test your knowledge of cabling LANs and WANs.

The Lab Exercises portion of this chapter includes all the online curriculum labs and a comprehensive lab to ensure that you have mastered the practical, hands-on skills needed to cable LANs and WANs.

As you work through this chapter, use Module 5 in the CCNA 1 online curriculum or use the corresponding Chapter 5 in the *Networking Basics CCNA 1 Companion Guide* for assistance.

Study Guide

Cabling LANs

Many organizations rely on the services made available through their LANs. These networks can be as simple as two computers directly connected by a crossover cable. More complex LANs include multiple client computers, servers, printers, and other information resources connected using network devices. Understanding the fundamentals of LAN cabling is essential to creating an effective network.

In this section, you find exercises to help you learn the terminology associated with LANs, compare and contrast peer-to-peer and client/server networks, identify LAN components, and investigate server types. These exercises focus on the key areas of LAN cabling.

Vocabulary Exercise: Completion

Complete the following statements by using the proper terms to fill in the blanks.

In a _____ environment, each network device runs both client and server portions of an application.

A _____ can regenerate and retime network signals at the bit level to allow them to travel a longer distance on the media.

A multiport network device that filters, forwards, and floods frames based on the destination address of each frame is known as a _____.

_____ uses a dual-ring fiber-optic architecture to provide redundancy in a token-passing environment.

Also known as a multiport repeater, an active _____ repeats signals that come in one and out all other interfaces.

A _____ is used in Ethernet and IEEE 802.3 networks to provide an interface between the attachment unit interface (AUI) port of a station and the common medium of the Ethernet.

In Ethernet, a _____ occurs when two nodes transmit simultaneously, which results in damaged frames on the physical medium.

Lightning bolts represent _____ in a network diagram.

A computer system receives its network communication capabilities from the _____ that it uses to connect to the network.

A _____ is a data link layer device that intelligently connects two network segments.

A system that provides requested services to client systems is known as a _____.

_____ is a baseband LAN specification invented by Xerox Corporation and developed jointly by Xerox, Intel, and Digital Equipment Corporation.

Compare and Contrast Exercise: Peer-to-Peer and Client/Server Networks

Two specific types of LANs include peer-to-peer and client/server networks. While unique in design and components, each network type can provide services, such as file transfer and resource sharing. Use Table 5-1 to compare and contrast peer-to-peer and client/server networks.

Table 5-1   Compare and Contrast Peer-to-Peer and Client/Server Networks

	Peer-to-Peer Network	Client/Server Network
What basic components are needed to create this type of network?		
Where is this network type commonly implemented?		
What level of networking knowledge is required to create this type of network?		
What are the advantages of this network type?		

continues

Table 5-1   Compare and Contrast Peer-to-Peer and Client/Server Networks *continued*

	Peer-to-Peer Network	Client/Server Network
What are the disadvantages of this network type?		

Note: Now is a good time to complete Lab 5-1, Lab 5-2, and Lab 5-3. Lab 5-1 focuses on the materials and tools used to create an RJ-45 jack. Lab 5-2 and Lab 5-3 ask you to investigate hubs, network interface cards (NIC), and switches.

Concept Questions

Completely answer the following questions:

1. Fast Ethernet and Gigabit Ethernet are quickly replacing 10-Mbps Ethernet in LANs. What are the driving forces behind these changes?

    _____
    _____
    _____
    _____

2. Two common UTP cable types include straight-through and crossover cables. Describe each cable in terms of its pinouts and list the typical uses of each in a LAN.

    _____
    _____
    _____
    _____
    _____
    _____
    _____
    _____
    _____
    _____

3. Why is it important to understand the concept of tip and ring when creating a communications cable? Where did this concept originate? What are the tip and ring colors?

    _____
    _____
    _____
    _____

_____

_____

Note: The use of tip and ring colors goes way beyond their use in telephone and four-pair cabling. Use the Internet to search for the 25-pair color code. Make a note of the five tip colors and the five ring colors.

4. What is the 5-4-3 rule?

_____

_____

_____

_____

_____

_____

_____

5. A bridge is an intelligent device that connects two segments of a network. How does a bridge make traffic forwarding or blocking decisions?

_____

_____

_____

_____

■ _____

_____

■ _____

_____

■ _____

_____

6. Why is a switch often referred to as a multiport bridge? What advantages does a switch have over a bridge?

_____

_____

_____

_____

_____

_____

■ _____

■ _____

_____

■ _____

_____

■ _____

7. List and describe the three types of hubs available today.

_____

■ _____

_____

_____

■ _____
_____
_____

■ _____
_____
_____

Identifying LAN Cables and Components Exercise

It is important to identify LAN components and the cables that connect the different devices in the network. Improper device placement and cabling can result in poor network performance or a complete lack of communication. Figure 5-1 shows a LAN with multiple devices, including clients, servers, printers, networking hardware, and cabling. Knowing that the network uses UTP four-pair cabling and functions properly, answer the following questions regarding the LAN cables and components.

Figure 5-1   Typical LAN

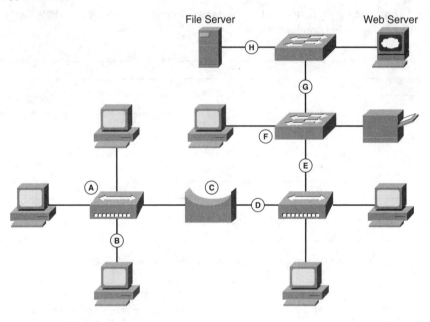

1. Device A is what type of networking hardware?

    _____

2. At what layer of the OSI model does device A operate?

    _____

3. What typical port types are found on device A?

    _____

4. What type of cable is cable B?

    _____

5. What does device C represent?

    _____

6. At what layer of the OSI model does device C operate?

    _____

7. What types of tables does device C maintain?

_____

8. What type of cable is cable D?

_____

9. What is the pinout of each end of cable D?

_____

_____

_____

_____

10. What type of cable is cable E?

_____

11. Device F is what type of networking hardware?

_____

12. At what layer of the OSI model does device F operate?

_____

13. What typical port types are found on device F?

_____

_____

14. What does device F use to make forwarding decisions?

_____

_____

15. What type of cable is cable G?

_____

16. What is the pinout of each end of cable G?

_____

_____

_____

17. What type of cable is cable H?

_____

Note: Now is a good time to work on Lab 5-4, Lab 5-5, and Lab 5-6. These labs focus on building LANs using various cables and devices. You use the ping command to verify connectivity.

Investigate Types of Servers Exercise

The most common type of network found in businesses today follows the client/server model. Client PCs access a dedicated server (or servers) for extended functionality. The services provided by the server might allow a client to print to a network printer, access a centralized application, or view a web page. Servers can provide many different types of services to the network. The functions of these network servers are central to the network's effectiveness.

Use Table 5-2 to investigate types of servers and services commonly used in a LAN. First, identify the type of server. Next, explain the service that is provided to the network clients. To get you started, three server types are identified in the first three rows of the table. Explain the services provided by each before identifying three more server types and their functions on your own.

Table 5-2   Identify Types of Servers and Their Functions

Type of Server	Services Provided to the Network Clients
Web server	
FTP server	
Print server	

Note: In Lab 5-11, you build a LAN made up of four PCs and interconnected switches. You can enhance the lab by adding a server to the topology.

Journal Entry

Each LAN is unique, and each computer network must be designed to meet the needs of its users. For example, look at a magazine-publishing company and a small doctor's office. Both businesses rely on the use of their LAN. The publishing company has multiple servers that host the large documents that make up the magazine. Writers access these servers to upload their materials, and editors access these servers to compile the writers' submissions into the next issue of the magazine. The publishing company also has high-speed, high-quality printers that use the resources of dedicated print servers. Because the files and print jobs that move across the LAN are rather large, high-speed connections to the client PCs, printers, and servers are required. This LAN uses switches throughout the infrastructure to keep data moving quickly.

The doctor's office uses a smaller LAN that consists of a few client PCs and a single server. Receptionists and office workers use clients to access the patient database on the server. The files are small, so a single server can maintain all the data. The office printer is directly connected to the server and is located centrally in the office for everyone to access. This LAN uses a Fast Ethernet hub to connect the client PCs to the server. At the doctor's office, a switch can easily replace the hub, but the network users might not see enough of an improvement to justify the cost of the new network device.

Your task is to find a nearby business or organization that uses a LAN, list the technologies and components used in their network, and identify the services used by the network.

Answer the following questions regarding the network:

1. What is the name of the business or organization?

2. What is the primary function of the organization?

3. What are the hardware components used in their LAN? Include PC hardware, networking devices, printer, and servers.

4. What types of services are available on the network? Include services such as addressing services, printing services, application access, file storage, and others.

5. Who designed or built the network?

6. Who maintains the network?

7. What type of connection do they have, if any, to the Internet?

Note: Many businesses will not share this type of information with anyone due to the nature of their operations. Local libraries and other municipal organizations are good options to investigate. Be sure to be courteous and explain the reason for the inquiry.

Cabling WANs

Routers are networking devices designed to connect LANs to WANs. Common WAN connections include serial interfaces, ISDN BRI interfaces, DSL interfaces, and cable interfaces. It is important to understand the physical characteristics of each type of interface and the cable used to connect the router interface to the WAN.

This section includes exercises that reinforce your knowledge of WAN cabling and communication types. These exercises include identifying acronyms associated with WANs, understanding router services and connection types, and troubleshooting network communications.

Vocabulary Exercise: Identifying Acronyms and Initialisms

An acronym is a word formed by the first letters in a multiword term. Initialisms are words made of initials pronounced separately. These are used extensively in the information technology (IT) field. Identify the terms associated with the following acronyms:

ARP _____

BRI _____

CSU/DSU _____

DCE _____

DSL _____

DTE _____

ISDN _____

RARP _____

WAN _____

Concept Questions

Completely answer the following questions:

1. Routers are network devices that connect networks together. What are some of the services that a router can provide a LAN connecting to a WAN?

    _____
    _____
    _____
    _____
    _____

2. Routers require configuration to function properly. How does a network professional initially connect to a router to configure it? What type of cable is required? What software and settings communicate from a PC to a router management interface?

    _____
    _____
    _____
    _____
    _____
    _____
    _____
    _____

3. Small office/home office (SOHO) routers connect to various broadband options. What is the primary type of connector used to connect a router to a DSL service? What is the primary type of connector to connect a router to a cable television Internet service?

    _____
    _____
    _____

4. What is the primary difference between an ISDN BRI U interface and an ISDN BRI S/T interface?

    _____
    _____
    _____
    _____

5. Why is it important to understand the role of DTE and DCE in serial communications?

    _____
    _____
    _____
    _____

Note: Now is a good time to work on Lab 5-7, Lab 5-8, and Lab 5-10. These labs focus on different types of router connections. Understanding LAN, WAN, and management router connections is required for network professionals.

Journal Entry

Troubleshooting network-connectivity problems begins with investigating the physical layer on the network because most connectivity problems arise from OSI Layer 1 issues. Understanding how to properly troubleshoot Layer 1 issues on LANs and WANs is extremely important.

Figure 5-2 shows a network made up of two LANs connected by a WAN serial link. This network is configured to allow all PCs to communicate with one another. To test the lower layer connectivity of the network, the **ping** command is used between the PCs. The results show that PC A cannot ping PC D. How would you troubleshoot this network problem? Be efficient yet thorough when listing your troubleshooting steps.

Figure 5-2   Two LANs Connected by a WAN Serial Link

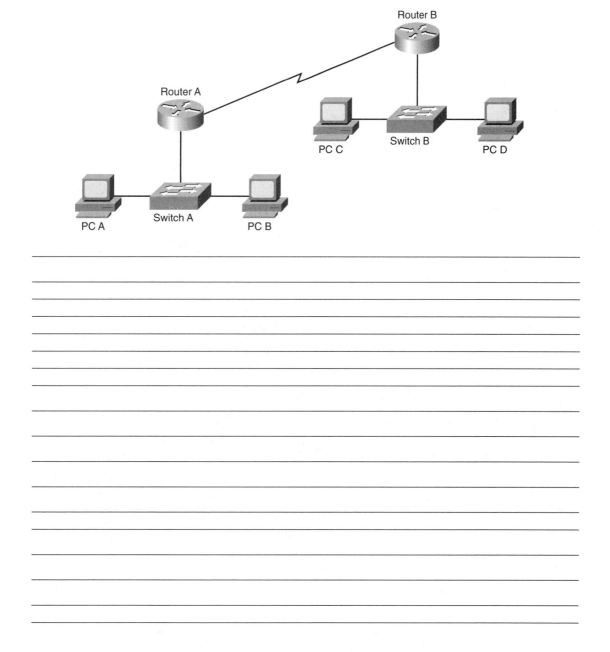

_____

_____

_____

_____

_____

_____

_____

_____

_____

_____

Note: Lab 5-9 focuses on troubleshooting network connectivity. Be sure to thoroughly document any errors you find in the network cabling and configuration.

Lab Exercises

Curriculum Lab 5-1: RJ-45 Jack Punch Down (5.1.5)

Objectives

- Learn the correct process for terminating (punching down) an RJ-45 jack.

- Learn the correct procedure for installing the jack in a wall plate.

Background/Preparation

In this lab, you learn to wire an RJ-45 data jack for installation in a wall plate using a punch-down tool. These skills are useful when you must install a small amount of cabling in an office or residence. A *punch tool* is a device that uses spring-loaded action to push wires between metal pins while at the same time skinning the sheath away from the wire. This process ensures that the wire makes a good electrical connection with the pins inside the jack. The punch tool also cuts off any extra wire.

You will work with Category 5 or 5e cabling and Category 5 or 5e T-568-B jacks. You normally plug a Category 5/5e straight-wired patch cable with an RJ-45 connector into the data jack (or outlet) to connect a PC in a work area to the network. It is important that you use Category 5 or 5e jacks and patch panels with Category 5 or 5e cabling to support Fast Ethernet (100 Mbps) and Gigabit Ethernet (1000 Mbps). The process of punching down wires into a data jack in an office area is the same as punching them down in a patch panel in a wiring closet. You need the following resources:

- Two- to 3-foot length of Category 5/5e cabling (one per person or one per team).

- Two Category 5/5e RJ-45 data jacks (one extra for a spare). If both ends of the cable have RJ-45 data jacks, you can test the installation by inserting cable with RJ-45 connectors and a simple cable continuity tester.

- Category 5/5e wall plate.

- 110 type punch-down tool.

- Wire cutters.

Use the following procedure to punch down the wires into the RJ-45 jack and install the jack into the wall plate:

Step 1.   Remove the jacket 1" from the end of the cable.

Step 2.   Hold the jack with the 8-pin jack receptacle (the part that the RJ-45 connector goes into) facing up or away from you while looking at the wire channels or slots. There should be four wire channels on each side. Match the wiring colors to the codes on the jack. Position wires in the proper channels on the jack, maintaining the twists as close as possible. Most jacks have the channels color-coded to indicate where the wires go. Jacks are typically stamped to indicate whether they are T-568-A or T-568-B, as Figure 5-3 shows.

Figure 5-3   RJ-45 Jack

Step 3.   Use the 110 punch-down tool (see Figure 5-4) to push conductors into the channels.

Make sure that you position the cut side of the punch-down tool so that it faces the outside of the jack, or you will cut the wire you are trying to punch down. (Note: If you tilt the handle of the punch tool a little to the outside, it will cut better.) If any wire remains attached after you use the punch tool, simply twist the ends gently to remove them, and then place the clips on the jack and tighten them.

Note: Make sure that no more than .5" of untwisted wire is between the end of the cable jacket and the channels on the jack.

Figure 5-4   Single-Wire Punch Tool

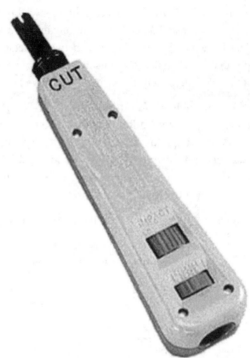

Step 4.   Snap the jack into its faceplate by pushing it in from the back side. When you do this, make sure that the jack is right-side up. (The clip faces down when the wall plate is mounted.)

Step 5.   Use the screws to attach the faceplate to either the box or the bracket. If you surface-mount the box, keep in mind that it might hold 1' or 2' of excess cable. Then, you need to either slide the cable through its tie-wraps or pull back the raceway that covers it to push the rest of the excess cable back into the wall. If you flush-mount the jack, all you need to do is push the excess cable back into the wall.

Curriculum Lab 5-2: Hub and NIC Purchase (5.1.7)

Objectives

- Introduce the variety and prices of network components in the market.

- Gather pricing information for hubs and Ethernet NICs for a small network.

Background/Preparation

A friend asks you to help him put together a price list for a small LAN to set up in his small business. Rapid growth is not really a concern. He has the computers, but he has not networked them. He is getting a

DSL connection so that he can access the Internet, and all he needs is a small hub and connections to each computer to complete the project. Each machine runs a version of Windows that will work on a peer-to-peer network. You can use any local source, catalog, or website. The requirements include the following:

- Ethernet hub

- Ethernet NICs for existing laptop PCs

- Ethernet NICs for existing desktop PCs

- Each computer will be close enough so that a 20' jumper would reach the hub. Price the Category 5 jumpers as well.

Task 1: Research Equipment Prices

Start by going to http://www.cisco.com, selecting **Products & Services**, and following the links to **Hubs and Concentrators** to gather basic information. The small list of choices should indicate something.

Use at least three other sources for technologies and pricing. If you do web searches, use http://www.cdw.com and http:// www.google.com, plus any others you prefer. As you look at the prices for small hubs, how much more would it cost to use a small switch? Compare the cost to a wireless implementation.

_____

_____

_____

_____

_____

_____

_____

_____

_____

_____

_____

_____

_____

_____

_____

_____

_____

_____

_____

_____

_____

_____

_____

_____

_____

_____

_____

_____

Task 2: Compile a One-Page Summary of Your Results

Use a spreadsheet or word processor to compile a one-page summary of your results. Use a table to show the choices and the features or factors that you compared (number of ports, features, price, performance, and so on).

Curriculum Lab 5-3: Purchasing LAN Switches (5.1.10)

Figure 5-5   Cisco Catalyst 2900 and 3550 Series Switches

Objectives

- Introduce the variety and prices of network components in the market.

- Gather pricing information for Ethernet switches and NICs for a network.

Background/Preparation

You are asked to put together a proposal for replacing a branch office's hubs with switches. You must research at least two different solutions and develop a proposal. The project details follow.

Your company has a branch location using an Ethernet hub network. Congestion issues are becoming a serious problem as the company adds more services to the network. Currently, each of the four floors has one or more hubs in a wiring closet supporting 30–35 computers except the ground floor, which has 65 computers.

The four floors plug in to an 8-port 10-Mbps switch that the company added earlier to reduce congestion problems. Although that solution was a major improvement, it can't keep up all the time. The two servers and router to the Internet also connect to the 8-port switch.

The branch cabling is relatively new and certified to Category 5 standards. The company is not interested in any major cabling changes at this time.

At least 75 percent of the 160 current workstations have NICs with 10/100, full-duplex capabilities. All laptop computers have the newer NICs. All new machines include similar NICs.

The requirements include the following:

- Replace all hubs with switches.

- Replace the 10-Mbps NICs for existing desktop PCs.

- Each host connection should be 10/100 Mbps minimum.

What should you do with the existing switch? Are there higher-bandwidth options for connecting the two servers?

Task 1: Research Equipment Prices

Start by going to http://www.cisco.com, selecting **Products & Solutions**, and following the links to **Switches** to gather basic information. Look specifically at the Catalyst 29xx and 35xx models.

Use at least three other sources for technologies and pricing. If you do web searches, use http://www.cdw.com and http://www.google.com, plus any others you prefer.

Task 2: Compile a Table of Your Results

Use a spreadsheet or word processor to compile a table of your results and the following:

- **Page 1**—An executive summary, where you recommend your choice of products and the total cost. Include a short reason (8–15 lines) why you selected this implementation.

- **Page 2**—A comparison table that shows the choices you worked from and the features or factors that you compared (price, performance, and so on).

- **Page 3**—A bulleted list of any security concerns you discovered. Summarize whether you think the concerns are serious and whether you can overcome them.

Optional Task 2: Create a Four- to Eight-Slide PowerPoint Presentation

Instead of creating Excel or Word documents, create a four- to eight-slide PowerPoint presentation that covers the same requirements.

Assume that you will present the material.

If time allows, perform both versions of Task 2, which is often standard.

Curriculum Lab 5-4: Building a Peer-to-Peer Network (5.1.12)

Figure 5-6   Peer-to-Peer Network Topology

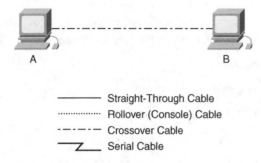

———— Straight-Through Cable

·············· Rollover (Console) Cable

– – – – – Crossover Cable

⎺⎺⏋⎺⎺ Serial Cable

Objectives

- Create a simple peer-to-peer network between two PCs.
- Identify the proper cable to connect the two PCs.
- Configure workstation IP address information.
- Test connectivity using the **ping** command.

Background/Preparation

This lab focuses on the ability to connect two PCs to create a simple hubless two-workstation peer-to-peer Ethernet LAN. In addition to the physical and data link (Layers 1 and 2) connections, you must also configure the computers with the correct IP network settings (Layer 3) so that they can communicate. This lab does not require a hub or any other interconnecting network device; all you need is a basic Category 5/5e UTP crossover cable. A crossover cable is the same type that you would use as backbone or vertical cabling to connect switches. Connecting the PCs in this manner can be useful for transferring files at high speed and for troubleshooting interconnecting devices between PCs. If you can connect the two PCs with a single cable and still communicate, any networking problems are not with the PCs themselves. Start this lab with the equipment turned off and with cabling disconnected. Work in teams of two (one person per PC). You need the following resources:

- Two workstations with an Ethernet 10/100 NIC installed
- Several Ethernet cables (straight-through and crossover) to connect the two workstations

Task 1: Identify the Proper Ethernet Cable and Connect the Two PCs

Step 1.   Make the connection between the two PCs using a Category 5 or 5e crossover cable. Locate a cable that is long enough to reach from one PC to the other and attach one end to the NIC in each of the PCs. Be sure to carefully examine the cable ends and select only a crossover cable.

What kind of cable do you need to connect from NIC to NIC?

_____

What is the category rating of the cable?

_____

What is the AWG wire-size designation of the cable?

_____

Task 2: Verify the Physical Connection

Plug in and turn on the computers. To verify the computer connections, ensure that the link lights on both NICs are lit. Are both link lights lit?

_____

Task 3: Access the IP Settings Window

_____

Note: Be sure to write down the existing IP settings so that you can restore them at the end of the lab. These settings include the IP address, subnet mask, default gateway, and DNS servers. If the workstation is a DHCP client, it is not necessary to record this information.

_____

Windows 95/98/Me users: Click **Start > Settings > Control Panel > Network**.

Select the TCP/IP protocol icon that is associated with the NIC in this PC, and click **Properties**. Click the **IP Address** tab and the **Gateway tab**.

Windows NT/2000 users: Click **Start > Settings > Control Panel > Network**.

Click the **Protocols** tab and select the TCP/IP protocol icon that is associated with the NIC in this PC. Click **Properties** and click **Specify an IP Address**.

Windows XP users: Click **Start > Control Panel > Network Connection**.

Select the **Local Area Network Connection** and click **Change Settings of This Connection** (see Figure 5-7).

Figure 5-7   TCP/IP Properties

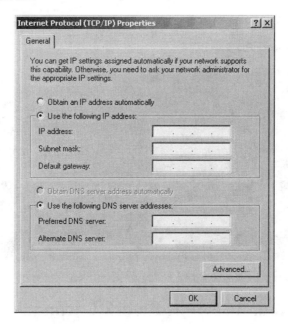

Task 4: Configure the TCP/IP Settings for the Two PCs

Set the IP address information for each PC according to the information in Table 5-3.

You do not need the default gateway IP address because these computers are directly connected. You only need the default gateway on LANs that are connected to a router.

Table 5-3   IP Address Settings for Both Peers

Computer	IP Address	Subnet Mask	Default Gateway
PC A	192.168.1.1	255.255.255.0	Not required
PC B	192.168.1.2	255.255.255.0	Not required

Task 5: Access the Command or MS-DOS Prompt

Use the Start menu to open the command prompt (MS-DOS–like) window.

Windows 95/98/Me users: Click **Start** > **Programs** > **MS-DOS Prompt**.

Windows NT/2000 users: Click **Start** > **Programs** > **Command Prompt**.

Windows XP users: Click **Start** > **Programs** > **Accessories** > **Command Prompt**.

Task 6: Verify That PCs Can Communicate

Step 1.   Test connectivity from one PC to the other by pinging the IP address of the opposite computer. Use the following command at the command prompt:

C:>**ping 192.168.1.1** (or 192.168.1.2)

Step 2.   You should get results similar to those shown in Figure 5-8. If not, check your PC connections and network TCP/IP settings for both PCs. What is the ping result?

_____

_____

Figure 5-8   Ping Results from PC B to PC A

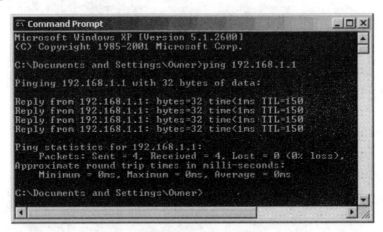

Task 7: Confirm Your TCP/IP Network Settings

Windows 95/98/Me users: Run the **winipcfg** command from the MS-DOS prompt. Record the results.

_____

_____

_____

_____

Windows NT/2000/XP users: Run the **ipconfig** command from the command prompt. Record the results.

_____

_____

_____

_____

_____

Task 8: Restore the PCs to Their Original IP Settings, Disconnect the Equipment, and Store the Cables

Curriculum Lab 5-5: Building a Hub-Based Network (5.1.13a)

Figure 5-9   Hub-Based Network Topology

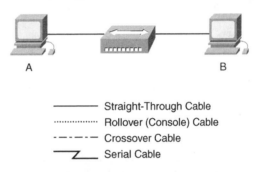

———————— Straight-Through Cable

················ Rollover (Console) Cable

- — - — - — Crossover Cable

⌐⎯Z⎯ Serial Cable

Objectives

- Create a simple network with two PCs using a hub.

- Identify the proper cable to connect the PCs to the hub.

- Configure workstation IP address information.

- Test connectivity using the **ping** command.

Background/Preparation

This lab focuses on the ability to connect two PCs to create a simple two-workstation, hub-based Ethernet LAN. A hub is a networking concentration device that is sometimes referred to as a *multiport repeater*. Hubs are inexpensive and easy to install, but they permit collisions to occur. They are appropriate for a small LAN with light traffic.

In addition to the physical and data link (Layers 1 and 2) connections, you must also configure the computers with the correct IP network settings (Layer 3) so that they can communicate. Because this lab uses a hub, you need a basic Category 5/5e UTP straight-through cable to connect each PC to the hub. This *patch cable* or horizontal cabling connects workstations and a typical LAN. Start this lab with the equipment turned off and with cabling disconnected. Work in teams of two (one person per PC). You need the following resources:

- Two workstations with an Ethernet 10/100 NIC installed

- An Ethernet 10BASE-T or Fast Ethernet hub

- Several Ethernet cables (straight-through and crossover) to connect the two workstations

Task 1: Identify the Proper Ethernet Cable and Connect the Two PCs to the Hub

You make the connection between the two PCs and the hub using a Category 5 or 5e straight-through patch cable. Locate two cables that are long enough to reach from each PC to the hub. Attach one end to the NIC and the other end to a port on the hub. Be sure to carefully examine the cable ends and select only a straight-through cable.

What kind of cable do you need to connect from NIC to hub?

_____

What is the category rating of the cable?

_____

What is the AWG wire-size designation of the cable?

_____

Task 2: Verify the Physical Connection

Plug in and turn on the computers. To verify the computer connections, ensure that the link lights on both PC NICs and the hub interfaces are lit. Are all link lights lit?

_____

Task 3: Access the IP Settings Window

Note: Write down the existing IP settings so that you can restore them at the end of the lab. These settings include the IP address, subnet mask, default gateway, and DNS servers. If the workstation is a DHCP client, it is not necessary to record this information.

Windows 95/98/Me users: Click **Start > Settings > Control Panel > Network**.

Select the TCP/IP protocol icon that is associated with the NIC in this PC and click **Properties**.

Click the **IP Address** tab and the **Gateway tab**.

Windows NT/2000 users: Click **Start > Settings > Control Panel > Network**.

Click the Protocols tab and select the TCP/IP protocol icon that is associated with the NIC in this PC. Click **Properties** and click **Specify** an IP Address.

Windows XP users: Click **Start > Control Panel > Network Connection**.

Select the **Local Area Network Connection** and click **Change Settings of This Connection** (see Figure 5-10).

Figure 5-10   TCP/IP Properties

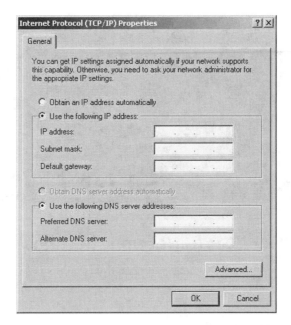

Task 4: Configure the TCP/IP Settings for the Two PCs

Set the IP address information for each PC according to the information in Table 5-4.

You do not need the default gateway IP address because these computers are directly connected. You only need the default gateway on LANs that are connected to a router.

Table 5-4   IP Address Settings for PCs in a Hub-Based Network

Computer	IP Address	Subnet Mask	Default Gateway
PC A	192.168.1.1	255.255.255.0	Not required
PC B	192.168.1.2	255.255.255.0	Not required

Task 5: Access the Command or MS-DOS Prompt

Use the Start menu to open the command prompt (MS-DOS–like) window.

Windows 95/98/Me users: Click **Start > Programs > MS-DOS Prompt**.

Windows NT/2000 users: Click **Start > Programs > Command Prompt**.

Windows XP users: Click **Start > Programs > Accessories > Command Prompt**.

Task 6: Verify That PCs Can Communicate

Step 1.   Test connectivity from one PC to the other through the hub by pinging the IP address of the opposite computer. Enter the following command at the command prompt:

C:>**ping 192.168.1.1** (or 192.168.1.2)

Step 2.   You should get results similar to those shown in Figure 5-11. If not, check your PC connections and network TCP/IP settings for both PCs. What is the ping result?

_____

_____

Figure 5-11   Ping Results from PC B to PC A

```
Command Prompt                                          _ □ X
Microsoft Windows XP [Version 5.1.2600]
(C) Copyright 1985-2001 Microsoft Corp.

C:\Documents and Settings\Owner>ping 192.168.1.1

Pinging 192.168.1.1 with 32 bytes of data:

Reply from 192.168.1.1: bytes=32 time<1ms TTL=150
Reply from 192.168.1.1: bytes=32 time<1ms TTL=150
Reply from 192.168.1.1: bytes=32 time<1ms TTL=150
Reply from 192.168.1.1: bytes=32 time<1ms TTL=150

Ping statistics for 192.168.1.1:
    Packets: Sent = 4, Received = 4, Lost = 0 (0% loss),
Approximate round trip times in milli-seconds:
    Minimum = 0ms, Maximum = 0ms, Average = 0ms

C:\Documents and Settings\Owner>
```

Task 7: Confirm Your TCP/IP Network Settings

Windows 95/98/Me users: Run the **winipcfg** command from the MS-DOS prompt. Record the results.

_____

_____

_____

_____

_____

Windows NT/2000/XP users: Run the **ipconfig** command from the command prompt. Record the results.

_____

_____

_____

_____

_____

Task 8: Restore the PCs to Their Original IP Settings, Disconnect the PCs from the Hub, and Store the Hub and Cables

Curriculum Lab 5-6: Building a Switch-Based Network (5.1.13b)

Figure 5-12   Switch-Based Network Topology

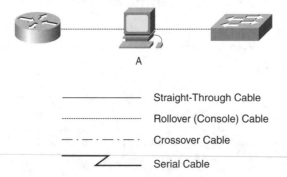

Objectives

- Create a simple network with two PCs using a switch.

- Identify the proper cable to connect the PCs to the switch.

- Configure workstation IP address information.

- Test connectivity using the **ping** command.

Background/Preparation

This lab focuses on the ability to connect two PCs to create a simple two-workstation, switch-based Ethernet LAN. A switch is a networking concentration device that is sometimes referred to as a *multiport bridge*. Switches are relatively inexpensive and easy to install. When operating in full-duplex mode, they provide dedicated bandwidth to workstations and eliminate collisions by creating two-workstation microsegments between ports. They are appropriate for small to large LANs with moderate to heavy traffic.

In addition to the physical and data link (Layers 1 and 2) connections, you must also configure the computers with the correct IP network settings (Layer 3) so that they can communicate. Because this lab uses a switch, you need a basic Category 5/5e UTP straight-through cable to connect each PC to the switch. This patch cable or horizontal cabling connects workstations and a typical LAN. Start this lab with the equipment turned off and with cabling disconnected. Work in teams of two (one person per PC). You need the following resources:

- Two workstations with an Ethernet 10/100 NIC installed

- An Ethernet 10BASE-T or Fast Ethernet switch

- Several Ethernet cables (straight-through and crossover) to connect the two workstations

Task 1: Identify the Proper Ethernet Cable and Connect the Two PCs to the Switch

Make the connection between the two PCs and the switch using a Category 5 or 5e straight-through patch cable. Locate two cables that are long enough to reach from each PC to the switch. Attach one end to the NIC and the other end to a port on the switch. Be sure to examine the cable ends carefully and select only a straight-through cable.

What kind of cable do you need to connect from a NIC to a switch?

_____

What is the category rating of the cable?

_____

What is the AWG wire-size designation of the cable?

_____

Task 2: Verify the Physical Connection

Plug in and turn on the computers. To verify the computer connections, ensure that the link lights on both PC NICs and the switch interfaces are lit. Are all link lights lit?

_____

Task 3: Access the IP Settings Window

Note: Write down the existing IP settings so that you can restore them at the end of the lab. These settings include the IP address, subnet mask, default gateway, and DNS servers. If the workstation is a DHCP client, it is not necessary to record this information.

Windows 95/98/Me users: Click **Start > Settings > Control Panel > Network**.

Select the TCP/IP protocol icon that is associated with the NIC in this PC and click Properties. Click the **IP Address** tab and the **Gateway** tab.

Windows NT/2000 users: Click **Start > Settings > Control Panel > Network**.

Click the **Protocols** tab and select the TCP/IP protocol icon that is associated with the NIC in this PC. Click **Properties** and click **Specify an IP Address**.

Windows XP users: Click **Start > Control Panel > Network Connection**.

Select the **Local Area Network Connection** and click **Change Settings of This Connection** (see Figure 5-13).

Figure 5-13   TCP/IP Settings

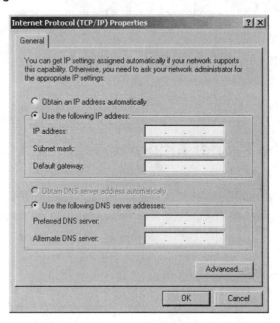

Task 4: Configure the TCP/IP Settings for the Two PCs

Set the IP address information for each PC according to the information in Table 5-5.

You do not need the default gateway IP address because these computers are directly connected. You only need the default gateway on LANs that are connected to a router.

Table 5-5   IP Address Settings for PCs

Computer	IP Address	Subnet Mask	Default Gateway
PC A	192.168.1.1	255.255.255.0	Not required
PC B	192.168.1.2	255.255.255.0	Not required

Task 5: Access the Command or MS-DOS Prompt

Use the Start menu to open the command prompt (MS-DOS–like) window.

Windows 95/98/Me users: Click **Start > Programs > MS-DOS Prompt**.

Windows NT/2000 users: Click **Start > Programs > Command Prompt**.

Windows XP users: Click **Start > Programs > Accessories > Command Prompt**.

Task 6: Verify That PCs Can Communicate

Step 1.   Test connectivity from one PC to the other through the switch by pinging the IP address of the opposite computer. Enter the following command at the command prompt:

C:>**ping 192.168.1.1** (or 192.168.1.2)

Step 2.   You should get results similar to those shown in Figure 5-14. If not, check your PC connections and network TCP/IP settings for both PCs. What is the ping result?

_____

_____

Figure 5-14   Ping Results from PC B to PC A

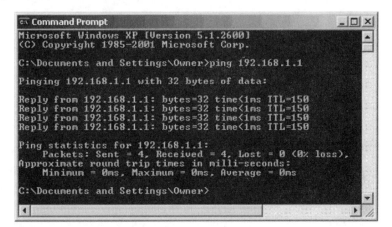

Task 7: Confirm Your TCP/IP Network Settings

Windows 95/98/Me users: Run the **winipcfg** command from the MS-DOS prompt. Record the results:

_____

_____

_____

_____

_____

Windows NT/2000/XP users: Run the **ipconfig** command from the command prompt. Record the results:

_____

_____

_____

_____

_____

Task 8: Restore the PCs to Their Original IP Settings, Disconnect the Equipment, and Store the Cables

Curriculum Lab 5-7: Connecting Router LAN Interfaces (5.2.3a)

Figure 5-15   Topology for Lab 5.2.3a

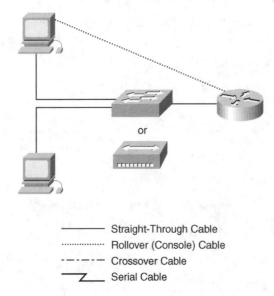

——————— Straight-Through Cable
.... Rollover (Console) Cable
— - — - — Crossover Cable
⎓⎓⎓⎓⎓ Serial Cable

Objectives

- Identify the Ethernet or Fast Ethernet interfaces on the router.

- Identify and locate the proper cables to connect the router and PC to a hub or switch.

- Use the cables to connect the router and PC to the hub or switch.

Background/Preparation

This lab focuses on the ability to connect the physical cabling between Ethernet LAN devices, such as hubs and switches, and the appropriate Ethernet interface on a router. The computers and router should have the correct IP network settings. Start this lab with the computers, router, and hub or switch turned off and unplugged. You need the following resources:

- At least one workstation with an Ethernet 10/100 NIC installed

- One Ethernet switch or hub

- One router with an RJ-45 Ethernet or Fast Ethernet interface (or an attachment unit interface [AUI])

- One 10BASE-T AUI transceiver (DB15-to-RJ-45) for a router with an AUI Ethernet interface (2500 series)

- Several Ethernet cables (straight-through and crossover) to connect the workstation and router to the hub or switch

Task 1: Identify the Ethernet or Fast Ethernet Interfaces on the Router

Step 1.   Examine the router. What is the model number of the router?

Step 2. Locate one or more RJ-45 connectors on the router labeled "10/100 Ethernet" (see Figure 5-16). This identifier can vary depending on the type of router. A 2500 series router has an AUI DB15 Ethernet port labeled AUI 0. This port requires a 10BASE-T transceiver to connect to the RJ-45 cable.

Figure 5-16 RJ-45 Connectors on the Router

Step 3. Identify the Ethernet ports that you can use to connect the routers. Record the information in the following chart. Record the AUI port numbers if you are working with a Cisco 2500 series router.

Router	Port	Port

Task 2: Identify the Proper Cables and Connect the Router

Step 1. Make the connection between the router and the hub using a Category 5 straight-through patch cable. Locate a patch cable that is long enough to reach from the router to the hub. Be sure to examine the cable ends carefully and select only straight-through cables.

Step 2. Use a cable to connect the Ethernet interface that uses the 0 (zero) designation on the router to a port on the hub or switch. Also, use the 10BASE-T AUI transceiver for the 2500 series.

Task 3: Connect the Workstation Ethernet Cabling

You will also connect the computers to the hub using a straight-through patch cable. Run Category 5 patch cables from each PC to where the switch or hub is located. Connect one end of these cables to the RJ-45 connector on the computer NIC and connect the other end to a port on the hub or switch. Be sure to carefully examine the cable ends and select only straight-through cables.

Task 4: Verify the Connection

Step 1. Plug in and turn on the routers, computers, and the hub or switch.

Step 2. To verify the router connections, ensure that the link lights on the router interface and the hub or switch interface are both lit.

Step 3. To verify the computer connections, ensure that the link lights on the NIC and the hub interface are both lit.

Curriculum Lab 5-8: Building a Basic Routed WAN (5.2.3b)

Figure 5-17   Basic Routed WAN Topology

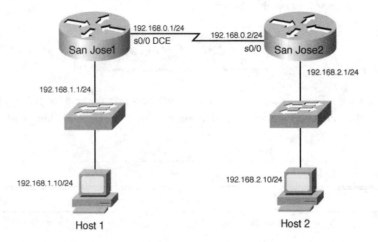

Objectives

- Create a simple routed WAN with two PCs, two switches or hubs, and two routers.
- Identify the proper cables to connect a PC and router to each switch.
- Identify the proper cables to connect the routers to form a WAN link.
- Configure workstation IP address information.
- Test connectivity using the **ping** command.

Background/Preparation

This lab focuses on the ability to connect two simple LANs, each consisting of a workstation and a switch (or hub), to form a basic router-to-router WAN. A router is a networking device that you can use to interconnect LANs; it routes packets between different networks using Layer 3 IP addressing. The Internet typically uses routers for its connections.

In addition to the physical and data link (Layers 1 and 2) connections, you must also configure the computers and routers with the correct IP network settings (Layer 3) so that they can communicate. Straight-through patch cables connect each PC and router to its switch (or hub). Two special V.35 cables create the simulated WAN link between the routers.

Note: The instructor or lab assistant must preconfigure the two routers to have the correct IP addresses on their LAN and WAN interfaces. Router A will provide the clocking signal as DCE.

Start this lab with the equipment turned off and with cabling disconnected. Work in teams of two (one person per LAN). You need the following resources:

- Two workstations with an Ethernet 10/100 NIC installed
- Two Ethernet 10BASE-T or Fast Ethernet switches or two hubs
- Two routers with an RJ-45 Ethernet or Fast Ethernet interface (or an AUI interface) and at least one serial interface
- A 10BASE-T AUI transceiver (DB15-to-RJ-45) for a router with an AUI Ethernet interface (2500 series)

- Four Ethernet straight-through cables to connect the workstations and routers to the hub or switch

- One female (DCE) and one male (DTE) V.35 cable for interconnecting the routers

Task 1: Identify and Connect the Proper Ethernet Cable from the PC to the Switch

Step 1.   Make the connection between the PC and the switch using a Category 5 or 5e straight-through patch cable. Attach one end to the NIC and the other end to a port on the switch or hub. Be sure to carefully examine the cable ends and select only a straight-through cable.

Step 2.   Examine the switch or hub.

What is the model number of the switch or hub?

Task 2: Identify the Ethernet or Fast Ethernet Interfaces on the Routers

Step 1.   Examine the routers.

What is the model number of router A?

What is the model number of router B?

Step 2.   Locate one or more RJ-45 connectors on each router labeled "10/100 Ethernet," as shown in Figure 5-18. This identifier can vary depending on the type of router. A 2500 series router has an AUI DB15 Ethernet port labeled AUI 0.

This port requires a 10BASE-T transceiver to connect to the RJ-45 cable.

Figure 5-18   10/100 Ethernet RJ-45 Connectors

Step 3.   Identify the Ethernet ports that you can use to connect the routers. Record the information in Table 5-6. If you are working with a Cisco 2500 series router, record the AUI port numbers.

Table 5-6   Router Port Identification

Router	Port	Port

Task 3: Cable the Router LAN Links

Step 1.   Configure the router.

The instructor or lab assistant should preconfigure the routers so that the Ethernet 0 interface on each router has the proper IP address and subnet mask, as indicated in Table 5-7. This setup allows the routers to route packets between LANs 192.168.1.0 and 192.168.2.0.

Table 5-7   Router IP Address and Subnet Mask Configuration Settings

Router	E0 Interface IP Address	Subnet Mask
Router A	192.168.1.1	255.255.255.0
Router B	192.168.2.1	255.255.255.0

Step 2.   Connect the cables.

Make the connection between the router and the hub or switch using a Category 5 straight-through patch cable. Locate a patch cable that is long enough to reach from the router to the hub. Be sure to examine the cable ends carefully and select only straight-through cables. Connect the Ethernet interface that uses the 0 (zero) designation on the router to a port on the hub or switch. Also, use the 10BASE-T AUI transceiver for the 2500 series routers.

Task 4: Verify the Physical Ethernet Connections

Plug in and turn on the computers, switches or hubs, and routers. To verify the connections, ensure that the link lights on both PC NICs, both switch or hub interfaces, and the router Ethernet interfaces are lit. Are all the link lights lit?

_____

If not, check the connections and cable types.

Task 5: Identify the Serial Interfaces on the Router

Step 1.   Examine the routers.

Step 2.   Identify the serial ports on each router that you could use to connect the routers to simulate a WAN link. Record the information in Table 5-8. If you have more than one serial interface, use Interface 0 on each router.

Table 5-8   Router Serial Port Identification

Router Name	Router Serial Port	Router Serial Port

Task 6: Identify and Locate the Proper V.35 Cables

Inspect the serial cables available in the lab. Depending on the type of router or serial card, the router can have different connectors.

Router Serial Port Characteristics

The two most common types are the DB60 connector and the smart serial, as Figure 5-19 illustrates. Use Table 5-9 to indicate which type your routers have.

Figure 5-19   Router Serial Port Connection Types

Smart Serial   DB60

Table 5-9   Router Serial Port Connectors

Router	Smart Serial Connector	DB60 Connector
A		
B		

Simulating the WAN Link: DCE/DTE and Clocking

Because this connection will not be through a live leased line, one of the routers needs to provide the clocking for the circuit. A CSU/DSU normally provides the clocking signal to each of the routers. To provide this clocking signal, one of the routers needs a DCE cable instead of the normal DTE that is used on the other router. Therefore, you must make the connection between routers using one DCE cable and one DTE cable. You will use a V.35 DCE cable and a V.35 DTE cable to simulate the WAN connection.

V.35 Cable Characteristics

The V.35 DCE connector is a large female V.35 (34-pin) connector. The DTE cable has a large male V.35 connector (see Figure 5-20). The cables are also labeled as DCE or DTE on the router ends. You will use the DCE cable on router A because it will provide the clock signal.

Figure 5-20   DTE (V.35 Male) and DCE (V.35 Female) Cables

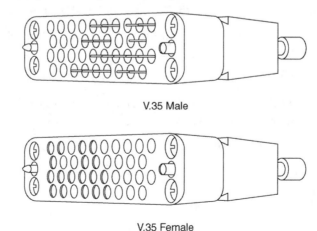

V.35 Male

V.35 Female

Task 7: Cable the Router WAN Link

Step 1. Configure the router.

The instructor or lab assistant needs to preconfigure router A to provide the DCE clock signal on a Serial 0 interface. The Serial 0 interface on each router should have the proper IP address and subnet mask, as indicated in Table 5-10.

The network interconnecting the router serial interfaces is 192.168.3.0.

Table 5-10   Router Serial 0 Interface IP Address/Subnet Mask Configuration Settings

Router	Clocking	S0 Interface IP Address	Subnet Mask
Router A	DCE	192.168.3.1	255.255.255.0
Router B	DTE	192.168.3.2	255.255.255.0

Step 2. Connect the cables.

The DCE cable will attach to the Serial 0 interface on router A. Attach the DTE cable to the Serial 0 interface on router B. First, make the connection between the two V.35 cables. There is only one proper way for the cables to fit together. Align the pins on the male cable with the sockets on the female cables and gently couple them. When they are joined, turn the thumbscrews (clockwise) to secure the connectors.

Make the connection to each of the routers. Holding the connector in one hand, properly orient the cable connector and the router connecter so that the tapers match. Push the cable connector partially into the router connector and tighten the thumbscrews to fully insert the cable into the connector.

Task 8: Configure Workstation IP Settings

Note: Write down the existing IP settings so that you can restore them at the end of the lab. These settings include the IP address, subnet mask, default gateway, and DNS servers. If the workstation is a DHCP client, it is not necessary to record this information.

Access the IP settings window.

Windows 95/98/Me users: Click **Start > Settings > Control Panel > Network**.

Select the TCP/IP protocol icon that is associated with the NIC in this PC and click **Properties**. Click the **IP Address** tab and the **Gateway** tab.

Windows NT/2000 users: Click **Start > Settings > Control Panel > Network**.

Click the **Protocols** tab and select the TCP/IP protocol icon that is associated with the NIC in this PC. Click **Properties** and click **Specify an IP Address**.

Windows XP users: Click **Start > Control Panel > Network Connection**.

Select the **Local Area Network Connection** and click **Change Settings of This Connection** (see Figure 5-21).

Figure 5-21   TCP/IP Settings

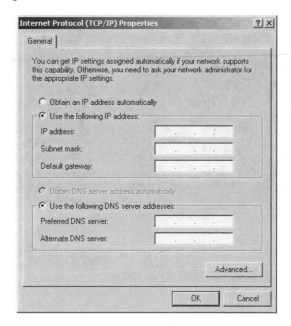

Set the IP address information for each PC according to the information in Table 5-11.

Note that the IP address of each PC is on the same network as the default gateway, which is the Ethernet interface of the connected router. You need the default gateway on LANs that are connected to a router.

Table 5-11   IP Address/Subnet Mask/Default Gateway Settings for PC A and PC B

Computer	IP Address	Subnet Mask	Default Gateway
PC A	192.168.1.2	255.255.255.0	192.168.1.1
PC B	192.168.2.2	255.255.255.0	192.168.2.1

Task 9: Verify That PCs Can Communicate Across the WAN

Step 1.   Access the command (MS-DOS–like) prompt.

Windows 95/98/Me users: Click **Start > Programs > MS-DOS Prompt**.

Windows NT/2000 users: Click **Start > Programs > Command Prompt**.

Windows XP users: Click **Start > Programs > Accessories > Command Prompt**.

Step 2.   Test connectivity. Ping the IP address of the computer on the other LAN. Enter the following command at the command prompt:

C:>**ping 192.168.1.2** (or 192.168.2.2)

This command tests IP connectivity from one workstation through its switch and router across the WAN link and through the other router and switch to the other PC.

You should get results similar to those shown in Figure 5-22. If not, check the PC connections and TCP/IP settings for both PCs. What is the ping result?

_____

_____

Figure 5-22   Ping Results from PC B to PC A

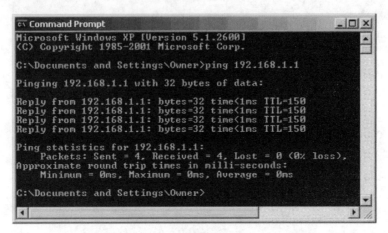

```
Command Prompt                                              _ □ ×
Microsoft Windows XP [Version 5.1.2600]
(C) Copyright 1985-2001 Microsoft Corp.

C:\Documents and Settings\Owner>ping 192.168.1.1

Pinging 192.168.1.1 with 32 bytes of data:

Reply from 192.168.1.1: bytes=32 time<1ms TTL=150
Reply from 192.168.1.1: bytes=32 time<1ms TTL=150
Reply from 192.168.1.1: bytes=32 time<1ms TTL=150
Reply from 192.168.1.1: bytes=32 time<1ms TTL=150

Ping statistics for 192.168.1.1:
    Packets: Sent = 4, Received = 4, Lost = 0 (0% loss),
Approximate round trip times in milli-seconds:
    Minimum = 0ms, Maximum = 0ms, Average = 0ms

C:\Documents and Settings\Owner>
```

Task 10: Restore the PCs to Their Original IP Settings, Disconnect the Equipment, and Store the Cables

Curriculum Lab 5-9: Troubleshooting Interconnected Devices (5.2.3c)

Figure 5-23   Network Topology for Lab 5.2.3c

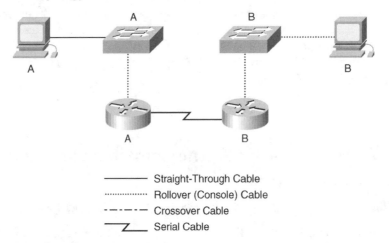

```
——————  Straight-Through Cable
·············  Rollover (Console) Cable
– – – –  Crossover Cable
——Z——  Serial Cable
```

Objectives

- Create a simple routed WAN with two PCs, two switches (or hubs), and two routers.

- Configure workstation IP address information.

- Identify and correct networking problems related to cabling issues.

- Identify and correct networking problems and workstation IP addressing issues.

Background/Preparation

This lab focuses on the ability to configure a basic router-to-router WAN and then troubleshoot Layer 1 cabling problems and workstation Layer 3 IP addressing problems.

Note: The instructor or lab assistant must preconfigure the two routers to have the correct IP addresses on their LAN and WAN interfaces. Router A will provide the clocking signal as DCE.

Refer to Lab 5.2.3b, "Building a Basic Routed WAN," to set up this lab before starting the troubleshooting. As you set up the configuration shown, you should introduce problems with cabling and workstation IP addressing into the network setup. Working in teams of two, one person can set up the configuration and introduce some errors, and the other person can troubleshoot the setup to determine the problems. This lab requires the following:

- Two Ethernet 10BASE-T or Fast Ethernet switches or two hubs

- Two routers with an RJ-45 Ethernet or Fast Ethernet interface (or an AUI interface) and at least one serial interface

- A 10BASE-T AUI transceiver (DB15-to-RJ-45) for a router with an AUI Ethernet interface (2500 series)

- Several straight-through, crossover, and improperly wired or bad cables for connecting the workstations and routers to the hub or switch

- One female (DCE) and one male (DTE) V.35 cable to interconnect the routers

Task 1: Set Up the Lab Configuration (Team Member A)

Step 1.   Set up the lab according to the specifications of Lab 5.2.3b.

Step 2.   As you connect the components, use a variety of Category 5 cables, including at least one crossover cable and a cable that is improperly wired.

Step 3.   When configuring the workstations, introduce at least one misconfiguration of IP address information per PC.

Step 4.   Record the problems in Table 5-12. The table provides space for up to three cabling problems and three IP problems. For a cabling problem, indicate the location of the problem (for example, PC A to Switch A). For an IP-related problem, indicate which PC has the problem. In the third column, describe the problem you introduced (such as a crossover cable, incorrect IP address, or incorrect default gateway).

Table 5-12   Network Cabling Problems (Team A)

Type of Problem	Location of Problem	Problem Introduced
Cabling related		
Cabling related		
Cabling related		
IP related		
IP related		
IP related		

Task 2: Troubleshoot the Lab Configuration (Team Member B)

Step 1.   Check workstation to workstation connectivity.

Ping from the command prompt on workstation A to the IP address of workstation B. If the first team member introduced problems, the ping attempt should fail.

Step 2.   Check physical layer integrity.

Start with Layer 1 issues and check cabling between the PCs and the switch. Check for the proper type of cable and good connections. Check the cabling between the routers and the switches for connections. Replace cables and ensure good connections as necessary.

Step 3.   Check network layer integrity.

Check for Layer 3 configuration problems with the workstations. (Note that the router should be preconfigured and should not have problems.) Use the command prompt or the **run** command to check the IP configuration of each workstation. You can also use the Control Panel network application to check IP settings. Verify the IP address, subnet mask, and default gateway for each workstation.

Task 3: Record the Problems Found in Table 5-13 (Team Member B)

Table 5-13   Network Cabling Problems (Team B)

Type of Problem	Location of Problem	Corrective Action Taken
Cabling related		
Cabling related		
Cabling related		
IP related		
IP related		
IP related		

Task 4: Team Members A and B Switch Roles and Repeat Lab

Task 5: Restore the PCs to Their Original IP Settings, Disconnect the Equipment, and Store the Cables

Curriculum Lab 5-10: Establishing a Console Connection to a Router or Switch (5.2.7)

Figure 5-24   Console Connection to Router or Switch

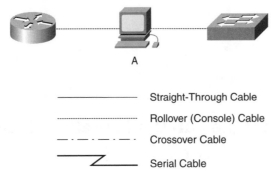

A

——————————   Straight-Through Cable

- - - - - - - - - - - -   Rollover (Console) Cable

— · — · — · — ·   Crossover Cable

——————Z——   Serial Cable

Objectives

- Create a console connection from a PC to a router and switch using the proper cable.

- Configure HyperTerminal on the PC.

- Observe the router and switch user interface.

Background/Preparation

This lab focuses on the ability to connect a PC to a router or a switch so you can establish a console session and observe the user interface. A console session lets you check or change the configuration of the switch or router; it is the simplest method of connecting to one of these devices.

Perform this lab twice, once with a router and once with a switch, to see the differences between the user interfaces. Start this lab with the equipment turned off and with cabling disconnected. Work in teams of two (one for the router and one for the switch). You need the following resources:

- A workstation with a serial interface and HyperTerminal installed

- An Ethernet 10BASE-T or Fast Ethernet switch

- A Cisco router

- Crossover (console) cable for connecting the workstation to the router or switch

Task 1: Identify the Router and Switch Console Connectors

Examine the router or switch and locate the RJ-45 connector labeled "Console," as indicated in Figure 5-25.

Figure 5-25   Router Console RJ-45 Connector

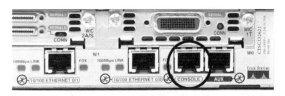

Task 2: Identify the Computer Serial Interface (COM 1 or 2)

The computer serial interface should be a 9- or 25-pin male connector labeled "serial" or "COM1." It might not have a label (see Figure 5-26).

Figure 5-26   9-Pin Serial Port

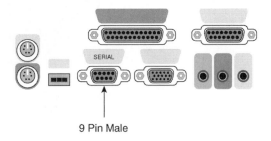

9 Pin Male

Task 3: Locate the RJ-45–to-DB9 Adapter

One side of the adapter connects to the PC's serial interface and the other to the RJ-45 rollover cable connector. If the serial interface on the PC or dumb terminal is a DB25, you need an RJ-45-to-DB25 adapter. Both the RJ-45-to-DB9 (see Figure 5-27) and RJ-45-to- DB25 adapters typically come with a Cisco router or switch.

Figure 5-27   RJ-45–to-DB9 Female Adapter

Task 4: Locate or Build a Rollover Cable

Use a rollover cable of adequate length, making one if necessary, to connect the router or switch to a workstation.

Task 5: Connect Cabling Components

Connect the rollover cable to the router or switch console port RJ-45 connector. Next, connect the other end of the rollover cable to the RJ-45-to-DB9 or -DB25 adapter. Attach the adapter to a PC serial port, either DB9 or DB25, depending on the computer (see Figure 5-28).

Figure 5-28   Router to PC Connection

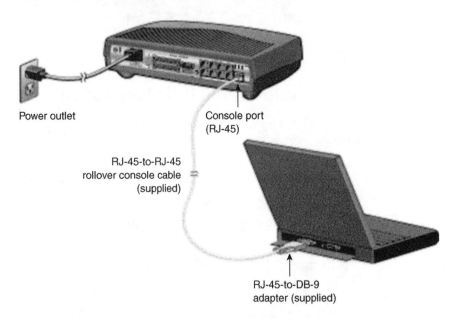

Power outlet

Console port
(RJ-45)

RJ-45-to-RJ-45
rollover console cable
(supplied)

RJ-45-to-DB-9
adapter (supplied)

Task 6: Start the PC HyperTerminal Program

Step 1.   Turn on the computer.

Step 2.   From the Windows taskbar, locate the HyperTerminal program (**Start > Programs > Accessories > Communications > HyperTerminal**).

Task 7: Name the HyperTerminal Session

In the Connection Description window, enter a name in the connection **Name** field and click **OK** (see Figure 5-29).

Figure 5-29   HyperTerminal Connection Description

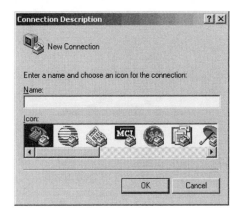

Task 8: Specify the Computer's Connecting Interface

In the Connect To window (see Figure 5-30), use the drop-down arrow in the Connect Using field to select **COM1** and click **OK**.

Note: Depending on which serial port you used on the PC, it might be necessary to set this to **COM2**.

Figure 5-30   HyperTerminal Connect To Dialog Box

Task 9: Specify the Interface Connection Properties

Step 1.   In the COM1 Properties window (see Figure 5-31), use the drop-down arrows to select the following:

Bits per second = **9600**

Data Bits = **8**

Parity = **None**

Stop bits = **1**

Flow control = **none**

Step 2.   Click **OK**.

Figure 5-31   HyperTerminal COM1 Properties

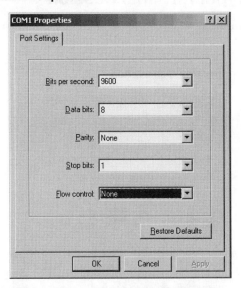

Step 3.   When the HyperTerminal session window opens, turn on the router or switch. If router or switch is already on, press **Enter**. You should see a response from the router or switch. If you do, you successfully completed the connection.

Task 10: Observe the Router or Switch User Interface

Observe the user interface.

If this is a router, what is the prompt?

_____

If this is a switch, what is the prompt?

_____

Task 11: Closing the Session

Step 1.   To end the console session from a HyperTerminal session, select **File > Exit**.

Step 2.   When the HyperTerminal disconnect warning window appears (see Figure 5-32), select **Yes**.

Figure 5-32   Closing a HyperTerminal Session

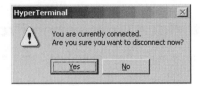

Step 3.   The computer will then ask whether you want to save the session. Select **No**.

Task 12: Shut Down the Router or Switch and Store the Cables

Comprehensive Lab 5-11: Building a Multiswitch Network

Figure 5-33   Multiswitch Network Topology

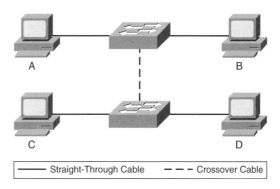

| —— Straight-Through Cable | – – – Crossover Cable |

Objectives

- Create a network with four PCs using two switches.

- Identify the proper cables to connect the PCs to the switches and the switches to one another.

- Configure workstation IP address information.

- Test connectivity using the **ping** command.

Background

This comprehensive lab focuses on the ability to connect two PC-populated switches to create a simple Ethernet LAN. Because switches eliminate collisions through microsegmentation, this is a practical way to expand the scope of a LAN.

In addition to the physical and data link connections, which are Layers 1 and 2, the computers must also be configured with the correct IP network settings, which is Layer 3, so that they can communicate. Because this lab requires connecting PCs to a switch and connecting two switches to one another, Category 5/5e UTP straight-through and crossover cables are needed. Start this lab with the equipment turned off and with cabling disconnected. Work in teams of four with one person per PC. The following resources will be required:

- Four workstations with an Ethernet 10/100 NIC installed

- Two Ethernet 10BASE-T or Fast Ethernet switches

- Several Ethernet cables (straight-through and crossover) to connect the devices

Task 1: Identify the Proper Ethernet Cables and Connect the Devices

Connect two of the PCs to one switch using straight-through cables. Connect the remaining two PCs to the other switch using straight-through cables. Connect the switches to one another using a crossover cable.

Task 2: Verify the Physical Connections

Plug in and turn on the PCs and switches. To verify connections, ensure that the link lights on all PC NICs and the connected switch interfaces are lit. What color are the LEDs on the connected switch ports?

_____

_____

Task 3: Access the IP Settings Window

Note: Write down the existing IP settings so you can restore them at the end of the lab.

Windows 95/98/Me users:

Step 1.   Click **Start > Settings > Control Panel > Network**.

Step 2.   Select the TCP/IP Protocol icon that is associated with the NIC in this PC and click **Properties**. Click the **IP Address** tab and the **Gateway** tab.

Windows NT/2000 users:

Step 1.   Click **Start > Settings > Control Panel > Network**.

Step 2.   Click the **Protocols** tab and select the TCP/IP Protocol icon that is associated with the NIC in this PC. Click **Properties** and click **Specify an IP Address**.

Windows XP users:

Step 1.   Click **Start > Control Panel > Network Connection**.

Step 2.   Select the **Local Area Network Connection** icon and click **Change Settings of This Connection**.

Task 4: Configure the TCP/IP Settings for the PCs

Set the IP address information for each PC according to the information in Table 5-14.

Table 5-14   IP Address Settings for PCs

Computer	IP Address	Subnet Mask	Default Gateway
PC A	192.168.1.1	255.255.255.0	Not required
PC B	192.168.1.2	255.255.255.0	Not required
PC C	192.168.1.3	255.255.255.0	Not required
PC D	192.168.1.4	255.255.255.0	Not required

Task 5: Access the Command Prompt

Use the Start menu to open the command prompt window.

Windows 95/98/ME users: Click **185Start > Programs > MS-DOS Prompt**.

Windows NT/2000 users: Click **Start > Programs > Command Prompt**.

Windows XP users: Click **Start > Programs > Accessories > Command Prompt**.

Task 6: Verify That the PCs Can Communicate

Test connectivity from one PC to the other PC on the same switch by pinging the IP address of the opposite computer. Was the ping successful?

_____

Test connectivity from one PC to another PC connected to the other switch by pinging the IP address of that computer. Was the ping successful?

_____

Task 7: Disconnect the Equipment

Disconnect and store the cables and switch.

Task 8: Restore the PCs to Their Original Configurations

Reconnect any cables that were originally connected to the PCs. Ensure that the original IP settings are restored to the PCs and verify that each is functioning properly.

CHAPTER 6

Ethernet Fundamentals

The Study Guide portion of this chapter uses a combination of matching, fill in the blank, compare and contrast, and open-ended question exercises to test your knowledge of Ethernet fundamentals.

The Lab Exercises portion of this chapter includes a challenge lab to ensure that you have mastered the practical, hands-on skills needed to use MAC addresses in an Ethernet LAN.

As you work through this chapter, use Module 6 in the CCNA 1 online curriculum or use the corresponding Chapter 6 in the *Networking Basics CCNA 1 Companion Guide* for assistance.

Study Guide

Ethernet Fundamentals

Engineers began developing Ethernet in the 1970s, and it is still being used today. The original concept grew from the need to allow two or more hosts to communicate across the same medium without interference between signals. The DIX consortium published the first Ethernet standard in 1980, which helped define the original IEEE 802.3 standard published in 1985. This standard has been amended and modified over the years, and it is the most popular LAN standard in the world.

Understanding Ethernet requires knowledge of its operations, how it relates to the OSI reference model, and the framing structure that is used. In this section, you find exercises that help you identify terminology associated with Ethernet, compare and contrast OSI model Layer 1 and Layer 2 functions, identify frame types, and understand MAC addresses. These exercises help you build and test your knowledge of Ethernet fundamentals.

Vocabulary Exercise: Matching

Match the definition on the left with a term on the right. This exercise does not necessarily use one-to-one matching. Some definitions might be used more than once and some terms might have multiple definitions.

Definitions

a. Media-access mechanism wherein devices ready to transmit data first check the channel for a carrier.

b. 100-Mbps Ethernet.

c. The network area within which frames that have collided are propagated.

d. The wrapping of data in a particular protocol header.

e. This message is sent to a single network destination.

f. A request sent to the sending station requesting that a frame be sent again because it was not received or received with errors.

g. Control information placed before data when encapsulating that data for network transmission.

h. 1000-Mbps Ethernet.

i. Logical grouping of information sent as a data link layer unit over a transmission medium.

j. Data packet that will be sent to all nodes on a network. Broadcasts are identified by a broadcast address.

k. A notification sent from one network device to another to acknowledge that some event has occurred.

l. 10-Mbps Ethernet.

m. These are single packets copied by the network and sent to a specific subset of network addresses.

n. The control information appended to the end of data when that data is encapsulated for network transmission.

o. An alternating pattern of 1s and 0s used to time synchronization in 10 Mbps and slower implementations of Ethernet.

p. The lower of the two sublayers of the data link layer defined by the Institute of Electrical and Electronics Engineers (IEEE).

q. An identifier assigned to an 802.3 standard supplement that contains a number representing the speed of the technology, the signaling type, and the medium used by the technology.

r. Higher of the two data link layer sublayers defined by the IEEE. This sublayer handles error control, flow control, framing, and MAC sublayer addressing.

Terms

___ frame

___ CSMA/CD

___ MAC

___ preamble

___ unicast

___ trailer

___ encapsulation

___ broadcast

___ collision domain

___ Legacy Ethernet

___ multicast

___ Gigabit Ethernet

___ header

___ acknowledgment

___ abbreviated description

___ LLC

___ Fast Ethernet

___ retransmission

Compare and Contrast Exercise: Layer 1 and Layer 2 Functions

Ethernet is a family of network technologies. Although multiple Ethernet implementations exist (Legacy, Fast Ethernet, Gigabit Ethernet, and so on), each type uses the same basic frame format and the functions of the IEEE sublayers of Layer 1 and Layer 2. Complete Table 6-1 to compare and contrast the OSI model Layer 1 and Layer 2 functions.

Table 6-1   Compare and Contrast Layer 1 and Layer 2 Functions

	Layer 1	Layer 2
How does this layer communicate with the upper layers of the OSI model?		
How does the layer identify hosts?		
How does the layer handle bits?		
How does the layer deal with multiple stations trying to transmit simultaneously?		

Concept Questions

Completely answer the following questions:

1. Ethernet was introduced in the 1970s and is still used today. What factors contribute to the success of Ethernet? Explain.

2. Explain how data is encapsulated as it passes through the OSI model from the user to the medium. What is the role of Ethernet in this process?

3. MAC addresses are data link layer identifiers that are hard-coded into network interface cards (NIC) and other communication adapters. What is the role of MAC addresses in Ethernet networks?

_____
_____
_____
_____
_____
_____
_____

4. The data link layer uses a frame to encapsulate upper-layer data as it passes through the OSI model. Briefly explain the framing process.

_____
_____
_____
_____
_____
_____

5. The Frame Check Sequence (FCS) field identifies errors in frames as they are transmitted from the source to a destination. What are some of the methods used to calculate the FCS number?

_____
_____
_____
_____
_____
_____
_____

Identifying Frame Types Exercise

A frame is a collection of bits organized into sections. The frame is the OSI model Layer 2 PDU. The structure of these sections, known as fields, is based on the framing standard that is being used by the network device. The two most common frame types include IEEE 802.3 and Ethernet II. Network professionals must understand each frame type and the information that is contained in each of the frame fields.

Use Figure 6-1 to label the field types and sizes for an IEEE 802.3 frame.

Figure 6-1   IEEE 802.3 Frame

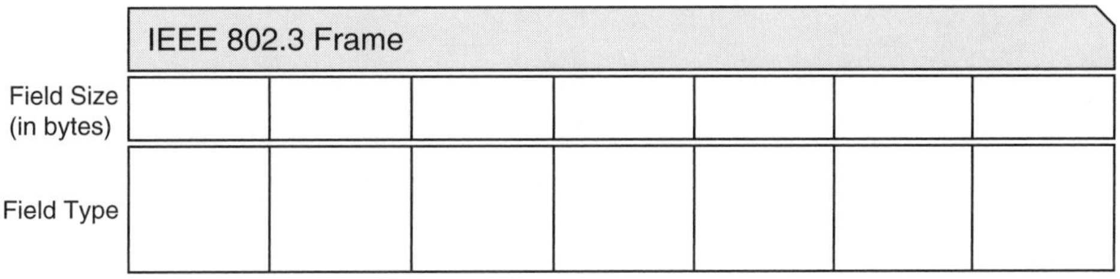

IEEE 802.3 Frame						
Field Size (in bytes)						
Field Type						

Use Figure 6-2 to label the field types and sizes for an Ethernet II frame.

Figure 6-2   Ethernet II Frame

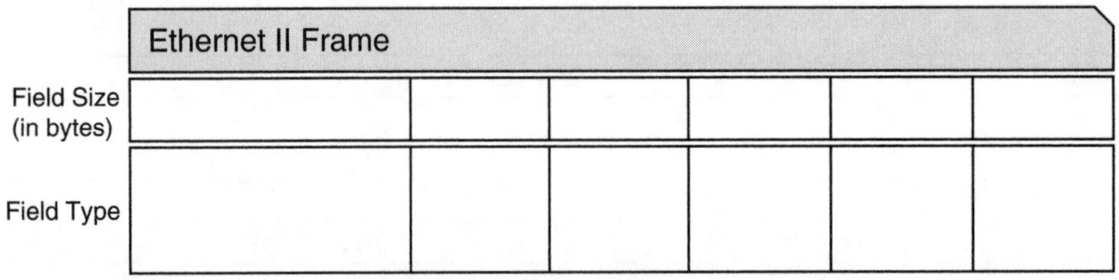

Ethernet II Frame					
Field Size (in bytes)					
Field Type					

Use Table 6-2 to describe each field type used within IEEE 802.3 and Ethernet II frames.

Table 6-2   IEEE 802.3 Frame Fields and Descriptions

IEEE 802.3 Frame Field	Field Description

Understanding MAC Addresses Exercise

Network communication requires naming or addressing systems to be in place. This system must have a global structure and the ability to uniquely address each device on the network. The MAC address system is an example of this type of system.

Answer the following questions about MAC addresses using the online curriculum or the *Networking Basics CCNA 1 Companion Guide*. You need Internet access to perform additional MAC address research.

1. What is the length of a MAC address?

_____

2. How are MAC addresses expressed? What is the format of a MAC address?

_____

_____

3. Where are MAC addresses located?

_____

_____

4. Is a MAC address flat or hierarchical? Explain.

_____

_____

5. What are the two components of a MAC address? What is the function of each?

_____

_____

_____

_____

6. Who maintains the official register of OUIs? What is the address of the website where this information can be viewed?

_____

_____

7. What is the price of registering a new public OUI?

_____

_____

8. List three public OUIs held by Cisco Systems.

_____

_____

Note: Now is a good time to challenge yourself with Lab 6-1. This lab focuses on building and configuring a LAN and gathering Layer 2 information. It also introduces Address Resolution Protocol (ARP).

Journal Entry

The Length/Type field in an IEEE 802.3 frame has two uses. If the value is less than 0x0600 hexadecimal, the value indicates the amount of data that follows the field (length). The type value is used to pass the frame's data to the appropriate upper-layer protocol after the Ethernet process is complete. This type value is often called the Ethernet number or EtherType.

EtherTypes, like OUIs, are registered through the IEEE Standards Association. If an individual or organization has a specialty application that requires a new EtherType, they must complete the registration process through the IEEE. Upon approval, the IEEE creates a unique EtherType for the applicant and this information is published publicly.

EtherTypes are referenced every time a frame is received. When a frame reaches its destination, the type value is evaluated and the data is handled by the appropriate protocols. Although this process takes place automatically at the network device, network administrators can also look at the frame types as they travel from source to destination. Frame-capturing software gives the administrator an opportunity to look at individual frames and frame fields, including the value of the Length/Type field. Using the Internet, network administrators can then compare the field value to a published list of EtherTypes to have a better idea of the frame types that travel the network.

Table 6-3 contains a list of well-known EtherTypes and their values, expressed in hexadecimal and binary. Complete the table by filling in the missing information in each row. To complete this assignment, you need to use the Internet to find a list of EtherTypes.

Table 6-3   EtherTypes

EtherType	Hexadecimal Value	Binary Value
ARP		
	8035	
		0000100000000000
	86DD	
PPP		
	809B	
		1000011101101011
	814C	

What is the URL of the website you used to find the EtherType information?

_____

_____

Ethernet Operation

Ethernet operates in shared-media environments and requires a mechanism to keep communications flowing smoothly with minimal interruptions. Carrier sense multiple access/collision detect (CSMA/CD) is a MAC protocol that Ethernet uses to listen to the line before transmitting data. Collisions occur when two stations simultaneously transmit data, which results in corrupted data. CSMA/CD minimizes collisions, but it does not completely eliminate them. When a collision is detected, other steps are taken to avoid further problems.

This section contains exercises that focus on Ethernet operation. These exercises increase your understanding of related vocabulary, deterministic and nondeterministic protocols, the functions of CSMA/CD, and recognizing collision domains. Additionally, you are asked to investigate another MAC protocol commonly used in wireless LANs (WLAN).

Vocabulary Exercise: Completion

Complete the following statements by using the proper terms to fill in the blanks.

In Ethernet, two nodes transmitting simultaneously on a common segment results in a _____.

When data is passed in one direction at a time between two hosts, _____ communication is being used.

CSMA/CD is a _____ MAC protocol because it uses a first-come, first-served approach.

A _____ generates a random transmission delay when a collision occurs.

The actual calculated _____ is just longer than the theoretical amount of time required to travel between the furthest points of the collision domain, collide with another transmission at the last possible instant, and then have the collision fragments return to the sending station and be detected.

_____ MAC protocols operate in a collisionless environment because only one host can transmit at a time.

_____ communications allow hosts to send and receive data at the same time.

The minimum spacing between two noncolliding frames is called _____.

As soon as a collision is detected, the sending stations transmit a 32-bit _____ to enforce the collision.

Network interfaces can use _____ to determine the best possible speed of the link and automatically configure the interface accordingly.

In IEEE 802.3, a data packet whose length exceeds that prescribed in the standard is known as _____.

_____ Ethernet uses extra timing information to synchronize the receive circuit to the incoming data.

Compare and Contrast Exercise: Deterministic and Nondeterministic MAC Protocols

MAC protocols determine which computer in a shared-media environment, or collision domain, is allowed to transmit data. The two major categories of MAC protocols handle this process in unique ways. Complete Table 6-4 to compare and contrast deterministic and nondeterministic MAC protocols.

Table 6-4   Compare and Contrast Deterministic and Nondeterministic MAC Protocols

	Deterministic	Nondeterministic
Provide a brief definition of the protocol.		
How does this protocol avoid and detect collisions?		
Provide specific examples of the protocol.		

Concept Questions

Completely answer the following questions:

1. CSMA/CD is a shared-media access method used in Ethernet. What are the primary functions of CSMA/CD?

    _____

    ■ _____

    ■ _____
    _____

    ■ _____

2. Bit times calculate the slot times necessary for proper frame timing. How is Ethernet bit time calculated?

    _____
    _____

3. A collision domain is a bounded area of a network that does not receive or pass collisions to other parts of the network. Which network devices can create additional collision domains?

    _____
    _____
    _____

4. Explain the concept of backoff after a collision is detected.

    _____
    _____
    _____
    _____
    _____

5. There are three types of collisions in Ethernet. List and briefly explain each collision type.

- _____
- _____
- _____

6. Collisions are a normal occurrence in Ethernet. When are collisions considered errors that require a network administrator to intervene?

_____

7. The FCS field ensures that the size of the frame at the destination is the size of the frame that was sent from the source. What is typically the problem if a high number of frames from a host or segment are discarded because of FCS errors?

_____

8. How does autonegotiation use link pulses to determine the best possible connection speed and duplex mode?

_____

Identifying Collision Domains Exercise

Collisions are a common occurrence in Ethernet implementations. A small number of collisions usually has little to no effect on network performance. A larger number of collisions, on the other hand, can negatively affect network communications and often points to a more serious problem within the infrastructure. Keeping collisions to a minimum is important. Keeping collisions contained within as small an area as possible is equally as important.

An area that contains a collision and does not pass it into other segments is known as a *collision domain*. Collision domains are created by defining network segment boundaries with devices and technologies that do not pass collisions.

Note: Having multiple, small collision domains is highly desirable. Network professionals need to take this into account when designing and configuring a LAN.

Identify the collision domains of the following networks by circling each of the domains. Record the number of collision domains for each network example.

Figure 6-3   Network Example 1

Number of
Collision Domains

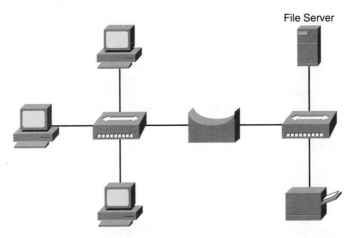

Figure 6-4   Network Example 2

Number of
Collision Domains

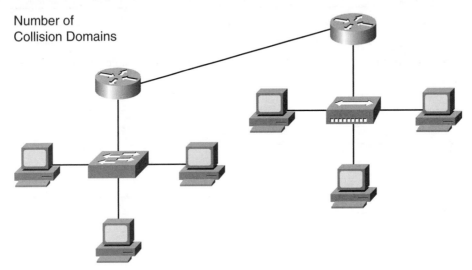

Figure 6-5   Network Example 3

Number of
Collision Domains

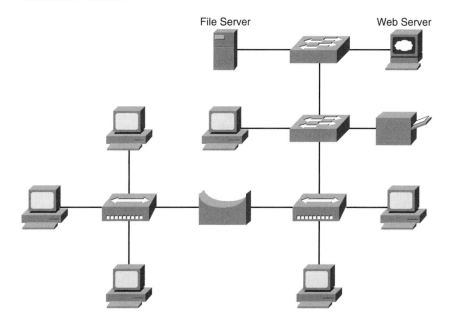

Journal Entry

WLANs are becoming increasingly popular because of their ease of setup and the convenience they provide users. Wireless segments often supplement existing Ethernet networks. IEEE 802.11 defines WLAN operating standards. Although the differences in media types are obvious, most WLANs and Ethernet implementations operate similarly. Each technology operates in a broadcast, shared-media environment. This requires a mechanism to avoid, detect, and properly handle collisions.

Use the Internet to research the MAC protocol used by IEEE 802.11 WLANs. Briefly describe the protocol and the way it operates.

_____

_____

_____

_____

_____

_____

_____

_____

_____

_____

Lab Exercises

Challenge Lab 6-1: Identifying MAC Addresses in a LAN

Figure 6-6   Four-Workstation LAN

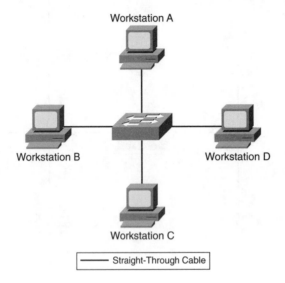

Workstation A

Workstation B

Workstation D

Workstation C

——— Straight-Through Cable

Objectives

- Create a small LAN with four PCs.

- Configure workstation IP address information.

- Test connectivity using the **ping** command.

- Gather the MAC addresses of remote PCs.

Background

Ethernet LANs use MAC addresses to communicate between LAN devices. These addresses are associated with a corresponding IP address, and this information is gathered and maintained by ARP. ARP requests are initiated by a source that needs to communicate with a destination but knows only the destination's IP address. The ARP request is broadcast to the LAN, and the destination replies with its MAC address. ARP then builds a table to associate the destination's IP address and MAC address on the source device. LAN communication requires a complete entry in the source's ARP table of the destination's addressing information.

This challenge lab focuses on building and configuring a LAN and gathering Layer 2 information. Work in teams of four with one person per PC. You need the following resources:

- Four workstations with an Ethernet 10/100 NIC installed

- One Ethernet switch or hub

- Several straight-through Ethernet cables to connect the PCs to the switch

Task 1: Build the LAN and Verify the Physical Connections

Connect all four PCs to the switch using straight-through cables. Plug in and turn on the devices. How can the physical connections be verified initially?

_____

Task 2: Configure the TCP/IP Settings on the PCs

Set the IP address information for each PC according to the information in Table 6-5.

_____

Note: Write down the existing IP settings so you can restore them at the end of the lab.

_____

Table 6-5   IP Address Settings for PCs

Computer	IP Address	Subnet Mask	Default Gateway
Workstation A	192.168.1.1	255.255.255.0	Not required
Workstation B	192.168.1.2	255.255.255.0	Not required
Workstation C	192.168.1.3	255.255.255.0	Not required
Workstation D	192.168.1.4	255.255.255.0	Not required

Task 3: Access the Command Prompt to Gather Information

Open a command prompt on your PC and gather the information to answer the following questions.

_____

Note: The steps used to open a command prompt can be different for each OS. Be familiar with the steps for the most common OSs.

_____

1. Which workstation are you working with?

_____

2. What OS is installed on the workstation?

_____

3. How did you access the command prompt?

_____

_____

_____

_____

4. What is the IP address of the workstation?

_____

5. What is the MAC address of the workstation NIC?

_____

6. What command did you use to see the MAC address?

_____

Task 4: View the Workstation ARP Table

At the command prompt, type **arp –a** and press **Enter** to view the contents of the workstation's ARP table. What are the contents of the ARP table?

Task 5: Verify Workstation Connectivity and Gather Layer 2 Addressing Information

Using the command prompt, **ping** one of the other workstations on the LAN. Use appropriate troubleshooting procedures if the ping was not successful.

1. Which workstation did you ping?

2. What is the IP address of that workstation?

3. After verifying Layer 3 connectivity to another workstation, check the contents of your workstation's ARP table. What has been added to the ARP table?

4. What information can be found in the ARP table for the new entry?

Ping the remaining workstations, view the updated ARP table, and complete Table 6-6.

Table 6-6   Workstation Layer 2 and 3 Information

	MAC Address	IP Address
Workstation A		192.168.1.1
Workstation B		192.168.1.2
Workstation C		192.168.1.3
Workstation D		192.168.1.4

Task 6: Disconnect the Equipment

Disconnect and store the cables and switch.

Task 7: Restore the PCs to Their Original Configuration

Reconnect any cables that were originally connected to the PCs. Ensure that the original IP settings are restored to the PCs and verify that each properly functions.

Task 7: Determine the EtherType Number for ARP Frames

LAN communications require the knowledge of Layer 2 and 3 addresses. MAC addresses are gathered dynamically as needed through the use of ARP requests, and the information is maintained in ARP tables on network devices. What is the EtherType for ARP frames?

_____

_____

Note: You learn more about the ARP process in Chapter 9 and in Curriculum Lab 9-3, "Workstation ARP (9.3.7)."

CHAPTER 7

Ethernet Technologies

The Study Guide portion of this chapter uses a combination of fill in the blank, compare and contrast, and open-ended question exercises to test your knowledge of Ethernet technologies.

The Lab Exercises portion of this chapter includes curriculum labs to ensure that you have mastered the practical, hands-on skills needed to use Ethernet technologies.

As you work through this chapter, use Module 7 in the CCNA 1 online curriculum or use the corresponding Chapter 7 in the *Networking Basics CCNA 1 Companion Guide* for assistance.

Study Guide

10-Mbps and 100-Mbps Ethernet

Ethernet is the dominant LAN technology today, and it will likely remain dominant in the near future. Reasons for Ethernet's success include simple implementation and its flexible framework. This framework allows Ethernet to continue to evolve and meet the changing needs of today's networks. 10-Mbps Ethernet, also known as Legacy Ethernet, is still used in networks but is normally not implemented in new installations. 100-Mbps Ethernet, or Fast Ethernet, is likely the slowest Ethernet technology being installed today. 1000-Mbps Ethernet, known as Gigabit Ethernet, and beyond is moving from the backbone into horizontal cabling and to end stations. Understanding today's Ethernet requires knowledge of the earlier implementations.

In this section, you find exercises that help you learn terminology associated with Legacy and Fast Ethernet, compare and contrast the varieties of Legacy Ethernet, and identify Ethernet parameters. These exercises focus on the key areas of the corresponding section of the curriculum.

Vocabulary Exercise: Completion

Complete the following statements by using the proper terms to fill in the blanks.

The _____, also called a heartbeat, is a transmission sent by a transceiver back to the controller to let the controller know whether the collision circuitry is functional.

_____ describes how bits are actually signaled on the wire.

In a 10BASE2 network, only _____ out of five consecutive segments between any two stations can be populated.

Any repeater that changes between one Ethernet implementation and another is a _____ repeater.

_____ encoding uses the transition in the middle of the timing window to determine the binary value for that bit period.

10BASE2 Ethernet devices connect to the media with _____
_____ connectors.

As part of the original IEEE 802.3 standard, _____ was the first medium used for Ethernet.

_____ is a Fast Ethernet technology that uses multimode optical fiber medium.

_____ encoding uses three voltage levels to signal binary 1s and 0s.

Compare and Contrast Exercise: Legacy Ethernet

Legacy Ethernet is the group of 10-Mbps Ethernet technologies, including 10BASE2, 10BASE5, and 10BASE-T. These technologies are grouped together because of their common features, including timing parameters, the frame format, transmission processes, and a basic design rule. What makes each technology unique is the media that it runs on, the media connectors, and the physical network configurations that are used. Use Table 7-1 to compare and contrast the three types of Legacy Ethernet.

Table 7-1   Compare and Contrast Legacy Ethernet Technologies

	10BASE2	10BASE5	10BASE-T
What is the media used by this type of Legacy Ethernet?			
What type of connector connects to the media?			
What is the maximum segment length?			
Is it capable of full-duplex operation?			
What are the advantages of this type of Legacy Ethernet when compared to the others?			
What are the disadvantages of this type of Legacy Ethernet when compared to the others?			

Concept Questions

Completely answer the following questions:

1. What types of Ethernet are considered Legacy Ethernet? What are the common features of Legacy Ethernet?

   _____
   _____
   _____

2. What is a line-encoding process? List some specific types of line encoding and their applications.

   _____
   _____
   _____

3. 10BASE-T usually runs across four-pair UTP cable but only uses four of the eight wires in the cable. Which pins are used, and what is the function of each?

_____

_____

_____

_____

_____

4. Although hubs can be added to extend the range of 10BASE-T networks, why is it best to keep from linking hubs to one another?

_____

_____

_____

5. 100BASE-TX is the standard desktop LAN connection in many organizations. What are the advantages of 100BASE-TX operating in full duplex as opposed to half duplex?

_____

_____

_____

6. Why was fiber Fast Ethernet never widely adopted?

_____

_____

_____

_____

7. What is the difference between a Class I and Class II repeater?

_____

_____

_____

_____

_____

Identifying Legacy and Fast Ethernet Parameters Exercise

Ethernet frame fields and sizes are common to all Ethernet technologies. The differences in the technologies lie within the parameters for transmitting frames. Timing plays a crucial role in each technology and strict adherence to timing parameters is essential to achieve the desired bandwidth and the proper functioning of carrier sense multiple access collision detect (CSMA/CD). It is important to understand these parameters when designing and troubleshooting an Ethernet installation.

Complete Figure 7-1 and Figure 7-2 by filling in the parameters used by Legacy Ethernet and Fast Ethernet, respectively. You can use the corresponding section of the curriculum to find many of the answers, but you need to calculate the time to send each type of frame.

Note: Calculate the time to send a frame by multiplying the number of bits in the frame by the bit time. Remember, 1 ns is equal to 10^{29} (.000000001 seconds).

Figure 7-1   10-Mbps Ethernet Parameters and Values

10-Mbps Ethernet	
Parameter	Value
Bit Time	
Slot Time	
Interframe Spacing	
Collision Attempt Limit	
Collision Backoff Limit	
Collision Jam Size	
Maximum Untagged Frame Size	
Time to Send a Maximum Frame	
Minimum Frame Size	
Time to Send a Minimum Frame	

Figure 7-2   100-Mbps Ethernet Parameters and Values

100-Mbps Ethernet	
Parameter	Value
Bit Time	
Slot Time	
Interframe Spacing	
Collision Attempt Limit	
Collision Backoff Limit	
Collision Jam Size	
Maximum Untagged Frame Size	
Time to Send a Maximum Frame	
Minimum Frame Size	
Time to Send a Minimum Frame	

Note: All network signals are sent in the form of waves, and it is important for networking professionals to understand how these waves are encoded and decoded. Now is a good time to begin Curriculum Lab 7-1.

Journal Entry

Ethernet is an effective and efficient network communications technology. Ethernet frames possess a small amount of overhead in comparison to the amount of data they contain. At even Legacy Ethernet speeds, generous amounts of data can be passed across a LAN at any given moment, provided the network is functioning properly. The amount of data that can be passed within a specific time can be calculated using bandwidth and framing data. Network professionals can benefit from the knowledge of this information.

Calculate the maximum amount of user data that can be passed across an optimally functioning 10-Mbps LAN in one second. Make the following assumptions in your calculation:

- The LAN is operating at half duplex.

- Only maximum-sized untagged frames will be sent.

- There are 1500 bytes of user data per frame.

- The network is collision free and has no other traffic.

1. How much user data can pass across this network in 1 second?

_____

_____

_____

_____

_____

_____

_____

_____

_____

_____

_____

2. In the real world, what factors would keep this network from functioning at this rate?

_____

_____

_____

_____

3. What can be done to increase the amount of user data passed across the network?

_____

_____

_____

Gigabit and 10-Gigabit Ethernet

1000-Mbps Ethernet, or Gigabit Ethernet, operates at 10 times the speed of Fast Ethernet and 100 times the speed of Legacy Ethernet. Obtaining this amount of bandwidth requires enhanced media properties and strict timing parameters. 10-Gigabit Ethernet and beyond are pushing the limits of current communications hardware even further.

This section includes exercises that reinforce your understanding of Gigabit and 10-Gigabit Ethernet. These exercises include identifying acronyms, understanding Gigabit and 10-Gigabit Ethernet parameters, and researching common IEEE 802.3 standards.

Vocabulary Exercise: Identifying Acronyms and Initialisms

An acronym is a word formed by the first letters in a multiword term. An initialism is a word made of initials pronounced separately. These are used extensively in the information technology (IT) field. Identify the terms associated with the following acronyms:

10GbE   _____

10GEA   _____

FEC   _____

LX   _____

NRZ   _____

PAM5 _____

QoS _____

SDH _____

SONET _____

SX _____

WWDM _____

Concept Questions

Completely answer the following questions:

1. Why are faster, copper-based Ethernet standards (Gigabit and beyond) more susceptible to noise and interference? What mechanisms are in place to ensure that bit streams are readable at the destination?

    _____
    _____
    _____
    _____
    _____
    _____

2. Fast Ethernet seemed to push the limits of four-pair copper cabling. How can Category 5e cable Gigabit Ethernet signals?

    _____
    _____
    _____
    _____

3. Why is Gigabit Ethernet over fiber the preferred backbone technology when compared to the copper variant?

    _____
    _____
    _____
    _____

4. When implementing Gigabit Ethernet across copper in an extended star topology, why is it recommended that all station to switch links be set to perform autoconfiguration?

    _____
    _____
    _____
    _____
    _____

5. 10-Gbps Ethernet (10GbE) operates at 1000 times the speed of Legacy Ethernet, yet they share many features. What are some features that are common to both 10GbE and Legacy Ethernet? What are some differences?

_____

_____

6. Ethernet is no longer a LAN-only technology. What allows Ethernet functionality to extend beyond the confines of a LAN and into MAN and WAN territories?

_____

_____

Identifying Gigabit and 10-Gigabit Ethernet Parameters Exercise

Ethernet frame fields and sizes are common to all Ethernet technologies. The differences in the technologies lie within the parameters for transmitting frames. Timing plays a crucial role in each of the technologies, and strict adherence to timing parameters is essential to achieve the desired bandwidth and the proper functioning of CSMA/CD. It is important to understand these parameters when designing and troubleshooting an Ethernet installation.

Complete Figure 7-3 and Figure 7-4 by filling in the parameters used by Gigabit Ethernet and 10-Gigabit Ethernet, respectively.

Figure 7-3   1-Gbps Ethernet Parameters and Values

1-Gbps Ethernet	
Parameter	Value
Bit Time	
Slot Time	
Interframe Spacing	
Collision Attempt Limit	
Collision Backoff Limit	
Collision Jam Size	
Maximum Untagged Frame Size	
Time to Send a Maximum Frame	
Minimum Frame Size	
Time to Send a Minimum Frame	

Figure 7-4   10-Gbps Ethernet Parameters and Values

10-Gbps Ethernet	
Parameter	Value
Bit Time	
Slot Time	
Interframe Spacing	
Collision Attempt Limit	
Collision Backoff Limit	
Collision Jam Size	
Maximum Untagged Frame Size	
Time to Send a Maximum Frame	
Minimum Frame Size	
Time to Send a Minimum Frame	

Note: Curriculum Labs 7-2 and 7-3 introduce you to network analysis software that you can use to discover network devices and gather information from traffic that passes across the network. Take your time when you work through these labs because you will be asked to use these applications in other labs and curriculums.

Journal Entry

The IEEE 802.3 collection of standards defines the current Ethernet technologies. The IEEE began creating these standards in the early 1980s and continues to do so today. They define the characteristics of the lower portions of the OSI model to include the MAC sublayer of the data link layer, the physical layer, as well as the medium. It is important for networking professionals to be familiar with the standards and the technologies they describe.

Table 7-2 contains a list of IEEE 802.3 standards and their technology descriptions. Complete the table by filling in the missing information in each row and listing two other standards and their descriptions that are not on the list. You might need to use the Internet to find the list of standards to complete this assignment.

Table 7-2   IEEE 802.3 Standards

IEEE 802.3 Standard	Technology Description
	10BASE5
802.3an	
	1000BASE-X
802.3u	
802.3a	
	10 GbE over fiber
802.3ab	
	10BASE-T

What is the URL of the website you used to find the list of IEEE 802.3 standards?

_____

_____

Lab Exercises

Curriculum Lab 7-1: Waveform Decoding (7.1.2)

Objective

The purpose of this lab is to integrate knowledge of networking media; OSI Layers 1, 2, and 3; and Ethernet by taking a digital waveform of an Ethernet frame and decoding it. Specifically, you will do the following:

- Review numbering systems, OSI concepts, and encoding methods as background.

- Learn to decode the waveform into binary, reorder the binary, and identify Ethernet field boundaries.

- Decode the Ethernet Length/Type field, locate and read RFCs, and decode Layer 3 of the waveform.

- Use a protocol analyzer.

Background/Preparation

As a networking student, you learn about many new concepts: the OSI model, networking media and signals, Ethernet, and the TCP/IP protocols. Network administrators, technicians, and engineers study and troubleshoot a network using protocol-analysis software. Protocol-analysis software facilitates the capture and interpretation of frame-level data, which is crucial to understand what happens on a live (and perhaps troublesome) network. Hand-decoding the signal gives you more insight into what the software is doing automatically for you. This lab provides an important foundation for future network troubleshooting.

A digital oscilloscope was attached to an Ethernet 10BASE2 coaxial cable to capture actual Ethernet waveforms. Although it is possible to capture waveforms on 10BASE-T and 100BASE-TX twisted-pair media, the coaxial cable gives the cleanest and most readable waveform data. This data is available from your instructor. Decoding the waveform is a crucial step in understanding how networks operate.

For the first part of the lab, all that you need is this lab companion and the printout of the waveform to "mark up" as you decode. The last task of the lab involves using a protocol analyzer, such as Fluke Protocol Inspector or the equivalent.

Task 1: Review Numbering Systems, OSI Concepts, and Encoding Methods as Background

In this section, you review decimal, binary, and hexadecimal numbering systems; the OSI seven-layer reference model; and signaling and encoding methods.

Counting Systems

Computers rely on the concept of *on* and *off* to perform any action. On and off is the equivalent of the *binary* counting system, which uses only the digits 0 and 1. Before describing how the binary counting system works, let's first review the decimal counting system that we use every day. The review provides a reference for the other counting systems.

Decimal

The *decimal* counting system is based on the numbers 0 through 9. You depict decimal by writing the number 10 in subscript immediately after the number. For example, you can clearly express the number 22_{10} as decimal in this way.

A single decimal digit can represent any quantity between 0 and 9. If the current number were 9, adding 1 changes the number from a single digit to two digits. Thus, groupings are based on sets of 10. You show a complete set of 10 by a change in columns, moving one column to the left.

A counting sequence follows:

0

1

2

3

4

5

6

7

8

9

10

11

12

Figure 7-5 provides a graphical representation of the placeholders represented by each digit in a given number. Because of size limitations, the figure depicts only the grouping increments of 1s, 10s, and 100s. If it helps, look upon the placeholder graphic as a method of counting beans, one bean per placeholder circle.

Notice how Figure 7-5 shows a placeholder for nine sets in each column. Zero is represented by a lack of any populated placeholder in that column. Populating more than nine placeholders in any column is not possible, because no placeholder is offered. To increase the number of placeholders, it is necessary to change columns. All the placeholders, plus the placeholder that forced the change in columns, move to the next column to the left as a single entry. The second column, the 10s column, is populated by completed sets of the 1s column. The 100s column is likewise populated with completed sets of the 10s column, and so on.

Figure 7-5   Set Groupings in the Decimal Counting System

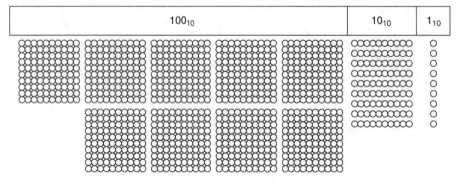

Populate the placeholders with values by using the decimal number 275. As indicated by the number itself, you have two populated placeholders in the 100s column, seven in the 10s column, and five in the 1s column. Although this result appears obvious because of your familiarity with the decimal counting system, try calculating the number of placeholders required, as shown in Figure 7-6. Again, this math is simple because you use the same counting system for the original number and the placeholders. This figure illustrates the concept that you will use shortly.

Figure 7-6   Required Number of Decimal Counting System Placeholders Populated by the Decimal Number 275

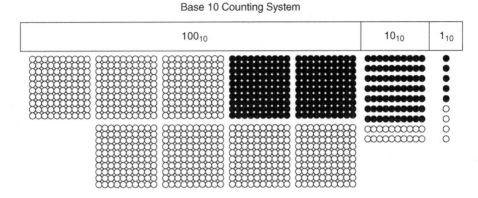

Base 10 Counting System

The largest column required to hold the current number is the 100s column. Thus, subtract 100 from the number until it no longer fits. This subtraction is possible twice, so you populate two placeholders in the 100s column. Subtract the next placeholder value from the number until that is no longer possible. It is possible seven times, so you populate seven placeholders. Repeating the process for the 1s column yields five populated placeholders.

Now that you have reviewed counting in decimal graphically, try the binary system using the same format.

Binary

The binary counting system is based on the numbers 0 and 1. You depict binary by writing the number 2 in subscript immediately after the number. For example, you can clearly express the number 1011_2 as binary in this way.

A single binary digit can represent 0 or 1. If the current number were 1, adding 1 changes the number from a single digit to two digits. Thus, groupings are based on sets of two. You show a complete set of two by a change in columns, moving one column to the left.

A counting sequence follows:

0

1

10

11

100

Notice that the column changes for every other increase in the count. Based on this observation, you can calculate the column values in the binary counting system for the decimal equivalent by repeatedly doubling the number. The first column is 1, so the second column is 2, followed by 4, 8, 16, and so on. Writing these doubled numbers in a row and using subtraction and addition as appropriate to make the conversion can create a quick conversion manual calculator. Figure 7-7 graphically represents the placeholders represented by each digit in a given number. Because of size limitations, the figure depicts only the first eight grouping increments. The decimal equivalent of each column value appears in the lower-left corner.

Figure 7-7   Set Groupings in the Binary Counting System

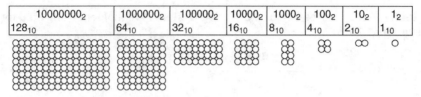

Base 2 Counting System

Notice how Figure 7-7 shows a placeholder for only one set in each column. Zero is represented by the lack of a populated placeholder in that column, and the only other value permitted is one. Populating more than one placeholder in any column is not possible, because no placeholder is offered. To increase the number of used placeholders, it is necessary to change columns. You move all the placeholders, plus the extra placeholder that forced the change in columns, to the next column to the left as a single entry. You populate the second column, the 2s column, with completed sets of the 1s column. You likewise populate the 4s column with completed sets of the 2s column, and so on.

Next, populate the placeholders with values using the decimal number 157, as Figure 7-8 illustrates. Deciding which columns to populate is slightly more difficult when you change numbering systems in the process. This example uses the process outlined in the decimal counting system example.

Figure 7-8   Required Number of Binary Counting System Placeholders Populated by the Decimal Number 157 (10011101)

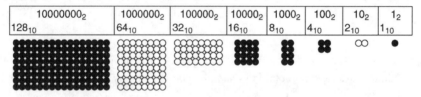

Base 2 Counting System

The largest column required to hold the current number is the 128s column. Thus, subtract 128 from the number until it no longer fits. This subtraction is possible once, so you populate the 128s column place-holder. The remainder is 29, which is already smaller than the next column to the right and the column after that. Both of those columns will have unpopulated placeholders representing 0. Subtract the next placeholder value from the number until that is no longer possible. It is possible once, so you populate the 16s column placeholder. The remainder is 13. Repeating the process for the remaining columns results in a placeholder populated in the 8s, 4s, and 1s columns.

Most people prefer the decimal counting system because we grew up working in that system. Computers will continue to operate on the binary counting system until quantum physics finds a way to cheaply build computers that can store more than *on* or *off* in a single location. Trying to count in binary or to write long strings of binary numbers is tedious at best, so we use hexadecimal notation to reduce the number of digits required for many computer-related activities.

Hexadecimal

The *hexadecimal* counting system is based on the numbers 0 through 15. Unfortunately, the numeric representation of 15 in decimal requires numbers in two columns, and those values all represent values in only a single hexadecimal column. For numbers larger than 9, you use the alphabetic characters of A through F so that only a single "digit" is present as a placeholder. You depict hexadecimal by writing the number 16 in subscript immediately after the number. For example, you can clearly express the number $6D_{16}$ as hexadecimal in this way.

As previously indicated, a single decimal digit can represent any quantity between 0 and F. If the current number were F, adding 1 changes the number from a single digit to two digits. Thus, groupings are based on sets of 16. You show a complete set of 16 by a change in columns, moving one column to the left.

A counting sequence follows:

0

1

2

3

4

5

6

7

8

9

A

B

C

D

E

F

Figure 7-9 shows a graphical representation of the placeholders represented by each digit in a given number. Because of size limitations, the figure depicts only the first three grouping increments.

The most obvious difference between hexadecimal and either binary or decimal is the quantity of placeholders represented in each column. Until you see it represented graphically, you cannot appreciate the significance of a few extra placeholders per set.

Notice how Figure 7-9 shows a placeholder for 15 sets in each column. Zero is represented by a lack of any populated placeholder in that column. Populating more than 16 (F_{16}) placeholders in any column is not possible, because no additional placeholder is offered. To increase the number of used placeholders, it is necessary to change columns. You move all the placeholders, plus the placeholder that forced the change in used columns, to the next column to the left as a single entry. You populate the second column, the 16s column, with completed sets of the 1s column. You likewise populate the 256s column with completed sets of the 16s column, and so on.

Figure 7-9   Set Groupings in the Hexadecimal Counting System

Base 16 Counting System

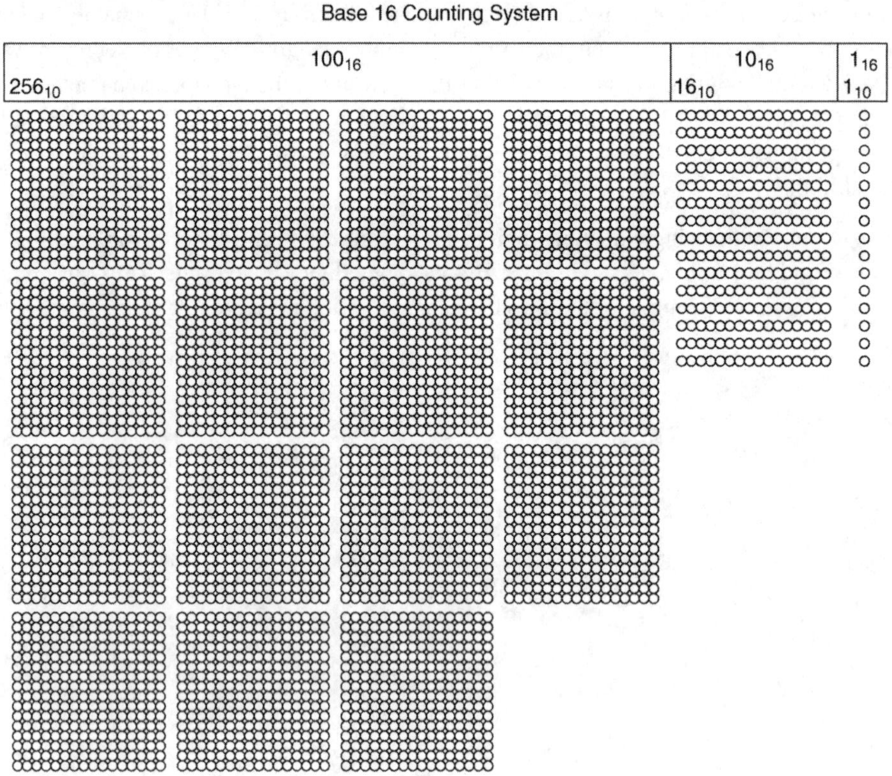

Populate the placeholders with values using the decimal number 157, as Figure 7-10 demonstrates. Deciding which columns you should populate is somewhat difficult because you are once more changing numbering systems in the process. Repeat the process outlined in the decimal counting system.

Figure 7-10   Required Number of Hexadecimal Counting System Placeholders Populated by the Decimal Number 157 (Binary 10011101_2 and Hexadecimal $9D_{16}$)

Base 16 Counting System

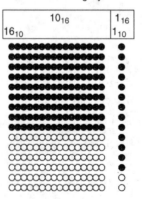

The largest column required to hold the current number is the 16s column because the number is less than the number of placeholders in the 256s column. Thus, subtract 16 from the number until it no longer fits. This subtraction is possible nine times, so you populate nine placeholders in the 16s column. The remainder is 13. The next column is the 1s column, and you use the entire remainder to populate placeholders.

That is a fast tour through counting systems, so look at Table 7-3 to help with the conversions. First, be aware that computer-related use of hexadecimal numbers virtually always represents octets, or groups of eight binary digits. This means that you will virtually never use the 256s column with hexadecimal conversions. Here is almost everything you need in one table.

Table 7-3   Conversion Between Hexadecimal, Decimal, and Binary Counting Systems

Hexadecimal	Decimal	Binary	Four-Digit Binary
0	0	0	0000
1	1	1	0001
2	2	10	0010
3	3	11	0011
4	4	100	0100
5	5	101	0101
6	6	110	0110
7	7	111	0111
8	8	1000	1000
9	9	1001	1001
A	10	1010	1010
B	11	1011	1011
C	12	1100	1100
D	13	1101	1101
E	14	1110	1110
F	15	1111	1111

Also, compare the calculation performed to obtain the binary conversion and the hexadecimal conversion in their respective sections. Notice especially that the left four binary digits convert to a hexadecimal 9 and the right four binary digits convert to a hexadecimal D. This conversion is always true: The left group of four binary digits converts to one hexadecimal number and the right to another. Thus, you only have to memorize how to convert the 1s column of hexadecimal. To simplify memorization, Table 7-3 shows a fourth column, which has leading 0s included for a total of four binary digits. That is how you usually see the binary when you are converting. After a surprisingly small number of calculations, converting between binary and hexadecimal becomes easy.

OSI Seven-Layer Model

You can best understand most issues related to networking when you align them with the OSI model for network communications. The International Organization for Standardization (ISO) created the OSI seven-layer basic reference model as standard ISO/IEC 7498. At the time of its creation, the various available networking protocols were proprietary and offered little or no interoperability. The OSI model, as outlined in Table 7-4, has since become the most common reference point for discussing network protocols, features, and hardware. For a complete description of each layer in the OSI model, see ISO/IEC 7498-1 or ITU-T X.200.

Table 7-4   Simple OSI Seven-Layer Model Description

Layer	Name	Purpose
7	Application	Provides interface with network users
6	Presentation	Performs format and code conversion
5	Session	Manages connections for application programs
4	Transport	Ensures error-free, end-to-end delivery
3	Network	Handles internetwork addressing and routing
2	Data link	Performs local addressing and error detection
1	Physical	Includes physical signaling and interfaces

Figure 7-11 provides a chart to aid in understanding the various concepts and relationships between the OSI reference model and internetworking devices. This chart condenses as much information as possible to provide a visual reference. This basic information should become second nature to any networking professional for that person to be effective.

Figure 7-11   OSI Model Compared to Various Device Functions and Protocols

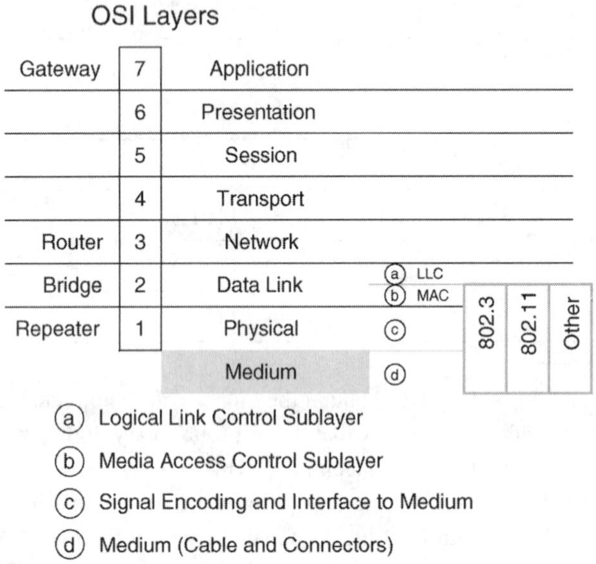

Each layer (except the physical layer) relies on the next lower layer to provide services as specified but to perform these services in a manner that is transparent to the next higher layer. Imagine a higher layer opening a trap door and dropping a request in the form of a package with a note attached into a dark hole. The higher layer neither knows nor cares how the needed services are accomplished, only that if it waits at the trap door long enough, a response will usually appear.

As you can see in Figure 7-12, each layer adds a bit of header information as it handles the request from the next higher layer. The added information is intended for the corresponding layer in the receiving station and is removed by that layer before it hands the data payload to the next higher layer. Almost everything received from or handed to the next higher layer is considered part of the data payload and holds no special meaning to the current layer. As previously mentioned, there is some interaction between adjacent layers, but most of the information is typically intended for the corresponding layer in the receiving station.

Figure 7-12 Conceptual View of the Layering Process Associated with the OSI Model

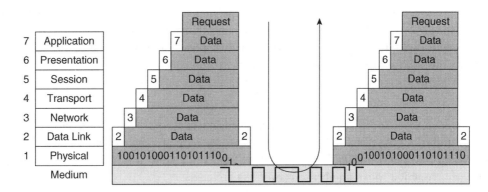

Even in the simplified conceptual depiction in Figure 7-12, it is evident that a small request from the user grows in size as each layer adds some handling information to the request. Each layer adds the same amount of overhead to the message whether it is large or small. The efficiency of a network is not good for small frames but improves considerably as the message approaches the maximum size.

OSI Layers 5 through 7 tend to be interested in handling the request, whereas Layers 4 and below are more interested in delivering the request across the network. Not indicated in the graphic is that each higher layer is usually able to work with a larger portion of a given request. The higher layer parcels out pieces of a request to the lower layer and reassembles the pieces upon reception. The data link layer is the only layer that places both a header and a trailer on the request, effectively framing it. The header includes addressing information for proper delivery, and the trailer holds error-checking information to ensure that the request arrives undamaged. Higher layers include any error-checking information in the header. The physical layer takes the binary string that results from the framed request from the data link layer and encodes it for transmission on the specified medium. The specified medium might be expecting light pulses, rising and falling electrical voltages, or radio waves.

For the receiving station to decode the request, it must be using the same encoding scheme and the same medium. This requirement might be fairly obvious. Not so obvious is that Ethernet uses signaling from one scheme to communicate link-partner capabilities before potentially switching to another encoding scheme. The 10BASE-T link pulse was adapted for use in autonegotiation between link partners on unshielded twisted-pair (UTP) cable. By transmitting coded groups of link pulses, the two link partners negotiate which is the fastest encoding scheme that both can support. Then, they switch to that scheme and proceed.

Once linked at the same speed and using the same encoding scheme, the two link partners are ready to service the user's requests. They do so using the process previously described and shown in Figure 7-12.

To decode a received request, each header includes a code that lets the next higher layer know how to decode the request. For example, in the Ethernet header is a field called Length/Type. If the value in that field is at least 0600_{16}, the data payload is interpreted according to the indicated EtherType. RFC 1700 includes a partial list of EtherType codes. In the header for Layer 3 is another protocol code, and so on.

If you were to hand-decode a single frame, you would need to manually repeat this process of identifying which code is in the header for each layer and finding the instructions for how to decode the protocol indicated by that code. In a computer, you install software drivers for the particular software you are using. The driver software has the encoding and decoding instructions for a limited set of protocols. If the received frame is not one of those known protocols, the first layer that cannot decode it discards the frame.

Signaling and Encoding Methods

Networking protocols use a considerable number of encoding and signaling schemes. The intent of a signaling scheme is to convey information across a given medium at the highest possible density, with the lowest acceptable error rate and cost. Because computers operate in binary, the signaling scheme represents binary information. You can describe this scheme electrically as *on* or *off* in the simplest terms. For an electrical signal to convey an alternating series of 1s and 0s, varying the voltage over time might produce the following signal.

Signals are often described by their *frequency*, or how many cycles per second they have. Figure 7-13 shows one cycle. In a complete cycle, the signal rises to the highest point, descends past the starting point to the lowest point, and returns to the starting point. This timing interval is one cycle period, and it is the basis for one bit-period with a number of networking protocols.

Figure 7-13   One Cycle Period

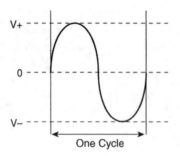

For most of the slower signaling schemes used in networking, one cycle also represents the time duration or interval for one bit period. For a few signaling schemes, the signal holds at a constant voltage for the duration of one period and then, if necessary, changes to the next voltage between periods.

The form of signaling in Figure 7-14 is adequate for any networking need, except that electrical behavior and the laws of physics start interfering. Transmitting signals involves a variety of problems. One obvious problem is that the interface components must be able to turn on and off or to transition fast enough to represent the signal. At lower speeds, this transition is not a problem. Another problem is that as the frequency of the signal (the number of cycles per second) increases, the maximum distance from the transmitter that you can reliably recover data decreases. Yet a third problem is that if the signal were to represent a single binary value for a length of time—say a long string of 1s—the interface electronics in the receiver sometimes begins to lose track of what voltage it is seeing. This loss is called *baseline wander*. In fiber-optic cables, the signals tend to spread out over distance because of the way they reflect down the fiber so that high-frequency pulses start blurring together. A fourth problem is how to synchronize the clock at both ends of a link so that the signal is sampled at the right times to allow reliable data recovery.

Figure 7-14   Simple Signaling Technique, Known as Nonreturn to Zero (NRZ), Where Zero Volts Equals a Binary 0 and V+ Equals a Binary 1

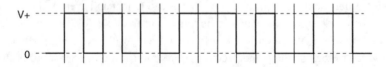

Networks must address two issues at the same time. First, methods to reduce the frequency help to increase the maximum transmission distance (and usually the amount of information contained in a single cycle at the same time). Second, transitions must be regular enough to establish and maintain clock synchronization (and avoid baseline wander).

In Figure 7-15, the signaling is called *level sensitive*. As long as the signal remains at V+, it is sampled as a binary 1. When it is sampled at zero volts, it is a binary 0. Another way that signals are often sampled is on an edge. If the signal is rising or falling at the moment it is sampled, it is interpreted according to the edge direction or the mere presence of an edge. For example, a rising edge might indicate a binary 1. This system requires good clocking and extremely small amounts of variation in the signal timing. If a transition takes place, but not at the exact moment when the signal is sampled, it does not produce the desired result. Variations in the timing, usually seen as oscillations between slightly too soon and slightly too late, are called *jitter*.

Figure 7-15   How Signal Jitter Causes Inaccurate Sampling of the Data (with X Indicating a Failure to Properly Sample the Edge-Sensitive Signal)

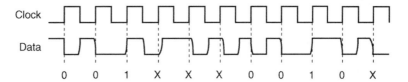

As Figure 7-16 suggests, other systems rely on the presence or absence of an edge transition instead of the direction the signal is headed during the transition.

Figure 7-16   Encoding Example Where a Transition in the Center of the Timing Window Represents a Binary 1 and the Absence of a Transition Indicates a Binary 0 (Nonreturn to Zero, Inverting on Ones [NRZI])

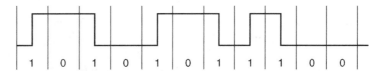

The example in Figure 7-17 shows the signaling system for Fast Ethernet, called Multilevel Transmit-3 (MLT-3), which transitions only the signal for a binary 1, but uses +1, 0, and -1 volts for signaling. Each transition carries only the signal half of the peak-to-peak distance. This system allows for the highest information density so far for a single cycle. Transmitting four consecutive 1s would occupy only a single cycle.

Figure 7-17   Encoding Example Where a Transition in the Center of the Timing Window Represents a Binary 1 and the Absence of a Transition Indicates a Binary 0

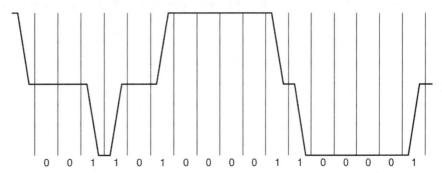

Many other and more complex signaling systems exist. However, this discussion is adequate for a simple overview of the process and some of the reasons for encoding the signal differently.

Task 2: Decode the Waveform into Binary, Reorder the Binary, and Identify Ethernet Field Boundaries

In this section, you review the 10-Mbps transmission process and take the first steps toward decoding a waveform.

10-Mbps Transmission Process

First, here is a quick description of the process used by the 10-Mbps versions of Ethernet to transmit a frame. Figure 7-18 shows the fields present in a simple 802.3 Ethernet frame.

Figure 7-18   Basic 802.3 Ethernet Frame Fields

Preamble 7	SFD 1	Destination 6	Source 6	Length Type 2	Data ┊ Pad 46 to 1500	FCS 4

Sample data for the first few fields in a frame might appear as shown in Figure 7-19. Each field is delineated above the sample hexadecimal data for that field and appears as it might appear at the MAC layer.

Figure 7-19   802.3 Ethernet Frame Fields with Sample Data

```
|      Preamble      | SFD |   Destination   |      Source      | Length/Type | ...
 55 55 55 55 55 55 55   D5   00 C0 17 A0 02 35   00 80 20 56 33 D4    08 06       ...
```

Using the hexadecimal-to-binary conversion process described in Task 1, Figure 7-20 demonstrates converting the hexadecimal data for the first two fields in the Ethernet frame to binary.

Figure 7-20   Converting the Hexadecimal Data in an Ethernet Frame to Binary

```
|                              Preamble                         |  SFD  | ...
 01010101 01010101 01010101 01010101 01010101 01010101 01010101 11010101 ...
```

Transmitting the frame involves passing it from the MAC layer to the physical layer. Ethernet encoding rules specify that each octet is transferred least-significant bit (LSB) first from the MAC layer to the physical layer, so the bits are reordered on a per-octet basis (see Figure 7-21). The Frame Check Sequence (FCS) field is not reordered.

Figure 7-21   Ethernet Requires That Each Octet Be Transferred LSB First, So the Order Is Reversed

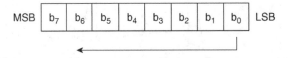

This concept is easiest to grasp as simply turning over each octet, as Figure 7-22 shows. The change is most identifiable in the start of frame delimiter (SFD) octet.

Figure 7-22   Reinterpretation of Figure 7-21

```
|                              Preamble                         |  SFD  | ...
 10101010 10101010 10101010 10101010 10101010 10101010 10101010 10101011 ...
```

```
 01010101 01010101 01010101 01010101 01010101 01010101 01010101 11010101 ...
```

Following the LSB reordering of each octet by the MAC layer, the octets are transferred to the physical layer. LSB-ordered octets received from the MAC layer are serialized from left-to-right using Manchester encoding rules.

Manchester encoding relies on the direction of the edge transition in the *middle* of the timing window to determine the binary value for that bit period.

The encoding example in Figure 7-23 has one timing window highlighted vertically through all four waveform examples; it is labeled as *one bit period*. The top waveform has a falling edge in the center of the timing window, so it is interpreted as a binary 0.

Figure 7-23   Manchester Encoding

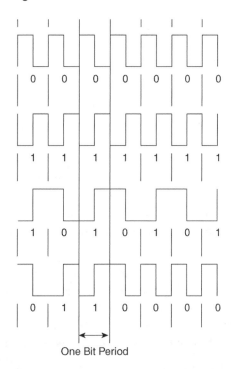

One Bit Period

Depending on how you view it, the second waveform is 180 degrees out of phase, or it is shifted half of one bit period to the side. It is otherwise identical. The result is that the center of the timing window for the second waveform has a rising edge, which is interpreted as a binary 1.

Instead of a repeating sequence of the same binary value, the third waveform example has an alternating binary sequence. In the first two examples, the signal must transition back between each bit period so that it can make the same-direction transition each time in the center of the timing window. With alternating binary data, there is no need to return to the previous voltage level in preparation for the next edge in the center of the timing window. Thus, any time a long separation exists between one edge and the next, you can be certain that *both edges represent the middle of a timing window*. (This tip will be useful later.) The fourth waveform example (see Figure 7-24) is random data, which allows you to verify that whenever a wide separation exists between two transitions, both edges are in the center of a timing window and represent the binary value for that timing window.

After encoding the binary into Manchester, the physical layer transmits the resulting signal onto the attached medium.

Figure 7-24 shows two vertical lines that clearly delineate the timing windows. In the center of both marked timing windows is an edge transition. The figure shows black dots at the boundaries of some other timing windows to aid in decoding the binary data. The decoded binary appears below the waveform along with the Ethernet field boundaries as appropriate.

Figure 7-24   Actual 10BASE5 Signal Decoded

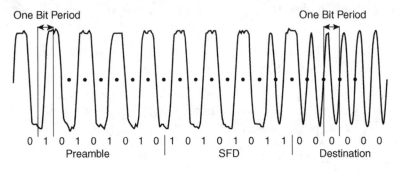

Now that you know the basic process, take out the lab sheet bearing the undecoded waveform.

Decoding the Waveform—Part A

Step 1.   Locate the boundaries of the timing windows. Your lab sheet has faint timing marks placed appropriately. Compare the locations of those timing marks with the Manchester-encoding examples in Figure 7-23 and the section of decoded waveform in Figure 7-24. Study the waveform and the examples until you feel that you could correctly annotate another sheet that did not have those timing marks. Remember the tip given previously: Whenever there are widely spaced edges in the waveform, both edges (rising and falling) represent the center of a timing window. It is not possible to locate the timing boundaries in areas where the waveform has closely spaced edges. In those areas is a consecutive pattern of the same binary value, but you have to look forward or backward along the waveform to find a widely spaced edge to determine which it is.

Step 2.   This step is only possible after you find and mark some of the timing-window boundaries. Using a pencil (because almost everyone makes mistakes), mark the direction of the edge in the center of the timing window, as shown in Step 3. After a short time, lean back and look at the spacing of the arrows you are using to mark the direction of the edge. Notice that despite how the waveform has narrow and widely spaced sections, your arrows are all evenly spaced.

Step 3.   Go back and write the binary value below each arrow, as shown in Figure 7-25, but only after you mark several feet of waveform in that manner. Do not mark the binary values as you go; you will make mistakes if you are not closely watching the waveform.

Figure 7-25   Appearance of the Waveform After Step 2 and During Step 3

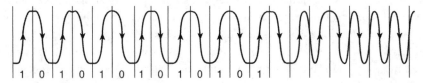

Step 4.   Look for the SFD, which appears at the end of the initial stretch of widely spaced waveform edges. You see a change in the pattern, and you should decode a binary 112 where the waveform pattern changes. Draw a vertical line through the waveform along the timing mark to the right of the binary 112 pattern and before the next timing window. That line separates the end of the SFD from the beginning of the destination address. Count back to the left eight bits, and draw another vertical line on the left-clocking line for the eighth bit. That line marks the end of the SFD (including the binary 112) and the beginning of the next field. Refer to Figure 7-22 to obtain the number of octets required for each Ethernet field. For example, the SFD in Figure 7-22 appears with the number 1 below it. That indicates one octet, or eight binary bits. Count bits, as indicated by Figure 7-25, until you draw vertical lines between each of the Ethernet fields

leading up to the Data field. You might want to make small marks along the way for each octet division, because you will find that useful in the next step.

Step 5. Convert the binary back to hexadecimal. But wait—there is a trick! Remember that the MAC layer reordered the bits before handing them to the physical layer. You must reverse that before you convert back to binary. Most people incorrectly perform the conversion the first time. See Figure 7-26 for a quick refresher on what happened. Unlike the example in Figure 7-26, you will not convert the hexadecimal into ASCII.

Figure 7-26   Reordering Example (LSB First)

Ethernet Data Transmission Order Example

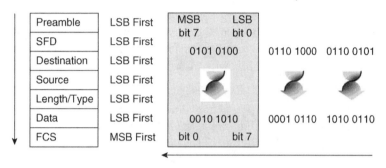

This example converts the word "The" from the appropriate ASCII hexadecimal codes into binary. The binary is then LSB reordered before passing from the MAC layer to the physical layer Ethernet implementation for transmission, as follows:

$$T = 54_{16} = 0101\ 0100_2 \quad h = 68_{16} = 0110\ 1000_2 \quad e = 65_{16} = 0110\ 0101_2$$

Step 6. Identify the Layer 3 protocol contained in the Length/Type field. You perform this step after you mark all the Ethernet header information into the correct fields and convert it into hexadecimal. If you do not perform the conversion correctly, the next operation results in the wrong answer for Module 3.

If the value in the Length/Type field is less than 0600_{16} (1536 in decimal), in most cases, the contents of the Data field are decoded according to the 802.2 protocol. If the value is less than 0600_{16}, the field indicates length.

If the value in the Length/Type field is equal to or greater than 0600_{16} (1536 in decimal), in most cases, the contents of the Data field are decoded according to the Ethernet II protocol. If the value is equal to or greater than 0600_{16}, the field indicates type.

If your Length/Type field indicated a type, you can look up the value in a table to learn which protocol is next in the Data field.

Task 3: Decode the Ethernet Length/Type Field, Locate and Read RFCs, and Decode Layer 3 of the Waveform

In this section, you review the process of publishing standards documents and continue the process of decoding a waveform.

Standards and RFCs

There are two processes in use to determine the structure and specifications of various networking aspects. One process is to go through the formal standards bodies, which produce documents such as the 802.3 Ethernet specifications and the ISO/IEC 7498 OSI basic model. These standards and RFC-issuing bodies include the ISO, the IEEE, the Internet Engineering Task Force (IETF), and the American National Standards Institute (ANSI).

The IETF publishes the specification documents of the Internet protocol suite as RFCs, but they can originate from anyone with a good idea. (Read RFC 2223 for instructions on how to submit one.) The RFC documents are subject to nearly the same level of scrutiny as the standards process before they are published, but they used to be more casual.

In 1969, when the RFC process started, the idea was to put a good proposal together, post it on the fledgling Internet, and wait to see what your peers thought of the idea. After the idea was vetted in this manner, your peers either implemented the proposal or not. No standards organization behind the proposal insisted that it be done in the prescribed manner, universally across all platforms. That is perhaps the single greatest difference between what is published as a standard and what is published as an RFC. Everyone must comply with the standards, but there is no obligation (except pressure from your customers and your peers) for compliance with an RFC.

As the RFC process becomes more structured, and more customers rely on the information available through compliance with published RFCs, the difference between being required by the standard and being pressured by your customer is growing narrower. To learn more about the standards development process, read RFC 2026.

RFCs are available from many sites on the Internet. The best site so far for obtaining published RFCs, and work in progress, is probably the RFC Editor site. Start at the URL http://www.rfc-editor.org/rfc.html.

Download the RFC index and save it on your local drive. It is handy to have around (http://www.rfc-editor.org/rfcindex.html).

In the index, each entry has some valuable information. Here is a sample entry:

0760 **DoD standard Internet Protocol** J. Postel [Jan-01-1980] (TXT = 81507 bytes)(Obsoletes IEN 123) (Obsoleted by RFC 0791) (Updated by RFC0777)

The most important information in this entry is that RFC 760 has been "obsoleted" and that the replacement is RFC 791. Other good information to know is in RFC 777, which in this case is related to the Internet Control Message Protocol (ICMP) error-messaging protocol for TCP/IP at Layer 3.

Decoding the Waveform—Part B

Step 1.   To proceed with the waveform-decoding exercise, search the RFC index for the phrase "assigned numbers." Make sure that you find the RFC number for the latest version of that document and then download it.

Step 2.   Search the RFC until you locate the section on EtherTypes. After you find that section, take the value that you decoded in Step 6 of Module 2 and find it in the list.

Step 3.   Go back to the RFC index and search on the protocol name that you found. Be sure to use the full name and not an acronym because the RFC you want defines that protocol and does not mention the acronym in the title.

Step 4.   Download the appropriate RFC for the protocol. Sometimes, it is necessary to check several RFCs for the information you seek. If you download the correct RFC, in Section 3, you find a table or chart that looks similar to Figure 7-27.

Figure 7-27   Data Field as Shown in RFCs

```
 0                   1                   2                   3
 0 1 2 3 4 5 6 7 8 9 0 1 2 3 4 5 6 7 8 9 0 1 2 3 4 5 6 7 8 9 0 1
+-+-+-+-+-+-+-+-+-+-+-+-+-+-+-+-+-+-+-+-+-+-+-+-+-+-+-+-+-+-+-+-+
|Version|  IHL  |Type of Service|          Total Length         |
+-+-+-+-+-+-+-+-+-+-+-+-+-+-+-+-+-+-+-+-+-+-+-+-+-+-+-+-+-+-+-+-+
```

This exact field listing shows you how to interpret the first part of the Data field. This document guides you through decoding Layer 3 of your waveform. The format in Figure 7-27 is common to the RFC documents. The numbers across the top represent bits. The 32 bits form four octets; you often see fields aligning on the octet boundaries, but not always.

Protocol-related RFCs typically provide a table or chart of the fields in a particular frame followed by a definition for and description of how to use each field depicted in the chart.

Step 5. Take the information from Step 4 and decode Layer 3 in your waveform. The portion of the table corresponds to the 32 bits immediately following the end of the MAC layer Length/Type field. The information appears in the order you see it in your waveform. The Version field follows as the next four bits after the Length/Type field.

Step 6. Find and decode the Protocol field from Layer 3. You use this value to find the field definitions for Layer 4. Be careful; there is another trick. Your clue is that when you look it up in the table of protocols, don't use the raw hexadecimal number.

Task 4: Use a Protocol Analyzer

Protocol analyzers let you view the contents of individual frames from the medium and offer functionality from Layer 2 up through Layer 7. They typically have a variety of built-in summary features that allow you to see who is talking to whom, by which protocol, and how much.

Protocol analyzers come in two general configurations: software-based and hardware-based. The software protocol analyzer is usually unable to detect or report upon MAC layer errors because it relies upon a standard network adapter. Software protocol analyzers tend to be somewhat limited in the amount of traffic that you can capture for the same reason. A typical network adapter is not well suited to capturing traffic at line rates because the typical workstation cannot process traffic at those rates. Dropped frames are not reported, and you cannot determine when a frame was missed. Hardware-based protocol analyzers usually have some level of integration to the front-end electronics and can show some or all the errors on a link. The level of error detection is often related to the price. Hardware protocol analyzers are more likely to be able to capture at line rates without dropping frames.

Both categories of protocol analyzer usually have several software modules that you can add for a price. These modules range from support for multiple network access protocols (Ethernet, Token Ring, Frame Relay, wireless, and so on) to an integrated *expert system* that compares the contents of a captured trace file against libraries of common symptoms related to specific faults or causes. Once beyond the built-in or automated test summary functions, the ability to obtain useful information from a protocol analyzer is directly related to the user's knowledge about the inner workings of the protocol in question. For that reason, protocol analysis is usually the domain of the senior network support staff.

Using a protocol analyzer as part of the instructional process greatly enhances the clarity of the topic of discussion. It is one thing to sit back and listen about a particular protocol or process, but it is another to take apart that process bit-by-bit at the same time.

The software protocol analyzer in the CCNA curriculum is the Protocol Inspector (educational version), or Protocol Inspector-EDV. The following is a quick way to begin exploring with a protocol analyzer without having to learn all the different functions.

Protocol Inspector in Five Buttons

This section provides a five-button quick start for Protocol Inspector. Figure 7-28 shows the Protocol Inspector startup screen.

Figure 7-28   Protocol Inspector Startup Screen

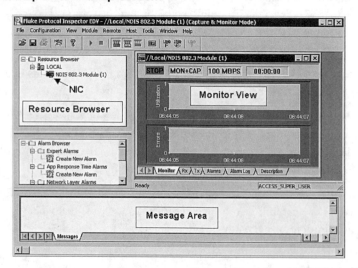

Step 1. Launch the application. Press the **Start** button, which appears on the toolbar at the top of the screen. One of the buttons looks like this and causes Protocol Inspector to begin capturing everything detected on the attached network adapter. If multiple network adapters are present, it might be necessary to select one from the Resource Browser first.

Step 2. Click the **Detail View** button in the toolbar or double-click anywhere on the Monitor View chart. This action opens another window and allows you to see what sort of traffic you have captured so far.

Step 3. To open an individual frame, you must first stop the capture. Press the **Stop** button.

Step 4. To open the captured trace file, press the **Capture View** button. With the educational version, a message box appears and tells you that the capture is limited to 250 packets. Just click **OK**. You see a three-window screen similar to what's shown in Figure 7-29. The top window shows a summary of all the captured frames. The middle window shows a field-by-field breakdown of the frame highlighted in the top window. The bottom windows show the raw, uninterpreted hexadecimal for the highlighted frame.

This screen shows plenty of information to absorb on the first visit.

Figure 7-29   Protocol Inspector Decode Screen

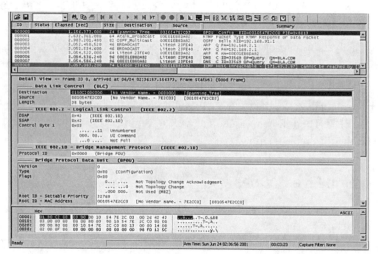

Step 5. Press the **Expert View** button on the toolbar at the top of the screen to examine the entire trace file for possible problems and warnings.

Congratulations! You have successfully used a protocol analyzer. For further exploration, Figure 7-30 and Figure 7-31 provide a quick summary of what some of the other toolbar buttons do.

Figure 7-30 shows the functionality of all the buttons on the toolbar for the first screen you see after launching the application.

Figure 7-30 Detail View Toolbar Menu Buttons

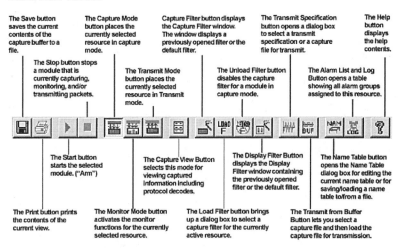

Figure 7-31 shows the functionality of all the buttons on the second screen, which is available after you press the **Capture View** button. Press each of these buttons to learn how each of these built-in summary tests operate and how you can view the contents of the capture file in different ways.

Figure 7-31 Data View Toolbar Menu Buttons

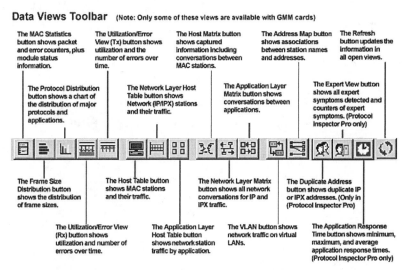

The Cisco Networking Academy Program website contains several labs, and you can use the linked Fluke Networks website to further explore Protocol Inspector in the classroom. Additional labs will be posted as they are completed.

Protocol Inspector Lab

As part of this lab, open the frame used to create the waveform lab on the linked Fluke Networks website. You can also capture a similar frame from the classroom network to use in this lab.

Step 1.   Open the Protocol Inspector application. Either open the trace file containing the frame used to create the waveform lab or capture a new trace file.

Step 2.   Press the **Capture View** button to open the Detail View window. If you capture a new trace file, look through the trace file for a frame of the same Layer 3 protocol as the Ethernet Length/Type field indicated at the end of Module 2 and highlight it. Click the middle window to freeze the top window on the frame in which you are interested. This step also allows you to scroll the middle window. Compare the decoded waveform field-by-field with the information in the middle window of the Detail View. Also, compare the hexadecimal data from the bottom window with the hexadecimal that you decoded from the waveform.

Step 3.   Compare the information in the middle window with the field descriptions in the RFC you used to decode Layer 3 of the waveform in Module 3. Having first hand-decoded this frame, you should be intimately familiar with the structure and contents of the frame. Comparing this new knowledge against what the protocol analyzer shows you about the same frame will usually take away all the fear and mystery about a protocol analyzer.

Congratulations! You now have a good understanding of what a protocol analyzer does! You should never have to hand-decode another frame—ever.

Use the protocol analyzer to capture each type of frame discussed in the lecture from this point forward. Compare the captured sample with the lecture material and the appropriate RFC for a better understanding of what is presented. The experience you gain from examining the behavior of a protocol using a protocol analyzer will place you several years ahead of your competition in the job market. Many networking professionals never master the protocol analyzer.

Curriculum Lab 7-2: Introduction to Fluke Network Inspector (7.1.9a)

Figure 7-32   Topology for Lab 7.1.9a

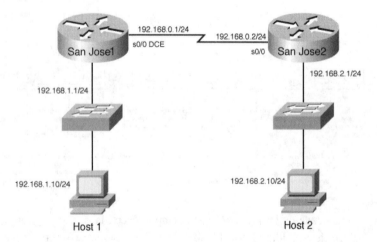

This lab is a tutorial that demonstrates how to use the Fluke Networks *Network Inspector* to discover and analyze network devices within a broadcast domain. This lab demonstrates the key features of the tool that you can incorporate into various troubleshooting efforts in the remaining labs.

Background/Preparation

The Network Inspector software can distinguish workstations, servers, network printers, switches, and managed hubs, if they have been assigned a network address.

Options for Conducting This Lab

You can use Network Inspector in a small controlled LAN that the instructor configures in a closed lab environment, as shown in Figure 7-32. The minimum equipment should include a workstation, switch, and router.

You might also perform the steps in a larger environment, such as the classroom or the school network to see more variety. Before attempting to run Network Inspector on the school LAN, check with your instructor and the network administrator.

You must consider the following points:

- Network Inspector detects the devices within a network subnet or VLAN. It does not search beyond a router. It will not inventory the school's entire network unless it is all on one subnet.

- Network Inspector is not a Cisco product nor is it limited to detecting only Cisco devices.

- Network Inspector is a detection tool, but it is not a configuration tool. You cannot use it to reconfigure any devices.

The output in this lab is only representative, and output varies depending on the number of devices, device MAC addresses, device host names, and LAN.

This lab introduces the Fluke Networks Network Inspector software, which can be useful in later troubleshooting labs and in the field. Although the Network Inspector software is a valuable part of the Networking Academy program, it is also representative of features available on other products in the market.

At least one host must have the Network Inspector software installed. If you perform the lab in pairs, having the software installed on both machines means that each person can run the lab steps. During installation, be sure to select both the Network Inspector and the Network Inspector Agent.

The console can be anywhere that has a valid IP path and security to allow the connection to an agent. In fact, it might be an interesting exercise to have the console reach across the serial link to load the database from the other agent. You can have the console reading from a different database than the one that is currently in use by the agent on the same PC.

Task 1: Configure the Lab or Attach the Workstation to the School LAN

Option 1. If you select the closed lab environment, cable the equipment as shown in Figure 7-32 and load the configuration files into the appropriate routers. These files might already be preloaded. If not, you can obtain them from your instructor. These files should support the IP addressing scheme, as shown in Figure 7-32 and Table 7-5.

Configure the workstations according to the specifications in Table 7-5.

Table 7-5   Workstation Configuration Settings

	Host #1	Host #2
IP Address	192.168.1.10	192.168.2.10
Subnet Mask	255.255.255.0	255.255.255.0
Default Gateway	192.168.1.1	192.168.2.1

Because the software discovers devices on the network, using additional devices provides a better demonstration. If available, add additional hosts to both LANs.

Option 2. If you select option 2 (connect to school LAN), simply connect the workstation, with Protocol Inspector or Protocol Expert installed, directly to a classroom switch or to a data jack connected to the school LAN.

Task 2: Start Network Inspector and the Agent

From the Start menu, choose **Network Inspector > Console**.

Click the **Agent** button at the left end of the toolbar (see Figure 7-33) to start the agent.

Figure 7-33   Launching the Network Inspector Agent

If necessary, select the **Agent** tab in the window, click the Start button, and watch the Status box until it shows that the agent is running (see Figure 7-34). This process might take several minutes to start.

Figure 7-34   Network Inspector Agent Status

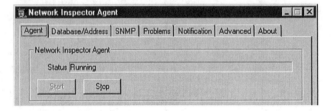

Task 3: Allow Network Discovery to Occur

The Network Inspector software is designed to quietly (passively and actively) collect network data. As such, it takes time for devices to appear. Network Inspector should discover this small network in a minute or so. The active collection of statistical data is delayed for the first 10 minutes. An actual production network might take 30 minutes or more before Network Inspector discovers most data.

Notice the agent status on the bottom of the console window in Figure 7-35. If you look closely, you notice that the agent has been running since 9:57 P.M.

After a few minutes, the console window should start showing information about the network. The example in Figure 7-35 added two workstations.

Figure 7-35   Network Inspector Active Session

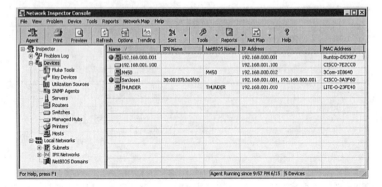

Use the **Close** button in the lower-right corner of the agent window to send the agent away. (Some versions might have a Hide button.) Do not use the Stop button or the discovery process will cease.

Note: You might see entries from previous sessions. It takes a few minutes for the entries to match the network. In the Agent window, under the Database/Address tab, is a checkbox for Overwrite (see Figure 7-36). If that box is checked, Network Inspector discards the current database content and loads a fresh data set as it is discovered when the agent starts. Otherwise, Network Inspector integrates any new data with the existing database as it is discovered.

Figure 7-36   Overwriting Previous Network Inspector Session Entries

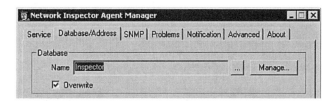

Notice the host names (M450, SanJose1, and THUNDER—PC host names will be different in student output), IP addresses, and MAC addresses for each discovered device in Figure 7-34. It is obvious that both SanJose1 and SanJose2 have two IP addresses assigned to the LAN interface.

Notice that Network Inspector does not investigate beyond the router interface. It only collects information on the devices that share the same broadcast domain as the computer's NIC.

Task 4: Investigate Device Properties

Double-click the router device's name and look over the available device properties, as shown in Figure 7-37. Remember that results depend on the devices included in the LAN's subnet.

The Overview tab in Figure 7-37 shows IP addresses, the Internetwork Packet Exchange (IPX) address, the IPX networks, the IPX data frame (802.3 here), and the MAC address. Notice that the organizational unique identifier (OUI) was converted to identify the manufacturer in this example.

Closest switches appear only if Network Inspector was provided a valid Simple Network Management Protocol (SNMP) community string for them.

Figure 7-37   Analyzing Router Properties

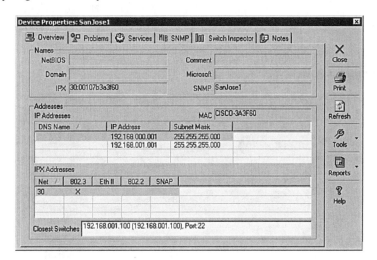

The Problems tab in Figure 7-38 reveals that one of the IP addresses is duplicated within the network. This duplication occurs if the student configured an optional host as defined in Task 1. The red ball to the left of the description indicates a problem.

Figure 7-38   Network Inspector Problems Tab

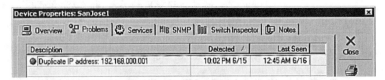

The Services tab in Figure 7-39 reveals the IP and IPX services running on the routers.

Figure 7-39   Network Inspector Services Tab

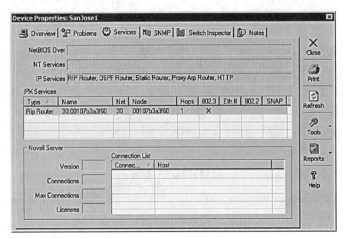

The IP Services field in Figure 7-40 reveals that the IP HTTP Server service is turned on, which means that you can access the router through a web browser.

The IPX Services shows the IPX network ID (30), the node address (MAC), the frame type, and that IPX Routing Information Protocol (RIP) is running.

The bottom third of the window shows the information that would have been revealed if the device had been a Novell server. A multihomed server, one with more than one NIC (connection) in separate networks, is working as a router or bridge. The MIB SNMP tab, shown in Figure 7-40, reveals SNMP information and the router Cisco IOS Software information.

Figure 7-40   Network Inspector MIB SNMP Tab

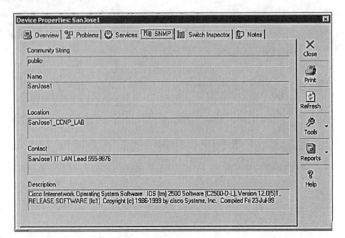

The Switch Inspector tab creates various charts of the switch interface data for the selected device. This data is not collected during the initial 10-minute period.

 The Switch Inspector test provides basic utilization graphs for any SNMP-enabled device. The level of information depends on which management information bases (MIB) are supported by the selected device. For example, because SanJose1 is a router, you cannot display the address of any directly connected devices for a highlighted port. The buttons on the left side of the window change the chart format. The Graph Legend button at the bottom-left corner displays the floating legend in Figure 7-41.

Figure 7-41   Network Inspector Switch Inspector Tab: Graph Legend

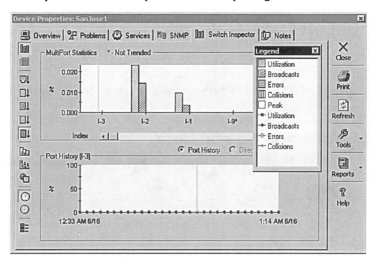

 The second button is the Tabular View; selecting it details each interface on the device, including whether the interface is up or down (see Figure 7-42). The checkbox at the left of each line determines whether statistics are gathered for trending on that interface. Scrolling to the right reveals maximum transmission unit (MTU) and description (FastEthernet0/0 or Token Ring 0/1) details.

Figure 7-42   Network Inspector Switch Inspector Tab: Tabular View

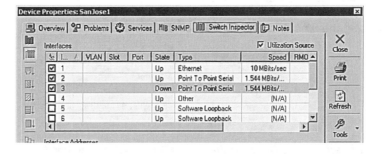

 The two clock-like buttons switch between a one-hour or 24-hour history, which can create an interesting comparison if the Network Inspector has been running for an extended time. The results will be the same in this short exercise.

While in the Switch Inspector, the Reports button on the right side of the screen expands to show two options (see Figure 7-43). Select **Switch Performance**, and a multipage report with various charts appears on the screen. Look over the results.

The Switch Detail option works only with a switch.

Figure 7-43   Network Inspector Switch Inspector Tab: Reports Options

After looking over the Device Properties window, click the **Close** button in the upper-right corner to return to the Network Inspector console.

Task 5: Explore Left Panel Options

At the Network Inspector console, experiment with expanding and contracting the choices in the left pane. As with the Explorer, if you select an item on the left side, the right side shows the details. In Figure 7-44, expanding the Problems Log and selecting **Errors** shows the devices on the right side with errors, which makes it easy to spot the duplicate IP address device.

Figure 7-44   Navigating the Network Inspector Console

Try different options on the left pane, and note the result in the right pane. Because of the limited number of devices, some will be empty. Try it later with a larger sample.

In the left pane, select **Devices** to show all devices in the right pane. Note the format of the MAC address.

Click the **Options** button in the toolbar (or choose **View > Options**) and note that you can choose between Manufacturer Prefix and Hex (see Figure 7-45). Select the one that is not chosen, look over the other options, and then click **OK**. Note the result.

Figure 7-45   Selecting the MAC Address Format for Display

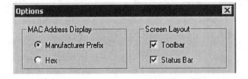

In the Console main screen, check that the Problems Log is selected and that a device in the detail window is highlighted. Press the **F1** (Help) function key to show a list of problems by category, as Figure 7-46 demonstrates.

Figure 7-46   Network Inspector Help

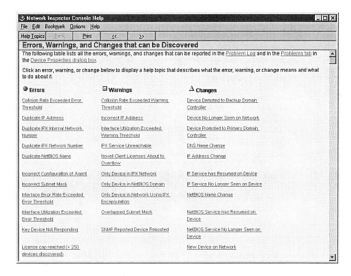

One of the problems created by the current lab configuration is a duplicate IP address. To learn about duplicate IP addresses, what the symptoms are, and what you can do about them, select the hyperlink listing for **Duplicate IP Address**. There is a wealth of information in the help for this software.

Take a minute and experiment with the Preview, Sort, and Reports buttons in the toolbar. The features should be obvious. Look particularly at the troubleshooting and documentation possibilities of the reports.

Select a host, open the **Tools** button in the toolbar, and select **Ping**.

The Select Parameter box (see Figure 7-47) includes the LAN IP addresses that you can ping. Select one and click **OK**. A command (MS-DOS) window appears to show the results.

When finished, type **exit** to close the new window.

Figure 7-47   Selecting Parameters to Ping

Use the **Telnet** and **Traceroute** options. Select a router or switch in the console display, choose **Tools > Telnet**, and a window with a Telnet session open appears. Trace works the same way.

The Web option on the Tools button opens a web session with a device if the IP HTTP server feature is turned on. If you want to try it, the username is the host name (SanJose1 or SanJose2), and the password is cisco.

In this lab, the switch is a Catalyst 1924 with an IP address assigned, so the screen shown in Figure 7-48 appears if you select the **Web** choice while the switch is highlighted.

Figure 7-48 Opening a Web Session

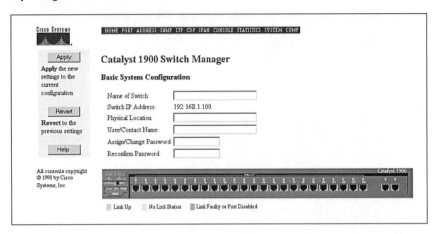

Experiment with the toolbar options until you are comfortable with the features.

Task 6: Use Net Map and Visio to Diagram the Network

If Visio is installed on the workstation, the Net Map button on the toolbar activates Visio and creates a network map of the broadcast domain. Figure 7-49 uses "Router Connections in a Switched Network" on the Net Map button. It draws the network whether or not it includes a switch.

Figure 7-49 Creating a Network Map with Visio

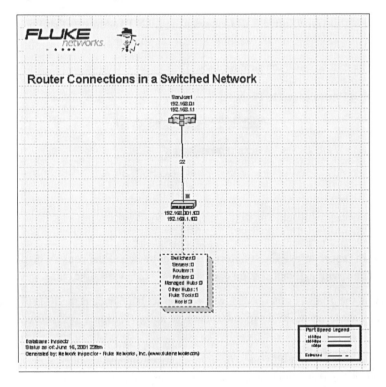

Visio is fully integrated into Network Inspector, which means that double-clicking one of the devices in the drawing calls up the Device Properties window that you used in Task 4.

Task 7: Document Router Information

Using the skills covered previously, select the router and document the following information where available:

1. What is the name of the device?

_____

2. What IP services is the device running?

_____

3. What IPX services is the device running?

_____

4. What is the SNMP community string?

_____

5. What is the location?

_____

6. Who is the contact?

_____

7. Which interfaces are available?

_____

8. Which interfaces are up?

_____

9. List any problem that the software has discovered.

_____

Task 8: Observe Device Discovery

If possible, connect the two switches with a crossover cable and watch the Network Inspector output as it discovers new devices. If a crossover cable is unavailable, remove one of the switches and plug the hosts and router into the second switch. Although you would not normally do this step in a production environment, do it now just to see how Network Inspector responds.

New devices should show up initially with blue triangles, which indicate that they are newly discovered. Many should eventually get a yellow warning rectangle, which indicates a potential problem. Remember that this process could take 10 or more minutes. Eventually, Network Inspector shows the other subnets and the second router.

Task 9: Stop the Capture and Access the Problems and Notification Tabs

Click the **Agent** button in the toolbar. The agent has been collecting data all this time. Click the **Stop** button and then confirm your intentions when prompted.

Look over the tabs to see the database options that you can set. Note the **Problems** tab and the choices for focusing the investigation (see Figure 7-50).

Figure 7-50   Network Inspector Agent Manager: Problems Tab

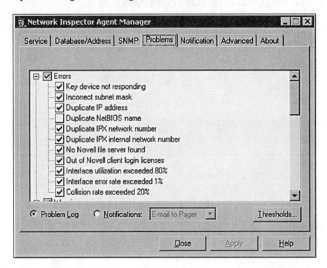

On the Notification tab (see Figure 7-51), notice that you can send out e-mail notifications. To use this feature, you need the same information as that required to set up an Internet e-mail account or an Outlook e-mail account.

Figure 7-51   Network Inspector Agent Manager: Notification Tab

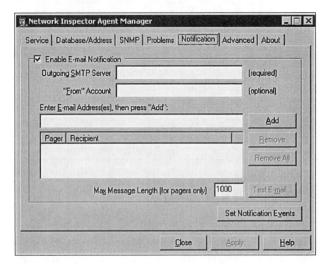

If you start the agent again, it might take a few minutes to detect any changes that occurred while the agent was off.

Task 10: Experiment with Network Inspector

Experiment with the Network Inspector tool by looking at the different devices.

If Network Inspector is installed on the classroom computers, investigate the devices on that larger network.

Reflection

1. How might you use this information in troubleshooting?

2. What advantages over HyperTerminal might Network Inspector have for troubleshooting documentation?

_____

_____

Curriculum Lab 7-3: Introduction to Fluke Protocol Inspector (7.1.9b)

Figure 7-52   Topology for Lab 7.1.9b

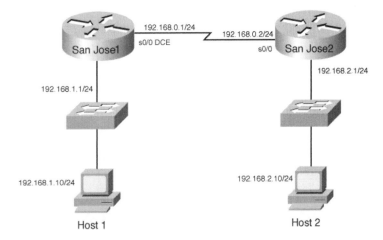

Objective

This lab is a tutorial that demonstrates how to use the Fluke Networks Protocol Inspector to analyze network traffic and data frames. Fluke OptiView Protocol Expert (PE) can also be used with this lab. Examples and screens shown in this lab are from Protocol Inspector. This lab demonstrates key features of the tool that you can incorporate into various troubleshooting efforts in the remaining labs.

Background/Preparation

The output in this lab is only representative and will vary depending on the number of devices, device MAC addresses, device host names, the LAN, and so on.

This lab is useful in later troubleshooting labs and in the field. Although the Protocol Inspector software is a valuable part of the Cisco Networking Academy Program, it also represents the features available on other products in the market.

Options for Conducting This Lab

You can use Protocol Inspector or PE in a small controlled LAN that is configured by the instructor in a closed lab environment, as shown in Figure 7-52. The minimum equipment should include a workstation, switch, and router.

You can also perform the steps in a larger environment, such as the classroom or the school network, to see more variety. Before attempting to run Protocol Inspector or PE on the school LAN, check with your instructor and the network administrator.

At least one host must have the Protocol Inspector software installed. If you perform the lab in pairs, having the software installed on both machines means that each person can run the lab steps, although each host can display slightly different results.

Task 1: Configure the Lab or Attach a Workstation to the School LAN

Option 1. If you select the closed lab environment, cable the equipment as shown in Figure 7-52 and load the configuration files into the appropriate routers. These files might be preloaded. If not, you can obtain them from your instructor. These files should support the IP addressing scheme, as shown in Figure 7-52 and Table 7-6.

Configure the workstations according to the specifications shown in Figure 7-52 and Table 7-6 (the same as those for Lab 7.1.9a).

Table 7-6   Workstation Configuration Settings

	Host #1	Host #2
IP Address	192.168.1.10	192.168.2.10
Subnet Mask	255.255.255.0	255.255.255.0
Default Gateway	192.168.1.1	192.168.2.1

Option 2. If you select option 2 (connect to school LAN), simply connect the workstation, with Protocol Inspector or PE installed, directly to a classroom switch or to a data jack connected to the school LAN.

Task 2: Start the Protocol Inspector EDV Program

From the Start menu, launch the Fluke Protocol Inspector EDV program, as shown in Figure 7-53.

Figure 7-53   Launching the Fluke Protocol Inspector EDV Program

Note: The first time the program runs, a message appears: Do you have any Fluke analyzer cards or Fluke taps in your local system?

If you are using the educational version, click **No**. If you answer Yes or if the following screen appears, just click **OK** without selecting any ports.

The four main Protocol Inspector views are

- Summary View
- Detail View
- Capture View of Capture Buffers
- Capture View of Capture Files

The program opens in the Summary View. This view shows several windows used by the tool. The Resource Browser window in the upper-left corner shows the only monitoring device that you have: the Network Driver Interface Specification (NDIS) 802.3 Module (NIC) of the host. If protocol media monitors existed, they would appear with the associated host devices. You will cover the Alarm Browser (left side) and Message Area (bottom) later.

The Monitor View (upper-right portion in the main window) monitors one resource per window in a variety of viewing options. Figure 7-54, and probably the startup screen, shows no information in the Monitor View window. (The Stop in the upper-left corner of the Monitor View window confirms that no monitoring is occurring.)

Figure 7-54   Monitor View Window in Protocol Inspector

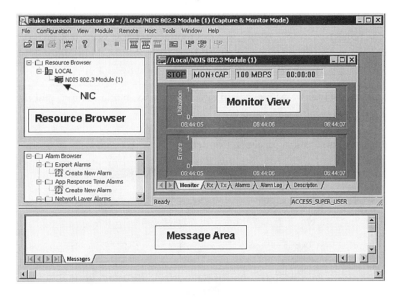

Task 3: Start the Monitor and Capture Process

To start the monitoring and capturing process, use the **Start** button or select **Module > Start**. The Utilization chart starts showing activity, as shown in Figure 7-55.

Figure 7-55   Activity in the Utilization Chart

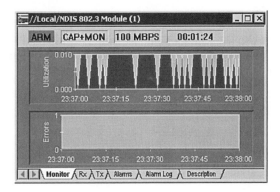

The word Arm should appear where Stop was before. If you open the Module menu, notice that Stop is an option, but Start is muted. Do not stop the process yet, or at least restart it again if it is stopped.

The tabs at the bottom of the window (refer to Figure 7-55) show the resulting data in various forms. Click each and note the results. (Transmit [Tx], Alarms, and Alarm Log will be blank.) Figure 7-56 shows the Received (Rx) frames, which indicate that broadcast and multicast frames are being received, but might not show any unicasts.

Figure 7-56   Tab Options for Data Reports

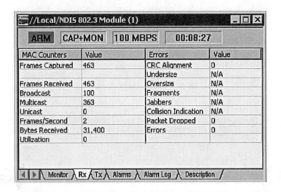

Using the console connection to the router, ping the monitoring host (192.168.1.10 or 192.168.2.10) and notice that Unicast frames appear. Unfortunately, the errors in the third column will not appear in the lab exercise unless you have a traffic generator, such as Fluke Networks OptiView.

The Description tab (see Figure 7-57) reveals the MAC address, manufacturer, and model of the NIC. It also shows which error counters are on.

Figure 7-57   Description Tab Option for Data Reports

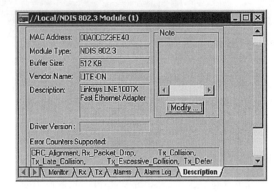

Take a few minutes to become familiar with the tabs and the scroll features of the window.

Task 4: View Details

 To go to the Detail View window, click the **Detail View** button in the toolbar or double-click anywhere on the Monitor View chart. This action opens a second window that looks something like Figure 7-58 after you maximize the Utilization/Errors Strip Chart (RX) window.

Figure 7-58   Detail View Window

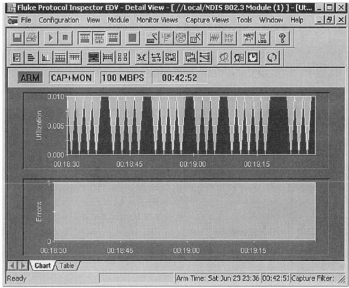

Note: If necessary, activate all toolbars on the View menu.

Initially, the chart output is the same as before, but there are more toolbar and menu options than in the Summary View. Before looking at these features, confirm that the Chart and Table tabs show the same information you previously saw.

Like all Windows-compliant programs, placing the mouse over a button brings up a screen tip that briefly identifies the button's purpose. As the mouse moves over the buttons, notice that some are muted, which means that the feature is not appropriate under current circumstances or, in some cases, not supported in the educational version.

Note: The Lab 7.1.9b Appendix, "Protocol Inspector Toolbars," at the end of this lab provides a complete display of the toolbars and what they do.

 Click the **Mac Statistics** button to see the Rx frame table data in another format. The result should be obvious. Maximize the resulting window. The one piece of new information is Speed, which shows the NIC transmission rate.

 Click the **Frame Size Distribution** button to see a distribution of the size frames received by the NIC. Placing the mouse over any bar displays a small summary, like the one shown in Figure 7-59. Maximize the resulting window.

Figure 7-59   Frame Size Distribution Window

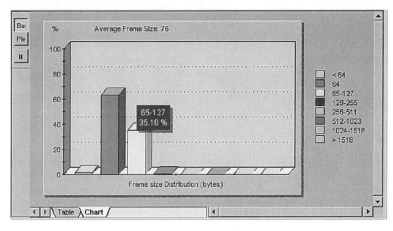

Click the **Pie**, **Bar**, and **Pause** buttons in the upper-left corner.

Note: Pause stops the capture, so click it again to resume the capture. Also, look at both the Table and Chart tab displays.

With the sample configurations, you should be getting mainly small frames because the only thing happening is routing updates. Use the extended ping feature from the router console connection, and specify 100 pings with a larger packet size. If you maximize each new display, return to any previous view by using the Window menu. You can also tile the windows. Experiment with the Window menu features and then close any unwanted views.

Click the **Protocol Distribution** button to see a distribution of the protocols received by the NIC. Placing the mouse over any bar displays a small summary panel. Maximize the resulting window, as shown in Figure 7-60.

Figure 7-60   Protocol Distribution Window

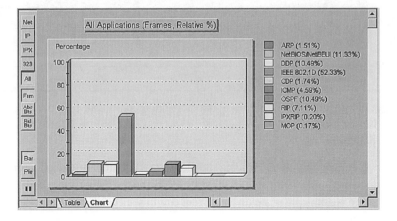

Click each of the buttons and tabs to see the results. The Net button shows only network protocols. The 323 button refers to the H323 voice over IP protocols. This button might also be labeled VoIP instead of 323. Look at Frm (frame), Abs Bts (absolute bytes), and Rel Bts (relative bytes) to see the results. Remember that the Pause button stops the capture.

Click the **Host Table** button to see the MAC stations and related traffic, as shown in Figure 7-61.

Figure 7-61   Viewing MAC Stations and Related Traffic

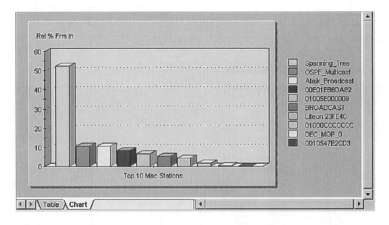

Notice the Spanning Tree, AppleTalk, and Open Shortest Path First (OSPF) protocol traffic. Be sure to look at the Table tab to see the actual values.

Click the **Network Layer Host Table** button to see the network (IP/IPX) stations and related traffic, as shown in Figure 7-62.

Figure 7-62   Viewing IP/IPX Stations and Related Traffic

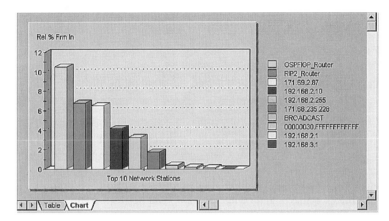

Any pings and any additional hosts that might have added to the configuration impact the actual addresses that appear on the right.

Click the **Application Layer Host Table** button to see the network station traffic by application, as shown in Figure 7-63.

Figure 7-63   Viewing Network Station Traffic by Application

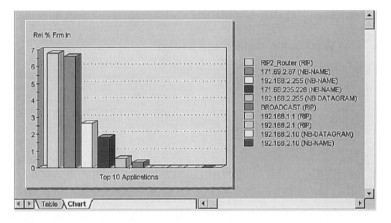

 Experiment with the next three buttons. They create host-to-host matrices for MAC, network, and application layer conversations. Figure 7-64 shows an example of the network layer (IP/IPX) conversations.

Of the next two buttons, the first is the VLAN button, which shows network traffic on VLANs. This sample does not use VLANs, but remember this button when troubleshooting VLANs later.

Figure 7-64   Viewing Network Layer Conversations

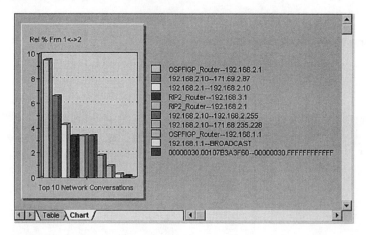

The second button creates a matrix that compares MAC and network-station addresses to names. In Figure 7-65, the second row is a Novell station.

Figure 7-65   Matrix to Compare MAC/Network-Station Addresses to Names

MAC Station Name	MAC Station Address	Network Station Name	Network Station Address
00107B3A3F60	00107B3A3F60	192.168.1.1	192.168.1.1
00107B3A3F60	00107B3A3F60	00000030.00107B3A3F60	00000030.00107B3A3F60
Liteon 23FE40	00A0CC23FE40	192.168.2.10	192.168.2.10
00E01EB6DA82	00E01EB6DA82	192.168.2.1	192.168.2.1
00E01EB6DA82	00E01EB6DA82	192.168.3.1	192.168.3.1

The Name Table button opens the current name table for viewing or editing, as shown in Figure 7-66.

Figure 7-66   Name Table Window for Viewing and Editing

Protocol	Name	Address
MAC	HP_Probe	090009000001
MAC	OSPF_Multicast	01005E000005
IP	IP_Station1	206.132.32.2
IP	BROADCAST	255.255.255.255
IP	IP_Multicast	224.0.0.0
IP	DVMRP_Router	224.0.0.4
IP	OSPFIGP_Router	224.0.0.5
IP	OSPFIGP_Router_0	224.0.0.6

 The Expert View button shows the expert symptoms (see Figure 7-67). These statistics are Protocol Inspector's way of pointing out potential problems. Clicking the underlined options brings up additional detail windows if any values are recorded. The sample for this lab does not show much, but it does look over the options for debugging Inter-Switch Link (ISL), Hot Standby Router Protocol (HSRP), and other types of problems that you will see in later labs.

Figure 7-67   Expert View Window

Expert Category	Value	Expert Category	Value
ICMP All Errors	368	Duplicate Network Address	0
ICMP Destination Unreachable	368	Unstable MST	0
ICMP Redirects	0	SAP Broadcast	0
Excessive Bootp	0	OSPF Broadcast	923
Excessive ARP	0	RIP Broadcast	25
NFS Retransmissions	0	ISL Illegal VLAN ID	0
TCP/IP SYN Attack	0	ISL BPDU/CDP Packets	0
TCP/IP RST Packets	0	IP Time to Live Expiring	0
TCP/IP Retransmissions	0	IP Checksum Errors	0
TCP/IP Zero Window	0	Illegal Network Source Address	0
TCP/IP Long Acks	0	Illegal MAC Source Address	0
TCP/IP Frozen Window	0	Total MAC Stations	11
Network Overload	0	Broadcast/Multicast Storm	0
Non Responsive Stations	0	Physical Errors	0
		HSRP Errors	0
		TCP Checksum Errors	0

Task 5: Stop the Capture Process

To stop the frame capture to look at individual frames, click the **Stop** button or choose **Module > Stop**.

After you stop the capture, click the **Capture View** button. With the education version, a message box announces that the capture is limited to 250 packets. Just click **OK**.

The resulting window, shown in Figure 7-68, can be overwhelming at first. Maximize the window to hide any other windows open in the background.

Figure 7-68   Capture View Window

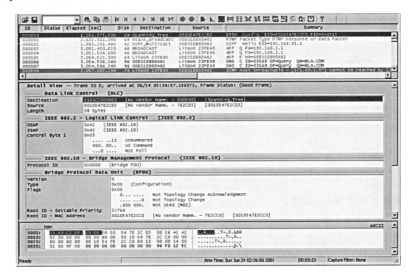

In the results, note that three horizontal windows are open. The top window lists the captured packets. The middle window shows the detail of the selected packet in the top window, and the bottom window shows the hexadecimal values for the packet.

If you position the mouse over the borders between the three windows, a "line mover" (two-headed arrow) appears, letting you change the distribution of space for each window. It might be advantageous to make the middle window as large as possible, leaving five or six rows in each of the other two, as shown in the figure.

Look over the packets in the top window. You should see Domain Name System (DNS), Address Resolution Protocol (ARP), Routing Table Maintenance Protocol (RTMP), and other types of packets. If you are using a switch, you should see Cisco Discovery Protocol (CDP) and spanning-tree packets. Notice that as you select rows in the top window, the contents of the other two windows change.

Select information in the middle window, and notice that the hexadecimal display in the bottom window changes to show where that specific information is stored. In Figure 7-69, selecting the source address (IP) shows hexadecimal values from the packet.

Figure 7-69   Viewing Hexadecimal Values from a Packet

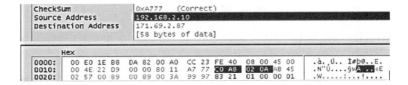

The color coding makes it easier to locate information from the middle window in the hexadecimal window. In Figure 7-70, with a DNS packet, the data in the Data Link Control (DLC) section of middle window is purple, whereas the IP section is green. The corresponding hexadecimal values are the same colors.

Figure 7-70   Color-Coded Packets and Hexadecimal Values

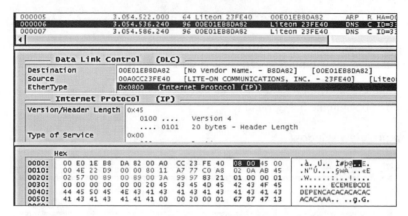

Notice in Figure 7-70, the EtherType is 0x0800, which indicates that it is an IP packet. You can also notice the MAC addresses for both the destination and source hosts as well as where that data is stored in the hexadecimal display.

In the same example, the next section in the middle window is the User Datagram Protocol (UDP) information, including the UDP port numbers (see Figure 7-71).

Figure 7-71   Viewing UDP Information

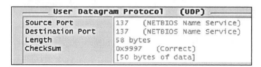

The structure of the middle window changes for each type of packet.

Take a few minutes to select different packet types in the top window and then look over the resulting display in the other two windows. Pay particular attention to the EtherType, any port numbers, and source and destination addresses (both MAC and network layer). You should see RIP, OSPF, and RTMP (AppleTalk) packets in the capture. Make sure that you can locate and interpret the important data. In the RIP capture in Figure 7-72, notice that it is a RIP version 2 packet; the multicast destination address is 224.0.0.9 (what would it be in version 1?); and that you can see the actual route table entries.

Figure 7-72   RIP Packet Information

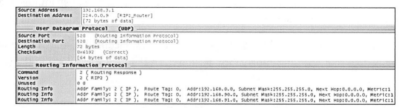

If you see any CDP packets, figure out the platform. Figure 7-73 is from a Catalyst 1900 switch.

Figure 7-73   Determining the Networking Device Platform Based on CDP Packet Information

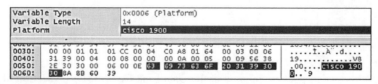

Experiment until you are comfortable with the tools.

Task 6: Save the Captured Data

Depending on the version of Protocol Expert/Inspector, File > Save Capture might be File > Save Current Section. To save captured data, click the **Save Capture** button or choose **File** > **Save Capture** to open the dialog box shown in Figure 7-74. Accept the **All** option by clicking the **Continue** button. You can save just a range of captured frames with this window.

Figure 7-74   Captured Data Save Options

Use a proper filename and store the file on the appropriate disk. If the CAP extension is showing when the window in Figure 7-75 opens, make sure it remains after you type the name.

Figure 7-75   Saving Captured Data to File

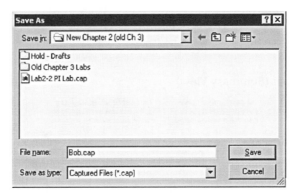

Click the **Open Capture File** button and open the file called Lab3-2 PI Lab.cap, or if it is not available, open the file that you just saved.

You are now using the Capture View of Capture Files. There is no difference in tools, but the title bar at the top of the screen indicates that you are viewing a file rather than a capture in memory.

Task 7: Examine Frames

Select a frame in the top window and click the buttons. The arrows by themselves move up or down one frame. The arrow with a single line jumps to the top or bottom of the current window, whereas the arrow with two arrows jumps to the top or bottom of the entire list. The arrow with the T also moves to the top of the list.

Click the **Search** buttons to perform searches. Type text such as OSPF in the list box, click the binoculars, and you can move from one OSPF entry to the next.

Experiment until you are comfortable with the tools.

Reflection

1. How might you use this tool in troubleshooting?

2. Is Protocol Inspector analyzing all the data on the network?

_____

3. What is the impact of being connected to a switch?

_____

Curriculum Lab 7-3 Appendix: Protocol Inspector Toolbars (7.1.9b)

Figure 7-76   Protocol Inspector Toolbar

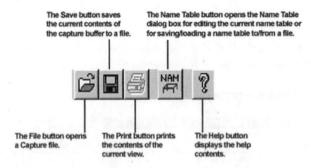

Figure 7-77   Module Toolbar (Summary View)

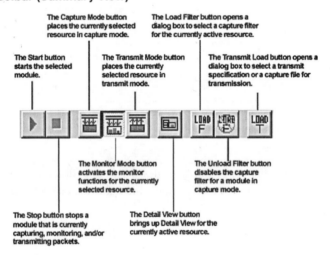

Figure 7-78   Detail View Toolbar

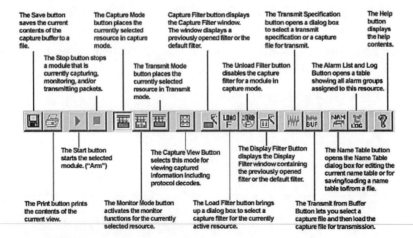

Figure 7-79   Data Views Toolbar (Note That Only Some of These Views Are Available with GMM Cards)

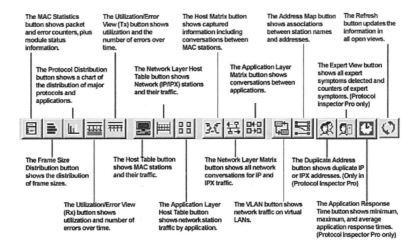

Figure 7-80   Create/Modify Filter Toolbar

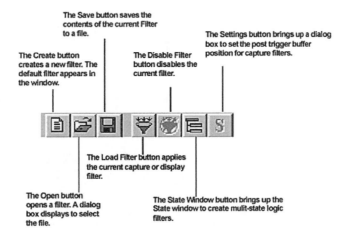

Figure 7-81   State Toolbar

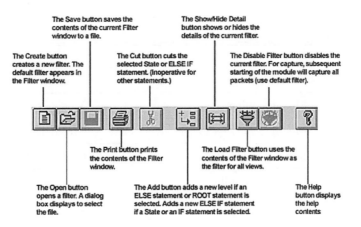

Figure 7-82   Capture View Toolbar

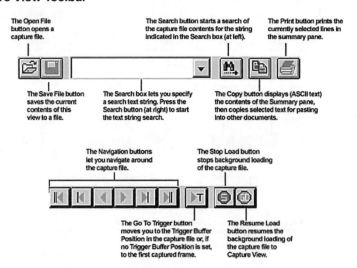

Figure 7-83   Capture View Toolbar, Continued

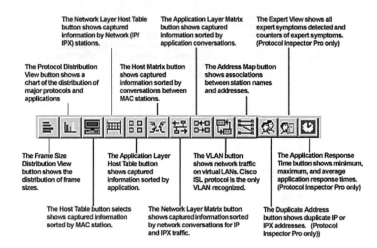

Table 7-7   Protocol Inspector Function Keys

Function Key	Summary View	Detail View
F1	Help	Help
F2	System settings	Capture view display options
F3	Module settings	Module settings
F4	Module monitor view preferences	Create display filter
F5	Connect to remote	Create capture filter
F6	Load capture filter	Load capture filter
F7	Open capture file	Expert summary view
F8	Save capture	Save capture
F9	Go to Detail view	Capture view
F10	Start/stop	Start/stop
F11	N/A	N/A
F12	N/A	N/A

Table 7-8   Protocol Inspector Keyboard Shortcuts

Key Combination	Action
Alt-F4	Close window
Ctrl-O	Open
Ctrl-S	Save
Ctrl-T	Start module
Ctrl-P	Stop module

CHAPTER 8

Ethernet Switching

The Study Guide portion of this chapter uses a combination of matching, fill in the blank, compare and contrast, and open-ended question exercises to test your knowledge of Ethernet switching.

The Lab Exercises portion of this chapter includes a challenge lab to ensure that you have mastered the practical, hands-on skills needed to build a multiswitch Ethernet network.

As you work through this chapter, use Module 8 in the CCNA 1 online curriculum or use the corresponding Chapter 8 in the *Networking Basics CCNA 1 Companion Guide* for assistance.

Study Guide

Ethernet Switching

In its most basic IT definition, switching involves receiving data on one interface and redirecting it to another interface. Ethernet switching is the process of receiving a frame, making a forwarding decision based on frame addressing, and redirecting the frame to the interface connected to the destination's segment. Ethernet switches are dominant LAN devices in today's networks. These switches segment networks into more manageable areas, provide dedicated bandwidth between communicating hosts, and make rapid frame forwarding decisions. Understanding the switching process is necessary for network professionals.

This section includes exercises that help you understand Ethernet switching terminology, identify switching modes, and recognize the steps in the switching process.

Vocabulary Exercise: Matching

Match the definition on the left with a term on the right. This exercise does not necessarily use one-to-one matching. Some definitions might be used more than once and some terms might have multiple definitions.

Definitions

a. A table built dynamically by a switch that contains MAC information for each switch port.

b. An electronic logic device that is custom designed to perform a particular function.

c. A switching method where the source port and destination port operate at different speeds.

d. A set of procedures that calculate the optimal path in a switched environment by identifying and shutting down redundant ports.

e. The ability of a switch to create a single, physical segment for each connected port.

f. A switching method where the source port and destination port operate at the same speed.

g. A standards-based protocol that is used to avoid switching loops.

h. Delay between the time when a device receives a frame and the time that frame is forwarded out the destination port.

i. Small messages used by switches to advertise information about ports and devices to other switches.

j. Access method in which network devices compete for permission to access the physical medium.

Terms

___ Spanning Tree Protocol (STP)

___ contention

___ symmetric switching

___ Content Addressable Memory (CAM)

___ latency

___ application-specific integrated circuit (ASIC)

___ asymmetric switching

___ microsegmentation

___ bridge protocol data units (BPDU)

___ spanning-tree algorithm

Compare and Contrast Exercise: Switch Modes

Ethernet switches are Layer 2 devices that make forwarding decisions based on MAC address information. Switches maintain a CAM table that contains a record of MAC addresses and associated interfaces. When a switch receives a frame, it checks the frame's destination MAC address against the table. After a match is found, the switch forwards the frame out the interface that is connected to the destination's segment. Although this is the basic operation of a switch, the exact method a switch uses to forward a frame varies.

Complete Table 8-1 to compare and contrast three switch modes.

Table 8-1   Compare and Contrast Switch Modes

	Store and Forward	Cut-Through	Fragment-Free
How are frames switched between interfaces in this mode?			
Relative to the other types, how much latency does this type of switch introduce to the network?			
Relative to the other types, how reliable is this type of switching?			
What are the advantages of this type of switching when compared to the other types?			
What are the disadvantages of this type of switching when compared to the other types?			

Concept Questions

Completely answer the following questions:

1. Bridges operate at Layer 2 of the OSI model. What type of information does a bridge use to make forwarding decisions? How is this information actually used in the bridging process?

    _____
    _____
    _____
    _____
    _____
    _____
    _____

2. Switches are often described as multiport bridges. Explain why switches operate faster and are more efficient than the bridges they are commonly compared to.

    _____
    _____
    _____
    _____
    _____
    _____
    _____
    _____

3. How does a switch provide microsegmentation?

    _____
    _____
    _____
    _____

4. All network devices contribute to the latency of frames traveling through a network. How do switches introduce latency?

    _____
    _____
    _____
    _____
    _____
    _____

5. Store and forward provides the greatest reliability while contributing the greatest amount of latency. Cut-through switching is fast and not as reliable. Explain how fragment-free switching offers a mix of reliability and speed.

    _____
    _____
    _____
    _____

6. List the five Spanning Tree Protocol (STP) switch port states in order. What is the purpose of each port state?

_____

■ _____

■ _____
  _____

■ _____
  _____

■ _____
  _____

■ _____
  _____

Note: Use Challenge Lab 8-1 to observe STP operations in a multiswitch network. You see how STP handles redundant interswitch connections and effectively eliminates switching loops.

Journal Entry

Figure 8-1 shows a small network that consists of four hosts linked to a switch. Table 8-2 lists each host's IP address, MAC address, and the switch port to which the host is connected.

Figure 8-1   Small, Switched Network

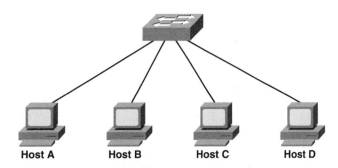

Host Name	MAC Address	IP Address	Switch Port
Host A	00-01-42-00-AA-BB	192.168.100.1	1
Host B	00-01-43-11-22-33	192.168.100.2	5
Host C	00-01-64-FF-EE-DD	192.168.100.3	9
Host D	00-01-C7-77-88-99	192.168.100.4	13

Table 8-2   Network Configuration

Hostname	MAC Address	IP Address	Switch Port
Host A	00-01-42-00-AA-BB	192.168.100.1	1
Host B	00-01-43-11-22-33	192.168.100.2	5
Host C	00-01-64-FF-EE-DD	192.168.100.3	9
Host D	00-01-C7-77-88-99	192.168.100.4	13

Assuming that the switch is working properly, has a populated CAM table, and that all ports are in the Forwarding state, how does the switch handle each of the following communications?

1. Host A pings 192.168.100.4. (The destination MAC address is in host A's ARP table.)

_____

_____

_____

_____

2. Host C sends a frame addressed to FF-FF-FF-FF-FF-FF.

_____

_____

3. Host B sends a frame addressed to 00-01-43-11-22-33.

_____

_____

_____

4. Host D sends a frame addressed to 00-01-42-00-AA-BB.

_____

_____

_____

_____

Collision Domains and Broadcast Domains

Collisions happen in shared-media environments. A small number of collisions is usually negligible, whereas a larger number of collisions can negatively affect network performance. Keeping collisions bounded in small areas can increase the efficiency of any network. The same is true for broadcast traffic. These bounded areas are known as collision and broadcast domains.

The exercises in this section are designed to increase your knowledge of network segmentation and the need for collision and broadcast domains. These exercises include identifying terms associated with segmentation, identifying collision and broadcast domains, and understanding data flow in a network.

Note: Packet Tracer is a learning tool that you can use to build and configure virtual networks. After a network is created, you can use Packet Tracer to simulate traffic on the network. This is an excellent tool to learn about the nature of collisions, broadcasts, and data flow.

Vocabulary Exercise: Completion

Complete the following statements by using the proper terms to fill in the blanks.

Layer 3 devices create _____ by defining bounded areas that restrict broadcast propagation.

Networking devices are used in _____ environments to broaden the scope of the network, which allows additional hosts to connect to the medium.

_____ are the connected physical network segments where collisions can occur and propagate.

Multiple hosts access the same medium in a _____ environment.

Creating smaller, more manageable collision domains by adding Layer 2 or 3 networking devices is known as _____.

A _____ can overwhelm a network with broadcast traffic to the point that no new connections can be made, and established network connections might be dropped.

In a _____ environment, a host or device connects only to one other host or device.

Concept Questions

Completely answer the following questions:

1. Routers are considered Layer 3 devices but actually perform functions at Layers 1, 2, and 3. Briefly explain these functions.

   _____

   _____

   _____

2. Which networking devices extend collision domains? Which devices segment collision domains?

   _____

   _____

   _____

3. Explain the four repeater rule. Why is this rule necessary?

   _____

   _____

   _____

   _____

   _____

   _____

4. Explain the concept of unicast, multicast, and broadcast frames. What is a common use for a broadcast frame?

   _____

   _____

   _____

   _____

   _____

   _____

5. Why must care be taken to contain broadcasts by creating broadcast domains?

   _____

   _____

   _____

   _____

   _____

   _____

   _____

6. As with many terms and acronyms, segment has multiple meanings. Explain the concept of a wire segment, LAN segment, and a TCP segment.

_____

_____

_____

_____

Identifying Collision and Broadcast Domains Exercise

Collision domains are the connected physical network segments where collisions can occur. A broadcast domain is a group of collision domains that are connected by Layer 2 devices. Identify the collision and broadcast domains in the following figures by circling each. Be sure to record the number of each type of domain in each figure.

Figure 8-2   Network Example 1

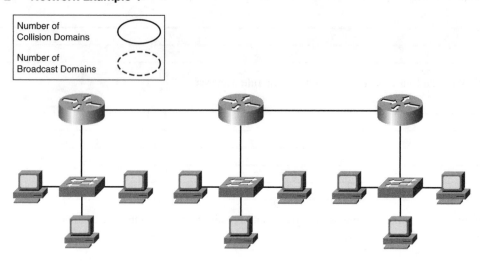

Figure 8-3   **Network Example 2**

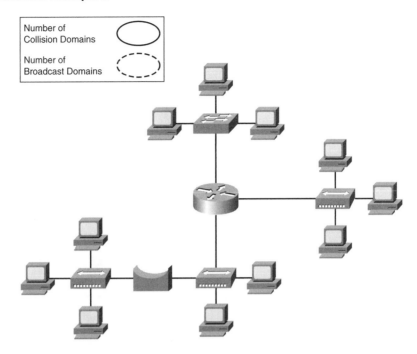

Figure 8-4   **Network Example 3**

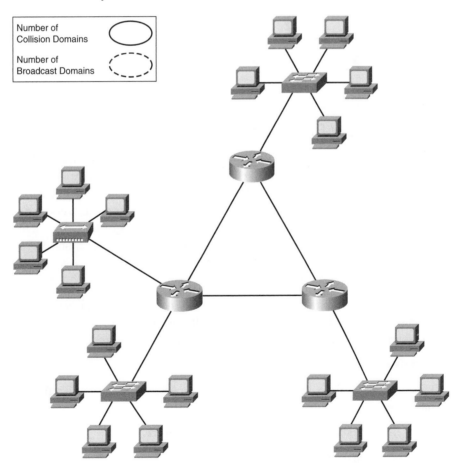

Figure 8-5   Network Example 4

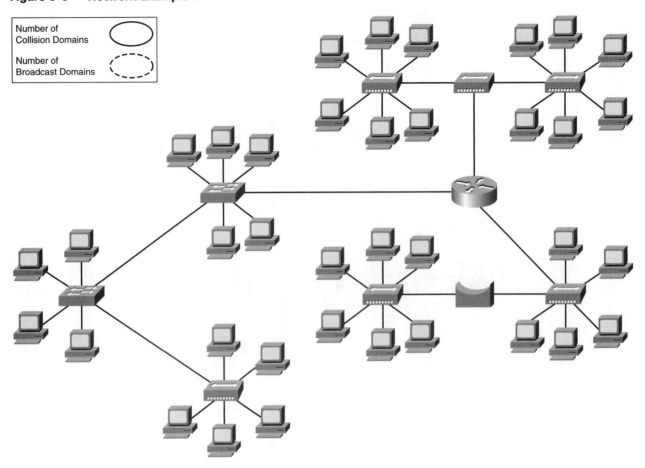

Illustrating Data Flow Exercise

Data flow is the movement of information in a network from a source to a destination. This includes traveling across the medium and through network devices. In an IP environment, data flow is also analyzed in relation to the OSI model. As IP traffic passes through networking devices, the information moves up and down the OSI model according to the device's layers of operation. For example, a bridge operates at Layer 2 of the OSI model. When a bridge receives a string of binary digits, it structures them in the form of a frame, the Layer 2 PDU. The bridge then analyzes the frame and makes a forwarding decision based on the framing information. If the frame is to be forwarded, the bridge passes the frame back to Layer 1 where the bits are placed on the medium.

Understanding the concept of data flows in a routed IP-based network is extremely important for network professionals. Figure 8-6 includes a diagram of a simple IP network. For the purpose of this exercise, device A is the source communicating with device E. To complete this exercise, follow these steps:

Step 1.   Identify each device in the network.

Step 2.   Label the layers of the corresponding networking device OSI models to reflect their layers of operation.

Step 3.   Draw arrows to show the data flow through the network.

Step 4.   Show how each device moves the information through its OSI model.

Figure 8-6 Data Flow in a Simple Network

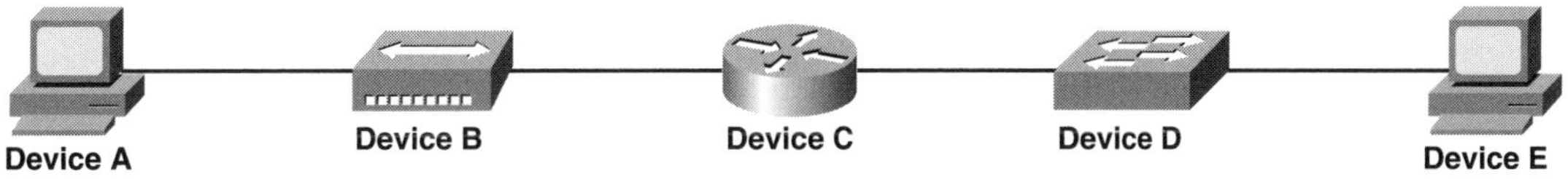

Device A	Device B	Device C	Device D	Device E
7 ____	7 ____	7 ____	7 ____	7 ____
6 ____	6 ____	6 ____	6 ____	6 ____
5 ____	5 ____	5 ____	5 ____	5 ____
4 ____	4 ____	4 ____	4 ____	4 ____
3 ____	3 ____	3 ____	3 ____	3 ____
2 ____	2 ____	2 ____	2 ____	2 ____
1 ____	1 ____	1 ____	1 ____	1 ____

Answer the following data flow questions:

1. What does device B use to make forwarding decisions?

   _____
   _____

2. What is the PDU used by device B?

   _____

3. What does device C use to make forwarding decisions?

   _____
   _____

4. What is the highest level PDU used by device C?

   _____

5. What does device D use to make forwarding decisions?

   _____
   _____

6. What is the highest level PDU used by device D?

   _____

7. Disregarding the source and destination, which device in the network introduces the greatest latency?
   Explain.

   _____
   _____
   _____
   _____

8. How many collision domains exist in the network?

_____

9. How many broadcast domains exist in the network?

_____

Journal Entry

Answer the following questions regarding the network illustrated in Figure 8-7.

Figure 8-7   Teaching Topology

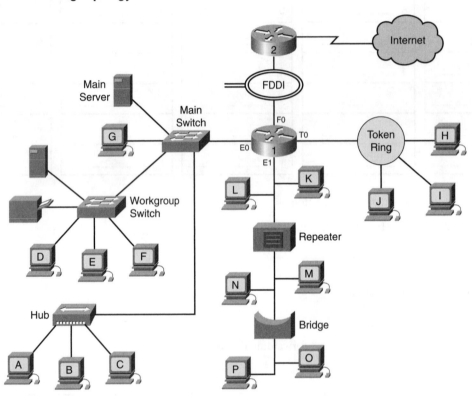

1. How many collision domains are in the network?

_____
_____

2. How many broadcast domains are in the network?

_____
_____

3. Explain the data flow from host A (source) to host D (destination).

_____
_____
_____
_____
_____
_____

4. Explain the data flow from host B (source) to host O (destination).

_____

_____

_____

_____

_____

_____

_____

_____

_____

_____

_____

_____

Lab Exercises

Challenge Lab 8-1: Building a Multiswitch Network with Redundant Links

Figure 8-8   Two Workstation, Two Switch Topology

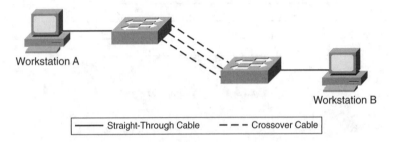

Objectives

- Create a small LAN with two PCs and two switches.

- Create redundant connections between the switches.

- Observe switch port state changes.

Background

Redundant Ethernet links can be used to increase reliability and fault tolerance by eliminating a single point of failure. If one link were to cease functioning, a second link can keep the communication path available. Although this is certainly advantageous, switching loops can keep a frame from ever reaching its intended destination. STP operates on switches and is designed to maintain redundant connections while eliminating the possibility of switching loops.

This challenge lab focuses on building a small multiswitch LAN to observe the way STP maintains redundant links. Work in teams of two (one person per PC). You need the following resources:

- Two workstations with an Ethernet 10/100 NIC installed

- Two Ethernet switches

- Two straight-through Ethernet cables to connect the PCs to the switches

- Three crossover cables to connect the switches to one another

Task 1: Build the LAN and Verify the Physical Connections

Initially, connect the two switches by using a single crossover cable (from port 1 to port 1). Connect one PC to each switch (on port 4 or above). Plug in and turn on the devices. How can the physical connections be verified initially?

Task 2: Configure the TCP/IP Settings on the PCs

Set the IP address information for each PC according to the information in Table 8-3.

Note: Write down the existing IP settings so you can restore them at the end of the lab.

Table 8-3   IP Address Settings for PCs

Computer	IP Address	Subnet Mask	Default Gateway
Workstation A	192.168.1.1	255.255.255.0	Not required
Workstation B	192.168.1.2	255.255.255.0	Not required

Task 3: Access the Command Prompt and Test Connectivity

Using the command prompt, **ping** the other workstation on the LAN. Use appropriate troubleshooting procedures if the ping is not successful.

Note: The steps used to open a command prompt can be different for each OS. Be familiar with the steps for the most common OSs.

Task 4: Add Redundant Links Between the Switches

Add two additional links between the switches by using crossover cables to connect port 2 to port 2 and port 3 to port 3. Observe the corresponding LEDs. Wait one minute and record the status of the LEDs for the switch link ports.

Switch A port 1 LED   _____

Switch B port 1 LED   _____

Switch A port 2 LED   _____

Switch B port 2 LED   _____

Switch A port 3 LED   _____

Switch B port 3 LED   _____

If STP is functioning, only one link will be active between the switches. Which is the active link? How can this be determined by observing the LEDs?

Task 5: Experiment with Redundant Links

Initiate a continuous ping from workstation A to workstation B by entering **ping –t 192.168.1.2**. Ensure that the ping attempts are successful.

Note: A continuous ping causes ping packets to be sent from the source to the destination until the operation is interrupted. To cancel a continuous ping, use **Ctrl+c**.

Next, break the active link between the switches by unplugging one end of the link cable. Observe the LEDs on the switches. Did a new link become active?

A few ping attempts might fail during the STP link changeover. After a new link becomes active, the ping attempts should be successful.

Experiment with the redundant links by disconnecting and reconnecting switch links and observe the port state changes.

Note: You learn more about STP functions in the Networking Academy CCNA 3 course.

Task 6: Disassemble the Lab Network

Restore the PCs to their original TCP/IP settings, disconnect the equipment, and store the cables.

TCP/IP Protocol Suite and IP Addressing

The Study Guide portion of this chapter uses a combination of matching, fill in the blank, compare and contrast, and open-ended question exercises to test your knowledge of the TCP/IP protocol suite and IP addressing.

The Lab Exercises portion of this chapter includes curriculum labs, a comprehensive lab, and a challenge lab to ensure that you have mastered the practical, hands-on skills needed to configure a DHCP client, identify internetworks, and monitor ARP messages.

As you work through this chapter, use Module 9 in the CCNA 1 online curriculum or use the corresponding Chapter 9 in the *Networking Basics CCNA 1 Companion Guide* for assistance.

Study Guide

Introduction to TCP/IP

The U.S. Department of Defense (DoD) created the Transmission Control Protocol/Internet Protocol (TCP/IP) reference model as a network model that provides reliable data communications across various network types under varying conditions. The four-layer TCP/IP model has become the standard on which the Internet is based.

In this section, you learn the function of each layer of the TCP/IP model, identify the protocols associated with each layer, and recognize the similarities and differences of the TCP/IP and OSI models.

Vocabulary Exercise: Completion

Complete the following statements by using the proper terms to fill in the blanks.

The _____ of the TCP/IP model handles high-level protocols, representation, encoding, and dialog control.

_____ is a network layer Internet protocol that reports errors and provides other information relevant to IP packet processing.

The purpose of the _____ layer is to select the best path through the network for packets to travel.

Networks that consist of many networks are called _____.

The _____ layer allows an IP packet to make a physical link to the network media and includes the LAN and WAN technology details and all the details contained in the OSI physical and data link layers.

_____ is a common name for the suite of protocols developed by the U.S. Department of Defense (DoD) in the 1970s to support the construction of world-wide internetworks.

The _____ layer provides a logical connection between a source host and a destination host and uses protocols to segment and reassemble data sent by upper-layer applications into the same data stream, or logical connection, between end points.

Compare and Contrast Exercise: Reference Models

It is important to understand the similarities and differences of the TCP/IP model and the Open Systems Interconnection (OSI) model because each model is referenced in many areas of internetworking. Complete Table 9-1 to compare and contrast these reference models.

Table 9-1   Compare and Contrast the TCP/IP and OSI Reference Models

TCP/IP Model Layer	TCP/IP Layer Function	OSI Model Layer	OSI Layer Function
		7	
		6	
		5	
		4	
		3	
		2	
		1	

Concept Questions

Completely answer the following questions:

1. What are the major categories of application layer protocols? Provide at least one specific protocol type per category.

    _____

    _____

    _____

    _____

    _____

    _____

2. What are the similar functions provided by TCP and UDP at the transport layer? What functions are unique to TCP?

    _____

    _____

    _____

    _____

    ■ _____

    ■ _____

    ■ _____

    ■ _____

    ■ _____

3. The main protocol that functions at the Internet layer is IP. Why is IP often referred to as an unreliable protocol? Where is reliability found in the TCP/IP model?

_____

_____

_____

_____

_____

4. Why are ARP and RARP considered Internet layer and network access layer protocols?

_____

_____

_____

5. An internetwork is a collection of networks interconnected by routers and other devices that function (generally) as a single network. What features must internetworks possess to remain effective today and in the future?

_____

■ _____

_____

■ _____

_____

■ _____

_____

Journal Entry

Internetworks are often complex systems that contain multiple networks consisting of thousands of network devices. When an internetwork diagram is created, clouds commonly represent complicated portions of the internetwork and areas that have not been documented completely.

List the typical components of these clouds. Also, identify the layer or layers of the TCP/IP model where each component operates.

_____

_____

■ _____

_____

■ _____

_____

■ _____

■ _____

_____

Internet Addresses

The Internet is based on the TCP/IP model and uses a universal, hierarchical addressing scheme to uniquely identify devices connected to the network. IP addresses are unique, logical addresses used by computers to locate and communicate with other computers on the network.

In this section, you learn the basics of IP addressing, identify the various classes of IP addresses, and understand the needs and uses of reserved, private, and public addresses. This section also introduces you to the next generation of IP (known as IPv6) and helps you discover its advantages over IPv4.

Vocabulary Exercise: Matching

Match the definition on the left with a term on the right. This exercise does not necessarily use one-to-one matching. Some definitions might be used more than once and some terms might have multiple definitions.

Definitions

a. A special address reserved for sending a message to all stations.

b. The first four bits of this address class are always set to 1s.

c. A single address that refers to multiple network devices.

d. A special address reserved for identifying the network itself.

e. A method of dividing and identifying separate networks throughout the LAN.

f. A 32-bit address assigned to hosts that use TCP/IP.

g. An IP address class that uses the first two of the four octets to indicate the network address.

h. An address space designed to support small networks with a maximum of 254 hosts.

i. Uses 128 bits to provide 640 sextillion addresses.

j. An address class designed to support extremely large networks with more than 16 million host addresses available.

k. An address class created to enable multicasting in an IP network.

Terms

___ Class C address

___ Class D address

___ multicast address

___ network address

___ broadcast address

___ Class E address

___ IPv4 address

___ Class B address

___ IPv6

___ subnetting

___ Class A address

Concept Questions

Completely answer the following questions:

1. Why is an IP address considered hierarchical? What two identifiers make up an IP address?

_____

_____

_____

_____

_____

_____

2. Each IP network contains at least two reserved addresses. What are these address types and why must they be reserved?

_____

_____

_____

_____

_____

3. Private address ranges exist in each of the three commercial IP address classes. How are private addresses used in today's networks?

_____

_____

_____

_____

_____

_____

_____

_____

4. What is subnetting and why is it needed? How is a subnet address created?

_____

_____

_____

_____

_____

_____

5. IPv6 will become the new standard for IP addressing on the Internet in the future. What are the advantages of IPv6 over IPv4? How are the address types similar? How are they different?

_____

_____

_____

_____

_____

_____

_____

_____

_____

IP Address Identification Exercise

You can identify each class of IP addresses by the significant bits of the first octet and the IP address range in dotted-decimal format. The three commercial classes also have unique structures with each octet designated as a network or host octet.

Complete Table 9-2 by identifying the significant bits of each class, the range of IP addresses, and the structure of network and host octets for each.

Table 9-2   Identify IP Address Class Attributes

IP Address Class	Significant Bits	Range in Dotted-Decimal Format	Class Structure
A			
B			
C			
D			
E			

Each of the three commercial classes includes a range of private addresses for network segments not connected to the Internet. Use Table 9-3 to list each private address range per class and calculate the number of addresses within each private address range.

Table 9-3   Identify Private IP Address Ranges

IP Address Class	Private Address Range	Number of Addresses Within Private Address Range
A		
B		
C		

Complete Table 9-4 by identifying the class of each IP address, determine if the address is public or private, and categorize each as an assignable address, network address, or broadcast address.

Table 9-4   Classify IP Addresses

IP Address	Class	Public or Private	Assignable, Network, or Broadcast Address
123.16.73.45			
192.168.10.0			
202.88.204.200			
172.31.255.0			
11.255.255.255			
192.168.95.255			

continues

Table 9-4   Classify IP Addresses   *continued*

IP Address	Class	Public or Private	Assignable, Network, or Broadcast Address
172.17.0.0			
172.35.1.0			

Note: Curriculum Lab 9-1 provides additional exercises in identifying IP addresses. Comprehensive Lab 9-4 asks you to identify address classes on the Internet. Now is a good time to complete these labs.

Journal Entry

IPv6 was designed to overcome the shortcomings of current IPv4 implementations. These shortcomings include limited scalability, a decreasing public address space, and rapidly growing Internet backbone routing tables. Making the move from a well-established IPv4 infrastructure to IPv6 poses many challenges to network administrators.

You are a network administrator of a large organization preparing to move to IPv6. Compile a list of potential challenges you might face when transitioning from IPv4 to IPv6. Focus on one of these challenge areas and formulate a strategy to ensure a smooth transition in this area.

Note: Use the Internet to research IPv4 to IPv6 transition issues and strategies.

Obtaining an IP Address

IP address calculation and assignment is a major task for every network administrator. Network hosts must have globally unique addresses to communicate with other hosts on the Internet.

In this section, you learn the two methods that network administrators use to assign IP addresses, discover three types of dynamic address assignment, and understand the need for Address Resolution Protocol (ARP).

Vocabulary Exercise: Define

Define the following terms:

Address Resolution Protocol (ARP) _____

_____

Bootstrap Protocol (BOOTP) _____

_____

default gateway _____

_____

_____

_____

_____

dynamic addressing _____

_____

Dynamic Host Configuration Protocol (DHCP) _____

_____

_____

proxy ARP _____

_____

_____

Reverse Address Resolution Protocol (RARP) _____

_____

static addressing _____

_____

_____

Concept Questions

Completely answer the following questions:

1. Network administrators use two methods for IP address assignment. Why are both methods used in most networks?

_____

_____

_____

_____

_____

_____

_____

_____

_____

_____

2. Dynamic Host Configuration Protocol (DHCP) is a popular method of dynamic IP address assignment. What are the steps in the DHCP process?

_____

_____

_____

_____

_____

_____

_____

_____

_____

3. Why is Address Resolution Protocol (ARP) a necessary LAN protocol? What type of information is contained in a host's ARP table?

_____

_____

_____

_____

_____

_____

_____

_____

_____

Note: Curriculum Labs 9-2 and 9-3 focus on the DHCP and ARP processes respectively. Complete these labs before moving to the Challenge Lab 9-5.

Journal Entry

Most networks use static and dynamic IP addressing methods. It is important to understand the strengths and proper uses of each.

You are a newly hired network administrator. Your first task is to evaluate the effectiveness of the current IP addressing methodology used by your organization. To accomplish this task, you need to complete the following steps:

Step 1.   Make a sketch of your computer lab. This needs to be a logical diagram that identifies each networked device in the lab.

Step 2.   Label each networked device. Use a naming scheme that others can easily follow.

Step 3.   Document the IP addressing mechanism used by each device. Is the IP address statically configured? Is the IP address obtained dynamically?

Step 4.   Evaluate the addressing system of the lab. Do you believe the addressing system is effective? Would there be any benefits from changing the way any of the devices are addressed? Be thorough with your answers.

Lab Exercises

Curriculum Lab 9-1: IP Addressing Basics (9.2.7)

Objectives

- Name the five different classes of IP addresses.

- Describe the characteristics and use of the different IP address classes.

- Identify the class of an IP address based on the network number.

- Determine which part (octet) of an IP address is the network ID and which part is the host ID.

- Identify valid and invalid IP host addresses based on the rules of IP addressing.

- Define the range of addresses and default subnet mask for each class.

Background/Preparation

This lab helps you develop an understanding of IP addresses and how TCP/IP networks operate. It is primarily a written exercise, but it would be worthwhile to review some real network IP addresses using the command-line utilities **ipcconfig** (Windows NT/2000/XP) or **winipcfg** (Windows 9x/Me). IP addresses uniquely identify individual TCP/IP networks and hosts (computers and printers) on those networks so devices can communicate. Workstations and servers on a TCP/IP network are called *hosts*, and each has a unique IP address, which is its *host address*. TCP/IP is the most widely used protocol in the world. The Internet, or World Wide Web, uses only IP addressing. For a host to access the Internet, it must have an IP address.

In its basic form, the IP address has two parts: a network address and a host address. The network portion of the IP address is assigned to a company or organization by the Internet Network Information Center (InterNIC). Routers use the IP address to move data packets between networks. IP addresses are 32 bits long (with the current version, IPv4) and have 4 octets of 8 bits each. They operate at the network Layer 3 of the OSI model (the internetwork layer of the TCP/IP model) and are assigned statically (manually) by a network administrator or dynamically (automatically) by a Dynamic Host Configuration Protocol (DHCP) server. The IP address of a workstation (host) is a *logical address*, which means that it can change. The MAC address of the workstation is a 48-bit *physical address*, which is burned into the NIC and cannot change unless you replace the NIC. The combination of the logical IP address and the physical MAC address helps route packets to their proper destinations.

There are five different classes of IP addresses, and depending on the class, the network and host part of the address will use a different number of bits. In this lab, you work with the different classes of IP addresses and become familiar with the characteristics of each. Understanding IP addresses is critical to understanding TCP/IP and internetworks in general. This lab requires a PC workstation with Windows 9x/NT/2000/XP and access to the Windows calculator.

Task 1: Review IP Address Classes and Their Characteristics

Step 1.   Address Classes

There are five classes of IP addresses (A through E). Only the first three classes are used commercially. Table 9-5 starts with a Class A network address. The first column is the class of IP address. The second column is the first octet, which must fall within the range shown for a given class of address. The Class A address must start with a number between 1 and 126. The first bit of a Class A address is always a 0, which means that you cannot use the high order bit (HOB), or the 128 bit. The 127 bit is reserved for loopback testing. The first octet alone defines the network ID for a Class A network address.

Step 2.   Default Subnet Mask

The default subnet mask uses all binary 1s (decimal 255) to mask the first 8 bits of the Class A address. The default subnet mask helps routers and hosts determine whether the destination host is on this network or another one. Because only 126 Class A networks exist, you can use the remaining 24 bits (3 octets) for hosts. Each Class A network can have 2^{24} (2 to the 24th power) or more than 16 million hosts. It is common to subdivide the network into smaller groupings called *subnets* by using a custom subnet mask, which is discussed in the next lab.

Step 3.   Network and Host Address

The network or host portion of the address cannot be all 1s or all 0s. For example, the Class A address of 118.0.0.5 is a valid IP address because the network portion (the first 8 bits, equal to 118) is not all 0s, and the host portion (the last 24 bits) is not all 0s or all 1s. If the host portion were all 0s, it would be the network address itself. If the host portion were all 1s, it would be a broadcast for the network address. The value of any octet can never be greater than decimal 255 or binary 11111111. Table 9-5 shows the information you should know about the five classes of IP addresses.

Table 9-5   IP Address Class Information

Class	First Octet Decimal Range	First Octet HOBs	Network/Host ID (N = Network, H = Host)	Default Subnet Mask	Number of Networks	Hosts per Network (Usable Addresses)
A	1–126*	0	N.H.H.H	255.0.0.0	126 ($2^7 - 2$)	16,777,214 ($2^{24} - 2$)
B	128–191	1 0	N.N.H.H	255.255.0.0	16,382 ($2^{14} - 2$)	65,534 ($2^{16} - 2$)
C	192–223	1 1 0	N.N.N.H	255.255.255.0	2,097,150 ($2^{21} - 2$)	254 ($2^8 - 2$)
D	224–239	1 1 1 0	Reserved for multicasting			
E	240–254	1 1 1 1 0	Experimental; used for research			

* You cannot use Class A address 127, which is reserved for loopback and diagnostic functions.

Task 2: Determine Basic IP Addressing

Use the IP address chart in Table 9-5 and your knowledge of IP address classes to answer the following questions:

1.   What is the decimal and binary range of the first octet of all possible Class B IP addresses?

Decimal: From: _____ To: _____

Binary: From: _____ To: _____

2.   Which octets represent the network portion of a Class C IP address?

_____

3.   Which octets represent the host portion of a Class A IP address?

_____

4.   What is the maximum number of hosts you can have with a Class C network address?

_____

5.   How many Class B networks are there?

_____

6. How many hosts can each Class B network have?

_____

7. How many octets does an IP address have?

_____

8. How many bits per octet?

_____

Task 3: Determine the Host and Network Portions of the IP Address

With the following IP host addresses, indicate the class of each address, the network address or ID, the host portion, the broadcast address for this network, and the default subnet mask. The host portion will be all 0s for the network ID. Enter only the octets that make up the host. The host portion will be all 1s for a broadcast. The network portion of the address will be all 1s for the subnet mask. Fill in Table 9-6.

Table 9-6   Determining IP Address Network and Host Portions

Host IP Address	Address Class	Network Address	Host Address	Network Broadcast Address	Default Subnet Mask
216.14.55.137					
123.1.1.15					
150.127.221.244					
194.125.35.199					
175.12.239.244					

Task 4: Given an IP Address of 142.226.0.15, Answer the Following Questions

1. What is the binary equivalent of the second octet?

_____

2. What is the class of the address?

_____

3. What is the network address of this IP address?

_____

4. Is this a valid IP host address (yes/no)?

_____

5. Why or why not?

_____

Task 5: Determine Which IP Host Addresses Are Valid for Commercial Networks

For the following IP host addresses, determine which are valid for commercial networks and indicate why or why not.

Valid means you could assign it to a workstation, server, printer, router interface, and so on. Fill in Table 9-7.

Table 9-7   Determining Valid IP Host Addresses for Commercial Networks

IP Host Address	Valid Address (Yes/No)?	Why or Why Not?
150.100.255.255		
175.100.255.18		
195.234.253.0		
100.0.0.23		
188.258.221.176		
127.34.25.189		
224.156.217.73		

Curriculum Lab 9-2: DHCP Client Setup (9.3.5)

Objective

The purpose of this lab is to introduce DHCP and the process for setting up a network computer as a DHCP client to use DHCP services.

Background/Preparation

Dynamic Host Configuration Protocol (DHCP) provides a mechanism for dynamically assigning IP addresses and other information. Instead of configuring a static IP address, subnet mask, default gateway, DNS server, and other resource addresses to each host, a DHCP server device located on the LAN or at the Internet service provider (ISP) can respond to a host request and furnish the required information. The DHCP device is typically a network server.

In small networks, including many home networks with DSL, cable, or wireless connections, a small router can provide DHCP services. Cisco Systems and many other manufacturers offer small routers that include an Internet (WAN) connection, a small built-in hub or switch, and DHCP server service. This lab focuses on setting up a computer to use the DHCP services provided.

This lab assumes that the PC is running any version of Windows. Ideally, perform this lab in a classroom or another LAN connected to the Internet. You can also perform it from a single remote connection through a modem or DSL-type connection.

Important Note: If the network connecting the computer uses static addressing, follow the lab and view the various screens. Do not change these machines to DHCP usage because you will lose the static settings, and a network administrator will need to reconfigure them.

Task 1: Establish a Network Connection

If the connection to the Internet is dialup, connect to the ISP to ensure that the computer has an IP address. In a TCP/IP LAN with a DHCP server, it is not necessary to do this step.

Task 2: Access a Command Prompt

Windows NT/2000/XP users: Use the Start menu to open the command prompt (MS-DOS-like) window (**Start > Programs > Accessories > Command Prompt** or **Start > Programs > Command Prompt**).

Windows 95/98/Me users: Use the Start menu to open the MS-DOS prompt window (**Start > Programs > Accessories > MS-DOS Prompt** or **Start > Programs > MS-DOS Prompt**).

Task 3: Display IP Settings to Determine Whether the Network Is Using DHCP

Windows 95/98/Me users: Type **winipcfg** and press **Enter**. Then, click the **More Info** button.

The example in Figure 9-1 indicates that DHCP is in use with the entries in the DHCP Server IP Address, Lease Obtained, and Lease Expires boxes. These entries would be blank in a "static" configured device. DHCP also supplied the DHCP and WINS server addresses. The missing default gateway indicates a proxy server.

Figure 9-1   IP Configuration Settings Help Determine DHCP Information

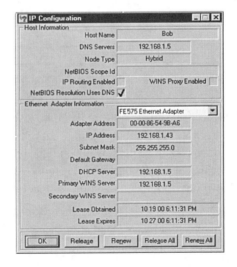

Windows NT/2000/XP users: Type **ipconfig /all** and press **Enter**.

The Windows NT/2000/XP example in Figure 9-2 indicates that DHCP is in use with the DHCP Enabled entry. The entries for DHCP Server, Lease Obtained, and Lease Expires confirm this fact. These last three entries would not exist in a "static" configured device, and DHCP Enabled would say No.

Figure 9-2   IP Configuration Settings Determine Whether DHCP Is Enabled

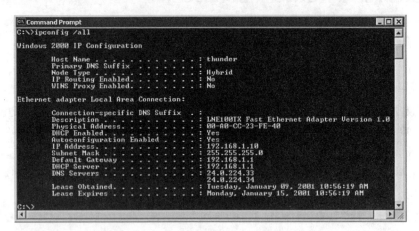

Very Important: Look over the results.

1. Is DHCP running on the network?

_____

_____

_____

Confirm this with a teacher or lab assistant if you are not sure.

2. What is the length of the DHCP lease?

_____

_____

_____

_____

_____

DHCP servers provide IP addresses for a limited time, in the same way a library checks out books. The network administrator can configure the actual length of time, but often, it is several days. If a lease expires, the IP address returns to the pool to be used by others. This process allows DHCP to recapture inactive IP addresses without needing humans to update the records. An organization that lacks enough IP addresses for every user might use very short lease durations so that the addresses are reused even during brief periods of inactivity.

The computer has an automatic method for requesting that the lease be extended, often avoiding an expired lease as long as the computer is used regularly.

If you move a computer from one network to another (a different network portion of the IP address), it might still retain its settings from the old network and be unable to connect to the new network. One solution is to release and renew the lease. Statically configured computers can do this, but there will be no change to the IP address. Computers connected directly to an ISP might lose connections and have to replace their calls, but no permanent changes occur. Follow the steps to release and renew the DHCP lease.

Windows NT/2000/XP users:

Type **ipconfig/release** and press **Enter**. Look over the results and then type **. ipconfig/renew**. You will probably get the same settings as before; had you changed networks, you would get new settings.

Windows 95/98/Me users:

Click the **Release All** button. Review the results and then click the **Renew All** button. You will probably get the same settings as before; had you changed networks, you would get new settings.

Task 4: Accessing the Network Configuration Window

Step 1.   On your desktop, right-click the **Network Neighborhood** or **My Network Places** icon and choose **Properties**. If you do not have either icon on this machine, use the Start button (**Start > Settings > Control Panel**), and double-click the **Network** icon.

Some users see a screen similar to the Network Properties dialog box shown in Figure 9-3.

Figure 9-3   Network Properties Dialog Box

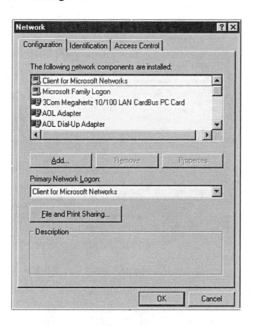

Step 2.   Different versions of Windows will have slightly different tabs, and the computer's current configuration will determine the items included in the Network Components box, but it should still look basically like Figure 9-3.

Most Windows 95, 98, and Me systems should see the network properties at this point. If you have a Network window similar to the one shown, skip to the next numbered step.

Windows 2000 and XP users need to do two more things:

In the window, double-click your **Local Area Connection**. When the Local Area Connection Status window appears, click the **Properties** button. That opens a Local Area Connection Properties dialog box similar to the one shown in Figure 9-4.

Figure 9-4   Local Area Connection Properties Window

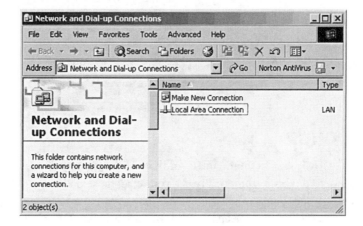

Step 3.   In the Network Properties dialog box, scroll through the listed components until you find TCP/IP. If you see more than one (older Windows), find the one for your current network connection, NIC, or modem. In Windows 2000 and XP, it will look like Figure 9-5.

Figure 9-5   Local Area Connection Properties Dialog Box: Network Connection Component

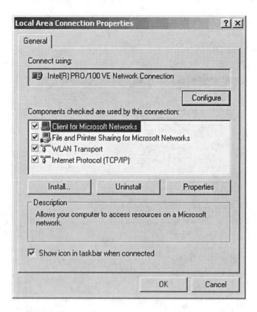

Step 4.   Either select the appropriate TCP/IP entry and click the **Properties** button or just double-click directly on the TCP/IP entry. The screen that appears next depends again on the version of Windows you are using, but the process and concepts are the same. The screen in Figure 9-6 should look similar to what Windows 2000/XP users see. The first thing you notice in the sample computer is that it is configured for static addressing.

Figure 9-6   TCP/IP Properties

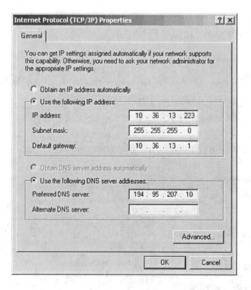

Task 5: Enable DHCP

Step 1.   To enable DHCP, select **Obtain an IP Address Automatically** and typically select **Obtain DNS Server Address Automatically**. As you select those options, you see the various settings blank out. If your computer had static addressing as in Figure 9-7, and you want it restored, click the **Cancel** button. To keep the changed settings, click **OK**. Older versions of Windows had multiple tabs and required that you select **Obtain an IP Address Automatically** on this tab, go to the **DNS Configuration** tab, and select **Obtain DNS Server Address Automatically**.

Step 2.   If you were really converting this computer from static to DHCP, you should also go to the Gateway and WINS Configuration tabs and remove any entries.

Step 3.   If your computer had static addressing and you want it restored, click the **Cancel** button.

Step 4.   To keep the settings, click **OK**.

Figure 9-7   **TCP/IP Properties: Static Addressing**

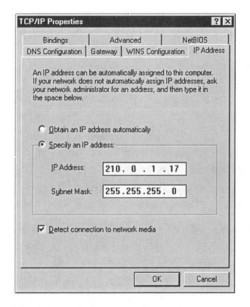

Task 6: Restart the Computer If Necessary

All older versions of Windows require that you restart the computer. Windows 2000 and XP typically do not require a restart.

On some old versions (Windows 95), you might even be asked for the installation CD-ROM to complete the process. If you were really changing over to DHCP, you would repeat Task 3 to confirm that you now have a valid set of configurations.

Reflection

1. As a network administrator, why might you prefer to use network profiles that hide the preceding options and screens, thereby preventing users from making these changes?

_____

_____

_____

2. As a network administrator, what are some of the potential benefits of using a DHCP server within your network?

_____

_____

_____

Note to home or small network users: Many small routers supplied for cable, DSL, or ISDN connections have DHCP configured by default. This configuration allows you to use the hub or switch ports (or add either device) so that additional computers can share the connection. You would configure each computer as you did in this lab. Typically, DHCP assigns addresses using one of the "private" networks (such as 192.168.1.0) that are set aside for this purpose. Although it is common to change these settings, read and understand the book first; learn the location of the Reset Defaults button.

Curriculum Lab 9-3: Workstation ARP (9.3.7)

Objective

The purpose of this lab is to introduce you to the Address Resolution Protocol (ARP) and the **arp -a** workstation command as a tool to confirm that your computer is successfully resolving network (Layer 3) addresses to MAC (Layer 2) addresses. You also explore the **arp** command help feature using the **-?** option.

Background/Preparation

The TCP/IP network protocol relies on IP addresses, such as 192.168.14.211, to identify individual devices and to assist in navigating data packets between networks. Although the IP address is essential for moving data from, say, Munich, Germany, to Seattle, Washington, it cannot deliver the data in the destination LAN by itself. Local network protocols, such as Ethernet or Token Ring, use the MAC (Layer 2) address to identify local devices and deliver all data. You saw your computer's MAC address in previous labs.

The MAC address looks something like this: **00-02-A5-9A-63-5C**. It is a 48-bit address displayed in hexadecimal format as six sets of two hexadecimal characters separated by dashes. (Each hexadecimal symbol represents four bits.) With some devices, the 12 hexadecimal characters can be displayed as three sets of four characters separated by periods or colons (**0002.A59A.635C**).

ARP maintains a table of IP and MAC address combinations, which tells what MAC address is associated with an IP address. If ARP does not know the MAC address of a local device, it issues a broadcast using the IP address, in essence saying, "Whose IP address is this?" If the IP address is active on the LAN, it sends a reply from which ARP extracts the MAC address. ARP then adds the address combination to the requesting computer's local ARP table.

Only the local network (LAN) uses MAC addresses and, therefore, ARP. When a computer prepares a packet for transmission, it checks the destination IP address to see whether it is part of the local network: Is the network portion of the IP address the same as that for the local network? If it is, the computer consults the ARP process to get the MAC address of the destination device using the IP address. It then applies the MAC address to the data packet and uses it for delivery.

If the destination IP address is not local, the computer needs the MAC address of the default gateway. The *default gateway* is the local network's router interface that provides connectivity with other networks. The computer uses the gateway's MAC address because after the packet arrives there, the router forwards it to its destination network.

If the computer does not receive any packets from an IP address after a few minutes, it drops the MAC/IP entry from the ARP table, assuming the device has logged off. Later attempts to access that IP address cause ARP to perform another broadcast and update the table.

This lab assumes that you are using any version of Windows. You can perform this nondestructive lab without changing anything in the system configuration. Ideally, perform this lab in a classroom or other LAN connected to the Internet. You can use a single remote connection through a modem or DSL-type connection.

Task 1: Establish a Network Connection

If the connection to the Internet is dialup, connect to the ISP to ensure that the computer has an IP address. In a TCP/IP LAN with a DHCP server, it should not be necessary to do this step.

Task 2: Access a Command Prompt

Windows NT/2000/XP users: Use the Start menu to open the command prompt (MS-DOS-like) window (**Start > Programs > Accessories > Command Prompt** or **Start > Programs > Command Prompt**).

Windows 95/98/Me users: Use the Start menu to open the MS-DOS prompt window (**Start > Programs > Accessories > MS-DOS Prompt** or **Start > Programs > MS-DOS Prompt**).

Task 3: Display the ARP Table

Step 1.   In the window, type **arp -a** and press **Enter**. Don't be surprised if you see no entries. The message would be "No ARP Entries Found." Windows computers remove any unused addresses after a few minutes.

Step 2.   Ping a few local addresses and a website URL and then rerun the command. Figure 9-8 shows a possible result of the **arp -a** command. The MAC address for the website appears because it isn't local, but the default gateway appears. In Figure 9-8, 10.36.13.1 is the default gateway, and 10.36.13.92 and 10.36.13.101 are other network computers. Notice that each IP address has a physical address (MAC) associated with it and a type that indicates how the address was learned.

Figure 9-8   TCP/IP Properties: Static Addressing

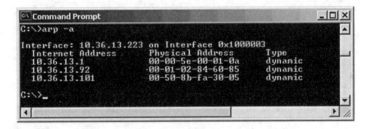

Step 3.   From Figure 9-8, you might logically conclude that the network is 10.36.13.0 and the host computers are represented by 223, 1, 92, and 101.

Task 4: Ping Several URLs

1. Ping the following URLs and note the IP address of each. Also, select one additional URL to ping and record it here. **http://www.cisco.com**:

   _____

   http://www.msn.de:

   _____

   _____

2. Run the **arp –a** command again and record the MAC addresses for each URL next to their IP addresses. Can you do it?

   _____

Why or why not?

_____

_____

3. What MAC address did the computer use to deliver each of the pings to the URLs?

_____

Why?

_____

_____

_____

_____

_____

Task 5: Use the ARP Help Feature

Type **arp -?** to see the help feature and look over the options, as shown in Figure 9-9.

Figure 9-9   arp Options

The purpose of this step is not to show the **arp** command options but to demonstrate using **?** to access help, if available. Help isn't always implemented uniformly. Some commands use **/?** instead of **-?**.

Task 6: Use Help with tracert and ping

Step 1.   Type **tracert -?** and then **ping -?** to see the options available for those commands. Figure 9-10 demonstrates the available **ping** options.

Figure 9-10   ping Options

```
Command Prompt                                              _ □ ×
C:\>ping -?

Usage: ping [-t] [-a] [-n count] [-l size] [-f] [-i TTL] [-v TOS]
            [-r count] [-s count] [[-j host-list] ! [-k host-list]]
            [-w timeout] destination-list

Options:
    -t                  Ping the specified host until stopped.
                        To see statistics and continue - type Control-Break;
                        To stop - type Control-C.
    -a                  Resolve addresses to hostnames.
    -n count            Number of echo requests to send.
    -l size             Send buffer size.
    -f                  Set Don't Fragment flag in packet.
    -i TTL              Time To Live.
    -v TOS              Type Of Service.
    -r count            Record route for count hops.
    -s count            Timestamp for count hops.
    -j host-list        Loose source route along host-list.
    -k host-list        Strict source route along host-list.
    -w timeout          Timeout in milliseconds to wait for each reply.
```

Step 2.   In the help for **ping**, notice the –t option, which sends continuous pings, not just four. More importantly, notice the two commands to stop it: **Ctrl-Break** and **Ctrl-C**. These commands are common for stopping runaway activities. Ping a neighboring computer with the **-t** option, and then use the **Ctrl-Break** and **Ctrl-C** features. An example in the network for this lab is typing **ping 10.36.13.101 -t** and then pressing **Enter**.

Step 3.   Be sure to use **Ctrl-C** to stop the pings.

Reflection

Based on today's observations, what can you deduce about the following results?

Computer 1

IP Address: 192.168.12.113

Subnet Mask: 255.255.255.0

Default Gateway: 192.168.12.1

Pings and tracert to 207.46.28.116 were both successful. What is the ARP table entry associated with this address, and why?

_____

_____

Comprehensive Lab 9-4: Identifying Internetworks

Objectives

- Identify and classify networks that packets cross on their way to a particular destination.

- Use **tracert** to gather valuable information about a route.

Background

tracert is a TCP/IP utility that reveals the route packets follow from the source to a destination. **tracert** provides round trip times (RTT) for each hop in the route, the fully qualified domain name (FQDN) of the device, and the IP address of the ingress interface of the device the packets pass through.

The **pathping** command is similar to **tracert** but is more useful for troubleshooting problem areas in the route because it pings each device periodically and computes statistics based on data returned by the ping packets.

This lab should be performed on a workstation that connects to the Internet through a LAN, home network, or dialup access.

Task 1: Access the Command Prompt

Note: The steps used to open a command prompt can be different for each operating system (OS). You should be familiar with the steps for the most common OSs.

Task 2: Verify Basic IP Connectivity to the Cisco Website

Type **ping www.cisco.com** and press **Enter**. Review the results and verify that the **ping** was successful. If the **ping** was not successful, use appropriate troubleshooting techniques. Remember that the network administrator might have disabled echo reply messages.

What is the IP address of the Cisco website?

_____

What class is the IP address?

_____

Task 3: Trace the Route to the Cisco Website

Type **tracert www.cisco.com** and press **Enter**.

What is the length of the logical path, measured in hops, between your workstation and the Cisco website?

_____

tracert in Microsoft Windows defaults to a maximum 30 hops per route. How can you change the maximum number of hops used in a **tracert**?

_____

_____

Figure 9-11   tracert Options

Task 4: Classify the Networks of a Route

Try **tracert** on another domain name. Set the maximum number of hops to 10 and record the results in the Table 9-8.

Table 9-8   Identifying Internetworks

Hop Number	IP Address of Network Device	Class of Device IP Address
1		
2		
3		
4		
5		
6		
7		
8		
9		
10		

How many Class A networks does the route pass through?

How many Class B networks does the route pass through?

How many Class C networks does the route pass through?

Reflection

Using **tracert** can provide valuable information about the route packets follow. What information can FQDN listings provide?

Challenge Lab 9-5: Using Fluke Protocol Inspector to Monitor ARP

Figure 9-12   Two Workstation, Single Switch Topology

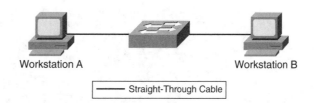

Workstation A   Workstation B

─────── Straight-Through Cable

Objectives

- Create a small LAN with two PCs and one switch.

- Observe ARP communications using Fluke Protocol Inspector.

Background

Layer 2 and 3 addressing must be known for devices to communicate using TCP/IP. Many devices maintain a table of IP addresses and associated MAC addresses by using ARP. When a device needs to communicate with another and the MAC address is unknown, an ARP request is sent, asking for a reply from the destination device containing the needed address.

This challenge lab focuses on using frame-capture software to observe the ARP process. Work in teams of two with one person per PC. The following resources are required:

- Two workstations with an Ethernet 10/100 NIC installed

- One Ethernet switch

- Two straight-through Ethernet cables to connect the PCs to the switches

- Fluke Protocol Inspector (or equivalent) installed on one or both workstations

Task 1: Build the LAN and Verify the Physical Connections

Connect the PCs to the switch. Plug in and turn on the devices. How can the physical connections be verified initially?

_____

Task 2: Configure the TCP/IP Settings on the PCs

Set the IP address information for each PC according to the information in Table 9-9.

Note: Be sure to write down the existing IP settings so you can restore them at the end of the lab.

Table 9-9   IP Address Settings for PCs

Computer	IP Address	Subnet Mask	Default Gateway
Workstation A	192.168.10.1	255.255.255.0	Not required
Workstation B	192.168.10.2	255.255.255.0	Not required

Task 3: Access the Command Prompt and Test Connectivity

Using the command prompt, **ping** the other workstation on the LAN. If the ping is not successful, use appropriate troubleshooting procedures. Figure 9-13 shows the results of a successful ping.

Figure 9-13   Successful Ping

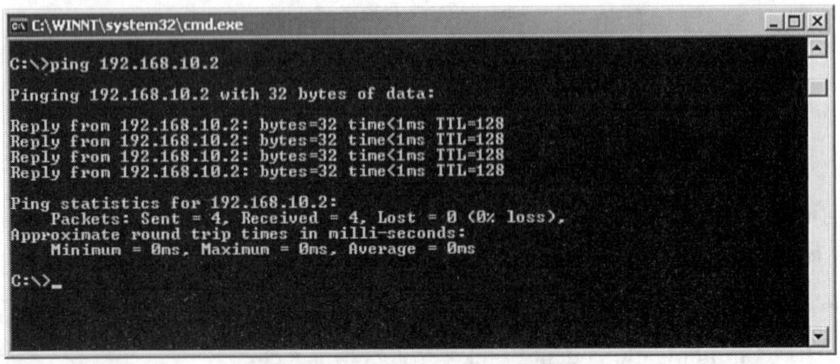

Note: The steps used to open a command prompt can be different for each OS. You should be familiar with the steps for the most common OSs.

Task 4: Record the MAC Address of Each Workstation

What command can be used to view the MAC address of the local workstation?

A successful ping to the other workstation ensures that the ARP learned the workstation's MAC address. What command can be used to see the ARP table of the local workstation?

What is the MAC address of workstation A?

What is the MAC address of workstation B?

Task 5: Clear the Workstation ARP Table

The **arp –a** command displays current ARP entries maintained by the local computer. These entries can be learned dynamically or through static configuration. Use the **arp /?** command to view other ARP options. How can a static entry be placed in the ARP table?

To ensure that an ARP request will be sent to the other workstation, the local workstation's ARP table needs to be cleared. Accomplish this by issuing the **arp –d *** command. This clears all entries in the ARP table. Verify that the table is empty by using the **arp –a** command.

Task 6: Start Fluke Protocol Inspector on Workstation A and Begin Capturing Frames

Use Fluke Protocol Inspector to gather information on the frames that are passing through the network.

Note: Refer to Lab 7-3, "Introduction to Fluke Protocol Inspector," for information on how to begin the frame-capture process.

Task 7: Initiate an ARP Request from Workstation A

Workstation A's ARP table is empty and must have an entry for workstation B before the PCs can communicate. Initiate an ARP request on workstation A by pinging workstation B.

Upon a successful ping, verify that workstation A's ARP table has the correct entry for workstation B. Figure 9-14 shows a workstation's ARP table entries.

Figure 9-14   Populated ARP Table

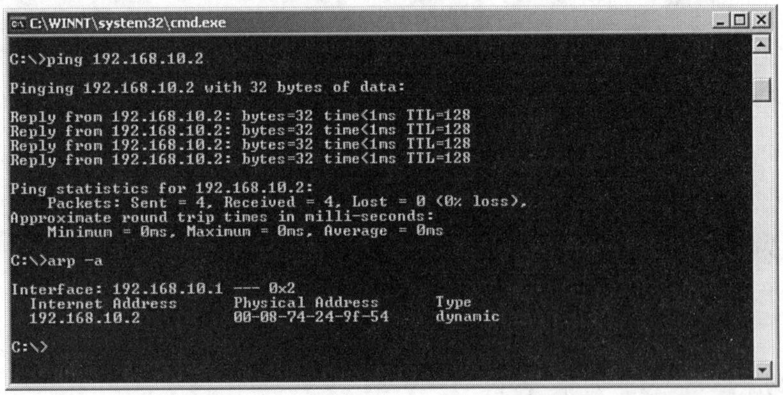

Task 8: Stop the Capture Process and Analyze the Frames

Click the **Capture View** button to see the list of captured frames near the top of the window. Look for workstation A's ARP request frame. It will be seen as a broadcast in the destination column and will begin with ARP Q in the summary column. Select this frame to see the frame details.

Why is this frame using a broadcast MAC address?

_____

What is the EtherType of the frame?

_____

What is the ARP operation number and to what type of message does it correspond?

_____

Next, look for the ARP reply sent from workstation B. Select this frame to see the frame details.

What is the ARP operation number and to what type of message does it correspond?

_____

What is the target Ethernet address of the frame?

_____

Do the source and destination addresses (both IP and MAC) match the addresses recorded in Task 4?

_____

Finally, look at the other frames that were captured. What other types of traffic occurred during the frame-capture process?

_____

Task 9: Disassemble the Lab Network

Restore the PCs to their original TCP/IP settings, disconnect the equipment, and store the cables.

Figure 9-15   ARP Request

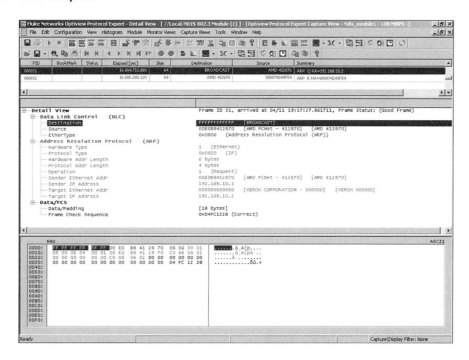

Figure 9-16   ARP Reply

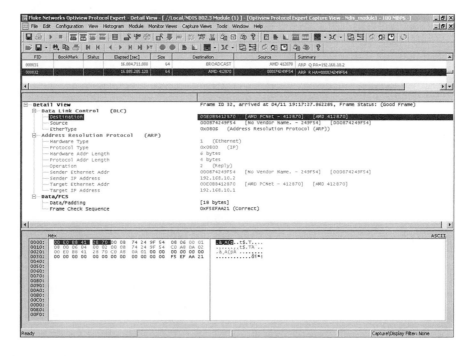

Challenge

Use Fluke Protocol Inspector to gather information on the DHCP process. This requires a DHCP client and server. Upon ensuring the client and server can communicate, release the DHCP assigned IP address on the client by typing the **ipconfig /release** command. Begin capturing frames on the client before issuing the **ipconfig /renew** command. This command requests an IP address from the DHCP server. After an address is obtained, stop the frame-capture process. Investigate the DHCP frames as they travel between the client and server.

Routing Fundamentals and Subnets

The Study Guide portion of this chapter uses a combination of matching, fill in the blank, compare and contrast, and open-ended question exercises to test your knowledge of routing and subnet fundamentals.

The Lab Exercises portion of this chapter includes curriculum labs and challenge lab to ensure that you have mastered the practical, hands-on skills needed to subnet all three IP address classes.

As you work through this chapter, use Module 10 in the CCNA 1 online curriculum or use the corresponding Chapter 10 in the *Networking Basics CCNA 1 Companion Guide* for assistance.

Study Guide

Routed Protocol

Protocols are the backbone of information networking. Protocols define the methods computers use to communicate with one another across networks. They set the format of messages and the rules for interpreting the message information. Routed protocols are responsible for end-to-end communication across networks. Routed protocols define hierarchical addressing information that is necessary for network path determination. Internet Protocol (IP) is the most popular routed protocol today.

In this section, you find exercises that help you learn terminology associated with routed protocols, compare and contrast routed and routing protocols, and identify the specifics of IP. These exercises focus on the key topics of the corresponding section of the curriculum.

Vocabulary Exercise: Completion

Complete the following statements by using the proper terms to fill in the blanks.

A packet is the Layer 3 _____.

The process of wrapping data in a particular protocol header as it moves through the OSI model is known as _____.

The network layer adds a _____ to the upper-layer data that includes source and destination IP address fields.

In a _____ communication system, data transfer requires the establishment of a dedicated virtual circuit.

In a _____ communication system, packets can take different routes through the network to reach the destination.

For a protocol to be _____, it must provide the capability to assign a network number and a host number to each device.

Compare and Contrast Exercise: Routed and Routing Protocols

Understanding the differences and functions of routed and routing protocols is critical in information networking. One protocol type is used for end-to-end communication, while the other protocol manages the paths that make communication possible. The proper implementation of each protocol type is required in all networks. Use Table 10-1 to compare and contrast these protocol types.

Table 10-1   Compare and Contrast Routed and Routing Protocols

	Routed Protocols	Routing Protocols
How is each protocol type defined?		

	Routed Protocols	Routing Protocols
What are the functions of each protocol type?		
Where do the protocols function in the OSI model?		
List some examples of each protocol type.		
What other network devices use this type of protocol?		

Concept Questions

Completely answer the following questions:

1. A protocol is a set of rules that determines how computers communicate with each other across networks. What does a protocol actually describe? Explain how routed protocols fit this description.

    _____

    _____

    _____

    _____

2. IP addresses consist of a network portion and host portion. Why is a network mask (or subnet mask) also required with IP addresses?

    _____

    _____

    _____

3. IP is considered a connectionless, unreliable, best-effort delivery routed protocol. What does each of these descriptions actually mean?

    _____

    _____

    _____

    _____

    _____

    _____

4. IP packets are made up of many fields. Describe the ToS, TTL, and protocol fields.

_____

_____

_____

_____

_____

_____

_____

Journal Entry

IP is the most widely used routed protocol today. Current-generation IP uses a 32-bit address expressed using four octets separated by dots. Each IP address consists of a network and host portion. The network portion of the address is used for path determination, and the host portion identifies the particular end device. A network mask (or subnet mask) distinguishes the portions from one another.

Use the Internet to research two other examples of routed protocols. Explain the format of each protocol's address. How long is the address? How is it usually written? How is the network and host portion defined?

_____

_____

_____

_____

_____

_____

_____

_____

_____

_____

_____

IP Routing Protocols

Routers are Layer 3 devices that connect internetworks. Routers receive incoming packets and make forwarding decisions based on the Layer 3 addressing contained in the packet. Forwarding decisions are made by evaluating entries in the local routing table. Routers use routing protocols to build and share table entries. IP routing protocols are used extensively on the Internet and in LANs and WANs. These protocols make use of specially designed algorithms that determine the best paths to destinations based on metrics. A thorough knowledge of routing protocols is required of all network professionals.

This section includes exercises that help you learn the terminology associated with IP routing protocols, understand the routing process, and recognize different types of routing protocols. You also learn the key role routing tables play in networking and the advantages and disadvantages of dynamic and static routing.

Vocabulary Exercise: Matching

Match the definition on the left with a term on the right. This exercise does not necessarily use one-to-one matching. Some definitions might be used more than once and some terms might have multiple definitions.

Definitions

a. A collection of data stored in a router that keeps track of routes to particular network destinations and, in some cases, metrics associated with those routes.

b. In a routing environment, this is a reference to the error rate of each network link.

c. Broadcast packets used by the receiving link-state routers to maintain their routing tables.

d. The speed and ability of a group of internetworking devices running a specific routing protocol to agree on the topology of an internetwork after a change in that topology.

e. A process to find a path to a destination host by using a hierarchical organizational scheme that allows individual addresses to be grouped together.

f. The router interface used by a segment to access other parts of the network.

g. Term describing the passage of a data packet between two network nodes (for example, between two routers).

h. A collection of networks under a common administration sharing a common routing strategy.

i. A routing protocol that operates between autonomous systems (AS).

j. A way to quantify the properties of a route for use by a routing algorithm to determine that one route is better than another.

k. A well-defined rule or process for arriving at a solution to a problem.

l. A routing protocol that operates within an AS.

m. Used by a router to compare a destination address to the available routes in its collection of known routes and select the best path.

Terms

___ routing

___ metrics

___ default gateway

___ autonomous system

___ hop

___ Interior Gateway Protocol

___ routing table

___ path determination

___ algorithm

___ convergence

___ reliability

___ Exterior Gateway Protocol

___ link-state advertisement

Compare and Contrast Exercise: Distance-Vector and Link-State Routing Protocols

Two types of routing protocols used within autonomous systems are distance-vector and link-state protocols. Each routing protocol performs the basic function of allowing routers to share information in a unique way. Use Table 10-2 to compare and contrast these types of routing protocols.

Table 10-2   Compare and Contrast Distance-Vector and Link-State Routing Protocols

	Distance-Vector Routing Protocols	Link-State Routing Protocols
What is the basic operating procedure used by this routing protocol?		
What metrics are commonly used by this routing protocol?		
What information is included in routing updates?		
How long is the convergence time relative to the other type of routing protocol?		
How difficult is the type of protocol to configure?		
What are some examples of this routing protocol?		

Concept Questions

Completely answer the following questions:

1. Routers operate at Layer 3 of the OSI model. What are the key functions of a router?

   _____

   ■ _____
   _____
   _____

   ■ _____
   _____
   _____

2. Routers and switches perform similar functions. Both devices maintain tables and make forwarding decisions based on table entries. What are the fundamental differences between these devices?

   _____
   _____
   _____
   _____
   _____

3. Routers maintain routing tables and use this information to make packet forwarding decisions. Briefly explain the path determination process that routers use.

   _____
   _____
   _____
   _____
   _____
   _____
   _____
   _____
   _____

4. Accurate and updated routing tables are necessary for efficient networking. What types of information are maintained for each entry in a routing table?

   _____

   ■ _____

   ■ _____
   _____

   ■ _____
   _____

   ■ _____

5. Routing algorithms use metrics for path determination and selecting the best route. List four common routing metrics and describe each.

   _____

   ■ _____

   ■ _____

- _____
- _____
- _____
- _____
- _____
  _____

6. Routing protocols are classified as either interior or exterior protocols. What are the differences between these protocol families? List an example of each protocol type.

_____
_____
_____
_____
_____
_____

Note: Now is a good time to complete Curriculum Lab 10-1. This exercise focuses on investigating small router options for use in a small office/home office (SOHO) environment.

Creating Routing Tables Exercise

Routers make packet-forwarding decisions based on routes stored in routing tables. Table entries identify destination networks and the information necessary to forward packets to these networks. Routing protocols determine best paths and share route information with other routers. When a network has converged, each router should have an entry in its routing table for all other segments in the network.

Complete the routing tables for the following networks. Figure 10-1 shows a two-router topology, and Figure 10-2 features a four-router network. Assume that each network has converged and that the network is stable. Entries in each router's routing table should include the following information:

- **Destination network**—Records the network address of the destination segment. The networks use classful routing so the routing protocol recognizes only Class A, B, and C network addresses.

- **Protocol type**—Determines the method the router used to learn about the destination network. All routers are running RIP that has been configured properly. Use **C** for directly connected networks and **R** for routes learned through RIP.

- **Next-hop association**—Identifies the IP address of the next closest router interface that is used to forward packets to the destination network.

- **Hop count**—Records the number of hops required to reach the destination network.

- **Outbound interface**—Identifies the local router interface that forwards packets to the destination network.

Figure 10-1   Two-Router Topology

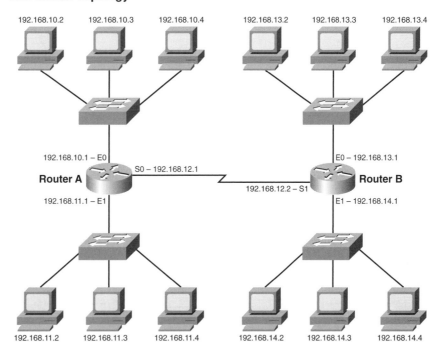

Table 10-3   Router A Routing Table

Destination Network	Protocol Type	Next-Hop Association	Hop Count	Outbound Interface

Table 10-4   Router B Routing Table

Destination Network	Protocol Type	Next-Hop Association	Hop Count	Outbound Interface

Figure 10-2   Four-Router Topology

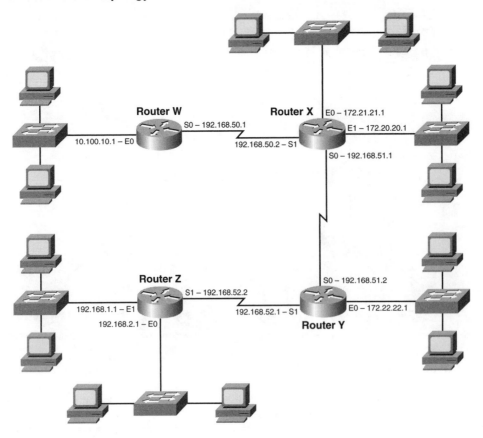

Table 10-5   Router W Routing Table

Destination Network	Protocol Type	Next-Hop Association	Hop Count	Outbound Interface

Table 10-6   Router X Routing Table

Destination Network	Protocol Type	Next-Hop Association	Hop Count	Outbound Interface

Destination Network	Protocol Type	Next-Hop Association	Hop Count	Outbound Interface

Table 10-7   Router Y Routing Table

Destination Network	Protocol Type	Next-Hop Association	Hop Count	Outbound Interface

Table 10-8   Router Z Routing Table

Destination Network	Protocol Type	Next-Hop Association	Hop Count	Outbound Interface

Journal Entry

Routing is the Layer 3 process used to determine network paths and forward packets across the best path to the destination. Routing protocols accomplish this task by using algorithms to evaluate metrics and define routes. These are also used to communicate between routers with information that can be used to update routing tables. New routes might be added and old routes might be discarded as changes occur in the network. The process of routing using routing protocols is known as dynamic routing.

Routing can also be performed using predefined routing tables that are configured by a network administrator. Known as static routing, this type of routing requires manual configuration to the routing table any time a change in the network occurs.

Most networks use a combination of dynamic and static routing because of the advantages that each routing method offers. What are the advantages of each type of routing? What are the disadvantages? Be sure to address configuration, scalability, bandwidth, and security issues of both methods. Describe a scenario where both routing methods would be used in the real world. Use the Internet to research dynamic and static routing methods.

Advantages of dynamic routing include the following:

■ _____
_____
_____

■ _____
_____

Disadvantages of dynamic routing include the following:

■ _____
_____
_____

■ _____
_____
_____

Advantages of static routing include the following:

■ _____
_____
_____

■ _____
_____

Disadvantages of static routing include the following:

■ _____
_____
_____

■ _____
_____

Mechanics of Subnetting

Subnetting is the process of subdividing networks into smaller, more manageable subnetworks. Subnetting requires an understanding of IP addresses and class information. Each address class is composed of network and host bits. Network bits are assigned, and the network administrator cannot manipulate them. Host bits are the assignable bits used for addressing end devices. Subnetting involves borrowing host bits to create manageable network bits to split the network into smaller sections.

This section includes exercises that reinforce your knowledge of subnetting and the techniques used to create effective subnets. These exercises include identifying key terms associated with subnets, understanding the role of subnetting in today's networks, and practicing the subnetting process.

Note: A theoretical and practical knowledge of subnetting is required for network professionals. The concepts and techniques take some time to master, so practice the subnetting process frequently.

Vocabulary Exercise: Completion

Complete the following statements by using the proper terms to fill in the blanks.

Subnets are created by borrowing _____ and changing them to network bits.

Routers use the ____ process to calculate the subnet address from the destination IP address and the subnet mask.

The _____ is located between the network and host fields and is created by borrowing bits from the host portion.

The formula used to calculate the number of usable hosts per subnet is 2 raised to the power of _____ _____ minus 2.

When subnets are created, a new _____ must be generated to denote the network and host portions of an IP address.

A subnetted IP address with 0s for each host bit is known as the _____ _____.

The _____ includes the host bits that remain after bits have been borrowed to create subnets.

_____ addresses require strict adherence to established network masks when subnetting.

A subnetted IP address with 1s for each host bit is known as the _____ _____.

The formula used to calculate the number of usable subnets is 2 raised to the power of _____ _____ minus 2.

Concept Questions

Completely answer the following questions:

1. Subnetting is the process of creating smaller networks by borrowing host bits to create additional network bits. What are the benefits of subnetting a network?

   _____

   _____

   _____

   _____

2. Subnetting a network requires the calculation of a new subnet mask. How is a subnet mask created? How is a subnet mask written? How is the subnet mask used by the router?

_____

_____

_____

_____

_____

_____

_____

3. Why must the last two bits of the last octet of an IP address class be left alone when creating subnets?

_____

_____

_____

_____

_____

4. Explain the process that routers use to determine subnet addresses using a subnet mask and IP address.

_____

_____

_____

Note: Curriculum Lab 10-2 is a good introduction to basic subnetting. Complete this lab before you move to the next exercise.

Subnetting Practice Exercise

The best way to learn subnetting is through practice. Answer the following questions regarding IP address classes and subnetting:

1. How many IP classes are available?

_____

2. Of these classes, how many are commercial classes?

_____

3. Describe the following IP classes by showing network (n) and host (h) octets in dotted-decimal format.

Class A: _____

Class B: _____

Class C: _____

4. What is the range of Class A IP addresses?

_____

5. What is the default subnet mask for a Class A network?

_____

6. What is the range of Class B IP addresses?

   _____

7. What is the default subnet mask for a Class B network?

   _____

8. What is the range of Class C IP addresses?

   _____

9. What is the default subnet mask for a Class C network?

   _____

10. What is the minimum number of bits that can be borrowed to create subnets?

    _____

11. What is the maximum number of bits that can be borrowed from a Class B network to create subnets?

    _____

12. If 4 bits are borrowed from a Class C address, how many usable subnets can be created? What is the subnet mask?

    _____

13. If 4 bits are borrowed from a Class A address, how many usable subnets can be created? What is the subnet mask?

    _____

14. If 8 bits are borrowed from a Class B address, how many usable subnets can be created? What is the subnet mask?

    _____

15. If 13 bits are borrowed from a Class B address, how many usable subnets can be created? What is the subnet mask?

    _____

16. If 4 bits are borrowed from a Class C address to create subnets, how many usable hosts can be placed on each subnet?

    _____

17. If 4 bits are borrowed from a Class B address to create subnets, how many usable hosts can be placed on each subnet?

    _____

18. How many usable hosts can be placed on a Class C network (not subnetted)?

    _____

19. Seven usable subnets are needed for a Class C network. What is the subnet mask?

    _____

20. Thirty-three usable subnets are needed for a Class B network. What is the subnet mask?

    _____

21. Sixty-one usable subnets are needed for a Class C network. How many usable hosts can be placed on each subnet?

_____

22. Seventy-seven usable subnets are needed for network 190.22.0.0. What is the subnet mask? How many usable hosts can be placed on each subnet?

_____

23. Fifty usable subnets are needed for network 192.2.8.0. What is the subnet mask? What is the subnet address of usable subnet #3 and usable subnet #4? How many usable hosts can be placed on each subnet?

_____

_____

_____

24. Twelve bits are borrowed to subnet network 129.3.0.0. What is the broadcast address of usable subnet #2 and usable subnet #6?

_____

_____

25. Three bits are borrowed to subnet network 207.98.6.0. What is the subnet mask? How many usable hosts can be placed on each subnet? What is the first assignable IP address subnet #1 and subnet #2?

_____

_____

_____

_____

26. You need to subnet network 178.99.0.0 so 4000 hosts can be placed on at least 13 subnets. What is your subnet mask?

_____

27. You are the network administrator of a rapidly growing company. Your first job is to subnet the company's network (133.9.0.0) so it meets future demands. Today, the company has need for 99 usable subnets. What is the subnet mask if you allow for 300 percent growth in the future? How many hosts can be placed on each subnet?

_____

You can use the Class C subnet table, which is shown in Table 10-9, to check many of the answers to the previous questions. Table 10-9 shows subnet addresses, usable address ranges, and subnet masks for every possible Class C subnet. The grayed-out portions of the table are unusable but are retained for references.

Table 10-9   Class C Subnet Table

Class C Subnet Table	.192 - /26 (11000000) 2 subnets/62 hosts	.224 - /27 (11100000) 6 subnets/30 hosts	.240 - /28 (11110000) 14 subnets/14 hosts	.248 - /29 (11111000) 30 subnets/6 hosts	.252 - /30 (11111100) 62 subnets/2 hosts
0	.0	.0	.0	.0	.0 (.1-.2)
4				(.1 - .6)	.4 (.5 - .6)
8			(.1 - .14)	.8	.8 (.9 - .10)
12				(.9 - .14)	.12 (.13 - .14)
16		(.1 - .30)	.16	.16	.16 (.17 - .18)
20				(.17 - .22)	.20 (.21- .22)
24			(.17 - .30)	.24	.24 (.25 - .26)
28	(.1 - .62)			(.25 - .30)	.28 (.29 - .30)
32		.32	.32	.32	.32 (.33 - .34)
36				(.33 - .38)	.36 (.37 - .38)
40			(.33 - .46)	.40	.40 (.41 - .42)
44		(.33 - .62)		(.41 - .46)	.44 (.45 - .46)
48			.48	.48	.48 (.49 - .50)
52				(.49 - .54)	.52 (.53 - .54)
56			(.49 - .62)	.56	.56 (.57 - .58)
60				(.57 - .62)	.60 (.61 - .62)
64	.64	.64	.64	.64	.64 (.65 - .66)
68				(.65 - .70)	.68 (.69 - .70)
72			(.65 - .78)	.72	.72 (.73 - .74)
76		(.65 - .94)		(.73 - .78)	.76 (.77 - .78)
80			.80	.80	.80 (.81 - .82)
84				(.81 - .86)	.84 (.85 - .86)
88			(.81 - .94)	.88	.88 (.89 - .90)
92	(.65 - .126)			(.89 - .94)	.92 (.93 - .94)
96		.96	.96	.96	.96 (.97 - .98)
100				(.97 - .102)	.100 (.101 - .102)
104			(.97 - .110)	.104	.104 (.105 - .106)
108		(.97 - .126)		(.105 - .110)	.108 (.109 - .110)
112			.112	.112	.112 (.113 - .114)
116				(.113 - .118)	.116 (.117 - .118)
120			(.113 - .126)	.120	.120 (.121 - .122)
124				(.121 - .126)	.124 (.125 - .126)
128	.128	.128	.128	.128	.128 (.129 - .130)
132				(.129 - .134)	.132 (.133 - .134)
136			(.129 - .142)	.136	.136 (.137 - .138)
140		(.129 - .158)		(.137 - .142)	.140 (.141 - .142)
144			.144	.144	.144 (.145 - .146)
148				(.145 - .149)	.148 (.149 - .150)
152			(.145 - .158)	.152	.152 (.153 - .154)
156	(.129 - .190)			(.153 - .158)	.156 (.157 - .158)
160		.160	.160	.160	.160 (.161 - .162)
164				(.161 - .166)	.164 (.165 - .166)
168			(.161 - .174)	.168	.168 (.169 - .170)
172		(.161 - .190)		(.169 -.174)	.172 (.173 - .174)
176			.176	.176	.176 (.177 - .178)
180				(.177 - .182)	.180 (.181 - .182)
184			(.177 - .190)	.184	.184 (.185 - .186)
188				(.185 - .190)	.188 (.189 - .190)
192	.192	.192	.192	.192	.192 (.193 - .194)
196				(.193 - .198)	.196 (.197 - .197)
200			(.193 - .206)	.200	.200 (.201 - .202)
204		(.193 - .222)		(.201 - .206)	.204 (.205 - .206)
208			.208	.208	.208 (.209 - .210)
212				(.209 - .214)	.212 (.213 - .214)
216			(.209 - .222)	.216	.216 (.217 - .218)
220	(.193 - .254)			(.217 - .222)	.220 (.221 - .222)
224		.224	.224	.224	.224 (.225 - .226)
228				(.225 - .230)	.228 (.229 - .230)
232			(.225 - .238)	.232	.232 (.233 - .234)
236		(.225 - .254)		(.233 - .238)	.236 (.237 - .238)
240			.240	.240	.240 (.241 - .242)
244				(.241 - .246)	.244 (.245 - .246)
248			(.241 - .254)	.248	.248 (.249 - .250)
252				(.249 - .254)	.252 (.253 - .254)

Note: The remaining labs focus on subnetting Class A, B, and C addresses. Take your time working through these labs to ensure accurate address assignments.

Journal Entry

Subnetting is a vital process in today's networks. Organizations secure IP addresses and must subnet these addresses to fit their networks. Subnetting offers many advantages, including greater addressing flexibility, broadcast containment, and low-level security, but it is not without some drawbacks.

Creating subnets removes assignable addresses from the network pool. An unsubnetted Class C address is capable of providing 254 assignable addresses. Creating six usable subnets in the Class C address decreases the number of assignable addresses to 180 (six subnets with up to 30 hosts per subnet). Also, subnets can be wasteful and further reduce the number of assignable addresses by "locking" addresses into subnets that will never use them. For example, a serial link between routers requires its own unique subnet, yet it needs only two IP addresses. If a Class C address is subnetted to create six subnets with up to 30 hosts per subnet, 28 of those addresses would go unused on the serial link subnet.

How can a network administrator emphasize the advantages of subnetting while minimizing its deficiencies? Use the Internet to research solutions to this problem.

Lab Exercises

Curriculum Lab 10-1: Small Router Purchase (10.2.9)

Figure 10-3   806 Router Components and Connections

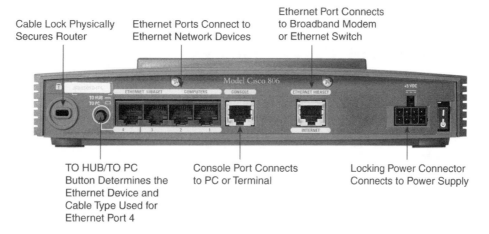

Cable Lock Physically
Secures Router

Ethernet Ports Connect to
Ethernet Network Devices

Ethernet Port Connects
to Broadband Modem
or Ethernet Switch

TO HUB/TO PC
Button Determines the
Ethernet Device and
Cable Type Used for
Ethernet Port 4

Console Port Connects
to PC or Terminal

Locking Power Connector
Connects to Power Supply

Objective

- The purpose of this lab is to introduce the variety and prices of network components in the market. This lab looks specifically at small routers that telecommuters use when working from home. The lab uses the website http://www.cdw.com, but you can use any local source, catalog, or website.

Background/Preparation

You are asked to put together a proposal for purchasing small routers that company executives will use for more secure connections when working with cable and digital subscriber line (DSL) connections from home. You are asked to research at least two different solutions and develop a proposal. The project details follow.

The company IT department is interested in reliability and concerned about working with and supporting too many models of devices. The company uses Cisco routers throughout the corporate network and wants to extend Cisco IOS Software features, such as virtual private networks (VPN) and firewalls to these remote users.

From talking to the executives and support personnel, you know that some live-in areas do not support either DSL or cable service, so you want to see if any models also support Integrated Services Digital Network (ISDN).

The requirements include the following:

- Twelve routers supporting DSL or cable connections

- Three routers supporting ISDN connections

- Support for IOS features

- The assumptions that the service provider supplies any required "modem" device and that the router will connect to it through an Ethernet interface

Several executives expressed an interest in connecting two or three computers to the same link. Assume that this setup will be the norm.

Task 1: Research Equipment Pricing

Step 1.   Go to **http://www.cisco.com**, select **Products & Services**, and following the links to Routers to gather basic information. Look specifically at the 700, 800, and SOHO models.

Step 2.   Look at the Overview option, particularly any white papers, presentations, and brochures. These documents might provide useful data and graphics for your final presentation.

Step 3.   Use at least three other sources for technologies and pricing. If you do web searches, use http://www.cdw.com and http://www.google.com, plus any others you prefer.

Task 2: Compile a One-Page Summary of Your Results

Use Microsoft Excel or Word (or any comparable products) to compile a summary of your results. Include a short explanation (8–15 lines) of why you selected this implementation. Include a simple diagram showing the router, PCs, power cord, and cable or DSL modem.

Optional Task 2

Instead of creating the Excel/Word documents, create a four- to eight-slide PowerPoint presentation that covers the same requirements.

Assume that you will be asked to present the material.

If time allows, perform both Step 2s, which is often the norm.

_____

_____

_____

_____

_____

_____

_____

Curriculum Lab 10-2: Basic Subnetting (10.3.5a)

Objectives

- Identify the reasons to use a subnet mask.

- Distinguish between a default subnet mask and a custom subnet mask.

- Given the requirements, determine the subnet mask, number of subnets, and hosts per subnet.

- Understand usable subnets and usable number of hosts.

- Use the ANDing process to determine whether a destination IP address is local or remote.

- Identify valid and invalid IP host addresses based on a network number and subnet mask.

Background/Preparation

This lab helps you understand the basics of IP subnet masks and their use with TCP/IP networks. You can use the subnet mask to split up an existing network into subnetworks or _subnets_. Some of the primary reasons for subnetting are as follows:

- Reduce the size of the broadcast domains. (Create smaller networks with less traffic.)

- Allow LANs in different geographical locations to communicate through routers.

- Provide improved security by separating one LAN from another.

Routers separate subnets, and the router determines when a packet can go from one subnet to another. Each router a packet goes through is considered a *hop*. Subnet masks help workstations, servers, and routers in an IP network determine whether the destination host for the packet they want to send is on their own network or another network. This lab reviews the default subnet mask and then focuses on custom subnet masks, which uses more bits than the default subnet mask by "borrowing" these bits from the host portion of the IP address. This process creates a three-part address:

- Original network address
- Subnet address consisting of the bits borrowed
- Host address that consists of the bits left after borrowing some for subnets

Task 1: Review IP Address Basics and Default Subnet Masks

Step 1. If your organization has a Class A IP network address, the first octet (8 bits) is assigned and does not change. Your organization can use the remaining 24 bits to define up to 16,777,214 hosts on your network. That is a lot of hosts! It is not possible to put all these hosts on one physical network without separating them with routers and subnets.

Step 2. It is common for a workstation to be on one network or subnet and a server to be on another. When the workstation needs to retrieve a file from the server, it must use its subnet mask to determine the network or subnet that the server is on. The purpose of a subnet mask is to help hosts and routers determine the network location where a destination host appears. See Table 10-10 to review IP address classes, default subnet masks, and the number of networks and hosts that you can create with each class of network address.

Table 10-10 IP Address Classes and Information

Address Class	First Octet Decimal Range	First Octet High Order Bits	Network/Host ID (N = Network, H = Host)	Default Subnet Mask	Number of Networks	Hosts per Network (Usable Addresses)
A	1–126*	0	N.H.H.H	255.0.0.0	126 ($2^7 - 2$)	16,777,214 ($2^{24} - 2$)
B	128–191	1 0	N.N.H.H	255.255.0.0	16,382 ($2^{14} - 2$)	65,534 ($2^{16} - 2$)
C	192–223	1 1 0	N.N.N.H	255.255.255.0	2,097,150 ($2^{21} - 2$)	254 ($2^8 - 2$)
D	224–239	1 1 1 0	Reserved for multicasting			
E	240–254	1 1 1 1 0	Experimental; used for research			

* You cannot use Class A address 127 because it is reserved for loopback and diagnostic functions.

Task 2: Review the ANDing Process

Hosts and routers use the ANDing process to determine whether a destination host is on the same network. The ANDing process happens each time a host wants to send a packet to another host on an IP network. To connect to a server, the host must know the IP address of the server or the hostname (for example, http://www.cisco.com). If the host uses the hostname, a Domain Name System (DNS) server converts it to an IP address.

First, the source host compares (ANDs) its own IP address to its own subnet mask. The result of the ANDing is to identify the network where the source host resides. It then compares the destination IP address to its own subnet mask. The result of the second ANDing is the network that the destination host is on. If the source network address and the destination network address are the same, they can communicate directly. If the results are different, they are on different networks or subnets, and they need to communicate through routers or they might not be able to communicate at all.

ANDing depends on the subnet mask. The subnet mask always uses all 1s to represent the network, or network plus subnet, portion of the IP address. A default subnet mask for a Class C network is 255.255.255.0 or 11111111.11111111.11111111.00000000. The host compares this mask to the source IP address bit for bit. It compares the first bit of the IP address to the first bit of the subnet mask, the second bit to the second, and so on. If the two bits are both 1s, the ANDing result is a 1. If the two bits are a 0 and a 1 or two 0s, the ANDing result is a 0. Basically, this rule means that a combination of two 1s results in a 1, but anything else is a 0. The result of the ANDing process is the network or subnet number that the source or destination address is on.

Task 3: Determine a Host Network Using Two Class C Default Subnet Masks

The example in Figure 10-4 shows how you can use a Class C default subnet mask to determine which network a host is on. A default subnet mask does not break an address into subnets. If you use the default subnet mask, the network is not being *subnetted*. Host X (source) on network 200.1.1.0 has an IP address of 200.1.1.5 and wants to send a packet to Host Z (destination) on network 200.1.2.0, which has an IP address of 200.1.2.8. All hosts on each network are connected to hubs or switches and then to a router. Remember that, with a Class C network address, the first three octets (24 bits) are assigned as the network address, so these are two different Class C networks. This requirement leaves one octet (8 bits) for hosts, so each Class C network can have up to 254 hosts ($2^8 = 256 - 2 = 254$).

Figure 10-4   Using a Class C Default Subnet Mask to Determine a Host's Network

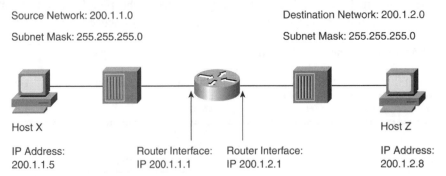

Source Network: 200.1.1.0   Destination Network: 200.1.2.0

Subnet Mask: 255.255.255.0   Subnet Mask: 255.255.255.0

Host X

IP Address: Router Interface: Router Interface: IP Address:
200.1.1.5   IP 200.1.1.1   IP 200.1.2.1   200.1.2.8

Host Z

The ANDing process helps the packet get from host 200.1.1.5 on network 200.1.1.0 to host 200.1.2.8 on network 200.1.2.0 by using the following steps:

Host X compares its own IP address to its own subnet mask using the ANDing process:

Host X IP address 200.1.1.5: 11001000.00000001.00000001.00000101

Subnet Mask 255.255.255.0: 11111111.11111111.11111111.00000000

ANDing Result (200.1.1.0): 11001000.00000001.00000001.00000000

Note: The result of Step 3a of the ANDing process is the network address of host X, which is 200.1.1.0.

Next, Host X compares the IP address of the host Z destination to its own subnet mask using the ANDing process.

Host Z IP address 200.1.2.8: 11001000.00000001.00000010.00001000

Subnet Mask 255.255.255.0: 11111111.11111111.11111111.00000000

ANDing Result (200.1.2.0): 11001000.00000001.00000010.00000000

Note: The result of Step 3b of the ANDing process is the network address of host Z, which is 200.1.2.0.

Host X compares the ANDing results from Step A and the ANDing results from Step B, and they are different. Host X now knows that host Z is not in its LAN, and it must send the packet to its default gateway, which is the IP address of the router interface of 200.1.1.1 on network 200.1.1.0. The router then repeats the ANDing process to determine which router interface to send the packet out.

Task 4: Determine the Host Subnet Using a Class C Network Custom Subnet Mask

This example uses a single Class C network address (200.1.1.0) and shows how you can use a Class C custom subnet mask to determine which subnetwork (or subnet) a host is on and to route packets from one subnetwork to another. Remember that, with a Class C network address, the first three octets (24 bits) are assigned as the network address. This requirement leaves 8 bits (one octet) for hosts, so each Class C network can have up to 254 hosts ($2^8 = 256 - 2 = 254$).

Perhaps you want fewer than 254 hosts (workstations and servers) all on one network, and you want to create two subnetworks and separate them with a router for security reasons or to reduce traffic. This setup creates smaller independent broadcast domains and can improve network performance and increase security because one or more routers separate these subnetworks. Assume that you need at least two subnetworks and at least 50 hosts per subnetwork. Because you have only one Class C network address, you have only 8 bits in the fourth octet available for a total of 254 possible hosts, so you must create a custom subnet mask. You use the custom subnet mask to "borrow" bits from the host portion of the address. Perform the following steps.

The first step to subnetting is to determine how many subnets you need. In this case, you need two subnetworks. To see how many bits you need to borrow from the host portion of the network address, add the bit values from right to left until the total is equal to or greater than the number of subnets you need. Because you need two subnets, add the one bit and the two bits, which equals three. This number is greater than the number of subnets you need, so you need to borrow at least two bits from the host address starting from the left side of the octet that contains the host address. Table 10-11 provides this information.

Table 10-11   Calculating Subnet Bits to Be Borrowed

Fourth Octet Host Address Bits	1	1	1	1	1	1	1	1
Host Address Bit Values (From Right)	128	64	32	16	8	4	2	1

(Add bits starting from the right side [the 1 and the 2] until you get more than the number of subnets you need.)

Note: An alternate way to calculate the number of bits to borrow for subnets is to take the number of bits borrowed to the power of 2. The result must be greater than the number of subnets you need. For example, if you borrow 2 bits, the calculation is 2 to the second power, which equals 4. Because the number of subnets you need is two, this result should be adequate.

After you know how many bits to borrow, you take them from the left side of the host address (the fourth octet). Every bit you borrow leaves fewer bits for the hosts. Although you increase the number of subnets, you decrease the number of hosts per subnet. Because you need to borrow two bits from the left side, you must show that new value in the subnet mask. The existing default subnet mask was 255.255.255.0, and the new "custom" subnet mask is 255.255.255.192. As Table 10-12 indicates, the 192 results from adding the first two bits from the left ($128 + 64 = 192$). These bits now become 1s and are part of the overall subnet mask. This change leaves 6 bits for host IP addresses, or $2^6 = 64$ hosts per subnet.

Table 10-12 Determining the "Custom" Subnet Mask

Fourth Octet Borrowed Bits for Subnet	1	1	0	0	0	0	0	0
Subnet Bit Values (From Left Side)	128	64	32	16	8	4	2	1

With this information, you can build Table 10-13. The first two bits are the subnet binary value. The last six bits are the host bits. By borrowing 2 bits from the 8 bits of the host address, you can create 4 subnets (2^2) with 64 hosts each. The four networks created are the 0 net, the 64 net, the 128 net, and the 192 net. The 0 net and the 192 net are unusable because the 0 net has all 0s in the host portion of the address and the 192 net has all 1s in the host portion of the address.

Table 10-13 Determining the Usable Subnets

Subnet Number	Subnet Bits Borrowed Binary Value	Subnet Bits Decimal Value	Host Bits Possible (Range) (6 Bits) Binary Values	Subnet/Host Decimal Range	Usable?
0 subnet	00	0	000000–111111	0–63	No
First subnet	01	64	000000–111111	64–127	Yes
Second subnet	10	128	000000–111111	128–191	Yes
Third subnet	11	192	000000–111111	192–254	No

Notice that the first subnet always starts at 0 and, in this case, increases by 64, which is the number of hosts on each subnet. One way to determine the number of hosts on each subnet or the start of each subnet is to take the remaining host bits to the power of 2. Because you borrowed 2 of the 8 bits for subnets and you have 6 bits left, the number of hosts per subnet is 2^6 or 64. Another way to figure the number of hosts per subnet or the "increment" from one subnet to the next is to subtract the subnet mask value in decimal (192 in the fourth octet) from 256 (which is the maximum number of possible combinations of 8 bits), which equals 64. This result means that you start at 0 for the first network and add 64 for each additional subnetwork. If you take the second subnet (the 64 net) as an example, you cannot use the IP address of 200.1.1.64 for a host ID because it is the network ID of the 64 subnet. (The host portion is all 0s.) You cannot use the IP address of 200.1.1.127 because it is the broadcast address for the 64 net. (The host portion is all 1s.)

Another common way to represent a subnet mask is through the use of the "slash/number" (/#), where the # following the slash is the number of bits used in the mask (network and subnet combined). As an example, a Class C network address such as 200.1.1.0 with a standard subnet mask (255.255.255.0) would be written as 200.1.1.0 /24, which indicates that 24 bits are used for the mask. The same network, when subnetted by using two host bits for subnets, would be written as 200.1.1.0 /26. This indicates that 24 bits are used for the network and 2 bits for the subnet. This would represent a custom subnet mask of 255.255.255.192 in dotted-decimal format.

A Class A network of 10.0.0.0 with a standard mask (255.0.0.0) would be written as 10.0.0.0/8. If 8 bits (the next octet) were being used for subnets, it would be written as 10.0.0.0/16. This would represent a custom subnet mask of 255.255.0.0 in dotted-decimal format. The "slash" number after the network number is an abbreviated method of indicating the subnet mask being used.

Task 5: Use the Following Information and the Previous Examples to Answer the Following Subnet-Related Questions

Your company has applied for and received a Class C network address of 197.15.22.0. You want to subdivide your physical network into four subnets, which will be interconnected by routers. You need at least 25 hosts per subnet. You need to use a Class C custom subnet mask and a router between the subnets to route packets from one subnet to another. Determine the number of bits you need to borrow from the host portion of the network address and then the number of bits left for host addresses.

(*Hint*: There will be eight possible subnets, of which six can be used.) Fill in Table 10-14 and answer the questions that follow.

Table 10-14   Creating a Class C Custom Subnet Mask to Support at Least 25 Hosts per Subnet

Subnet Number	Subnet Bits Borrowed Binary Value	Subnet Bits Decimal and Subnet Number	Host Bits Possible Binary Values (Range) (5 Bits)	Subnet/Host Decimal Range	Use?

Notes

Use the information you just developed in Table 10-14 to help answer the following questions:

1. Which octets represent the network portion of a Class C IP address?

2. Which octets represent the host portion of a Class C IP address?

3. What is the binary equivalent of the Class C network address in the scenario (197.15.22.0)?

   Decimal network address:

   Binary network address:

4. How many high order bits did you borrow from the host bits in the fourth octet?

_____

5. What subnet mask must you use? (Show the subnet mask in decimal and binary.)

Decimal subnet mask:

_____

Binary subnet mask:

_____

6. What is the maximum number of subnets that you can create with this subnet mask?

_____

7. What is the maximum number of usable subnets that you can create with this mask?

_____

8. How many bits were left in the fourth octet for host IDs?

_____

9. How many hosts per subnet can you define with this subnet mask?

_____

10. What is the maximum number of hosts that you can define for all subnets with this scenario (assuming that you cannot use the lowest and highest subnet numbers and cannot use the lowest and highest host ID on each subnet)?

_____

11. Is 197.15.22.63 a valid host IP address with this scenario?

_____

12. Why or why not?

_____

13. Is 197.15.22.160 a valid host IP address with this scenario?

_____

14. Why or why not?

_____

15. Host A has an IP address of 197.15.22.126. Host B has an IP address of 197.15.22.129. Are these hosts on the same subnet? No. Why?

_____

_____

Curriculum Lab 10-3: Subnetting a Class A Address (10.3.5b)

Objective

Analyze a Class A network address with the number of network bits specified to determine the subnet mask, number of subnets, hosts per subnet, and information about specific subnets.

Background/Preparation

Perform this written lab *without* the aid of an electronic calculator.

Task 1: Given a Class A Network Address of 10.0.0.0 /24, Answer the Following Questions

1. How many bits were borrowed from the host portion of this address?

   _____

2. What is the subnet mask for this network?

   Dotted decimal:

   _____

   Binary:

   _____

3. How many usable subnetworks?

   _____

4. How many usable hosts per subnet?

   _____

5. What is the host range for usable subnet 16?

   _____

6. What is the network address for usable subnet 16?

   _____

7. What is the broadcast address for usable subnet 16?

   _____

8. What is the broadcast address for the last usable subnet?

   _____

9. What is the broadcast address for the major network?

   _____

Curriculum Lab 10-4: Subnetting a Class B Address (10.3.5c)

Objective

- Provide a subnetting scheme using a Class B network.

Background/Preparation

Perform this written lab *without* the aid of an electronic calculator.

ABC Manufacturing has acquired a Class B address, 172.16.0.0, and needs to create a subnetting scheme to provide 36 subnets with at least 100 hosts, 24 subnets with at least 255 hosts, and 10 subnets with at least 50 hosts. It is not necessary to supply an address for the WAN connection because the ISP supplies it.

Task 1: Given This Class A Network Address and These Requirements, Answer the Following Questions

1. How many subnets do you need for this network?

   _____

2. What is the minimum number of bits that you can borrow?

   _____

3. What is the subnet mask for this network?

   Dotted decimal:

   _____

   Binary:

   _____

   Slash format:

   _____

4. How many usable subnetworks?

   _____

5. How many usable hosts per subnet?

   _____

Task 2: Complete the Chart in Table 10-15 Listing the First Three Subnets and the Last Four Subnets

Table 10-15   Subnetwork Chart

Subnetwork No.	Subnetwork ID	Host Range	Broadcast ID

1. What is the host range for subnet 2?

   _____

2. What is the broadcast address for the 126th subnet?

   _____

3. What is the broadcast address for the major network?

   _____

Curriculum Lab 10-5: Subnetting a Class C Address (10.3.5d)

Objective

- Provide a subnetting scheme using a Class C network.

Background/Preparation

Perform this written lab *without* the aid of an electronic calculator.

The Classical Academy has acquired a Class C address, 192.168.1.0, and needs to create subnets to provide low-level security and broadcast control on the LAN. It is not necessary to supply an address for the WAN connection because the ISP supplies it.

The LAN consists of the following, each of which will require its own subnet:

- Classroom #1: 28 nodes
- Classroom #2: 22 nodes
- Computer lab: 30 nodes
- Instructors: 12 nodes
- Administration: 8 nodes

Task 1: Given This Class C Network Address and These Requirements, Answer the Following Questions

1. How many subnets do you need for this network?

   _____

2. What is the subnet mask for this network?

   Dotted decimal:

   _____

   Binary:

   _____

   Slash format:

   _____

3. How many usable hosts per subnet?

   _____

Task 2: Complete the Chart in Table 10-16

Table 10-16   Subnetwork Chart

Subnetwork No.	Subnetwork IP	Host Range	Broadcast ID

1. What is the host range for subnet 6?

    _____

2. What is the broadcast address for the third subnet?

    _____

3. What is the broadcast address for the major network?

    _____

Comprehensive Lab 10-6: Subnetting a Network Using a Class C Address (1)

Objectives

-   Identify network segments.

-   Create an effective subnetting solution.

-   Assign addresses to appropriate devices.

Background

Subnetting a network is a multistep process. The first step is to calculate the number of needed subnets. This is determined by identifying the broadcast domains in the network. Each broadcast domain requires a unique subnet. For example, a network that consists of a router connected to two Ethernet segments has two broadcast domains and requires two subnets. A serial link between two routers is also a broadcast domain and needs a separate subnet.

After the number of required subnets is determined, the number of bits to be used to create subnets must be calculated. The formula to accomplish this is $2^n - 2 = USN$, where n is the number of host bits borrowed for subnetting and USN is the number of usable subnets created.

Next, the network must be evaluated to determine if the subnetting scheme will actually serve the network. The number of hosts in each broadcast domain needs to be counted. These host calculations need to include any interfaces within the domain that will be assigned an IP address. The host count per domain cannot be greater than the maximum number of allowable hosts per subnet. The formula to calculate the maximum number of hosts per subnet is $2^n - 2 = $ UHS, where n is the number of remaining host bits after bits were borrowed for subnetting and UHN is the number of usable hosts per subnet.

Finally, the subnetworks are defined and IP addresses are assigned to hosts and interfaces. The newly calculated subnet mask must be included with each address or the system will not function.

Note: Hosts and interfaces that share a broadcast domain share a subnet and must be addressed within the same usable host range. A serial link between two routers is a broadcast domain and requires its own subnet. The serial interfaces require addresses within the subnet's usable address range.

Using your knowledge of subnetting, provide an addressing solution for the network shown in Figure 10-5.

Figure 10-5   Two Router Network Topology Requiring Subnetting

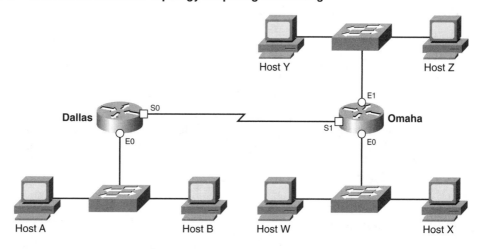

Task 1: Determine the Number of Subnets That Must Be Created

How many broadcast domains can be found in the network?

Task 2: Borrow Bits to Create the Required Subnets

The network has been assigned the 220.12.120.0 Class C address. How many bits need to be borrowed to create the needed subnets?

After creating subnets, what is the maximum amount of hosts that can be placed in each subnet?

If the network is built as pictured, will there be a problem with the subnet solution?

Task 3: Create the Subnets and Assign IP Addresses

What is the newly created subnet mask?

Complete the subnet chart shown in Table 10-17.

Table 10-17   Subnet Chart

Subnet Number	Subnet Address	Usable Address Range	Subnet Broadcast Address

Determine the subnet to broadcast domain assignment and apply addresses accordingly.

Note: Ethernet interfaces on routers act as the default gateway for the hosts connected to that segment. These interfaces are usually assigned the first usable address within the subnet address range.

What is the IP address of Dallas E0?

What is the IP address of Dallas S0?

What is the IP address of Omaha S1?

What is the IP address of Omaha E0?

What is the IP address of Omaha E1?

What is the IP address of Dallas host A?

What is the IP address of Dallas host B?

What is the IP address of Omaha host W?

What is the IP address of Omaha host Y?

Comprehensive Lab 10-7: Subnetting a Network Using a Class C Address (2)

Objectives

- Identify network segments.

- Create an effective subnetting solution.

- Assign addresses to appropriate devices.

Background

Using your knowledge of subnetting, provide an addressing solution for the network shown in Figure 10-6.

Figure 10-6   Three Router Network Topology Requiring Subnetting

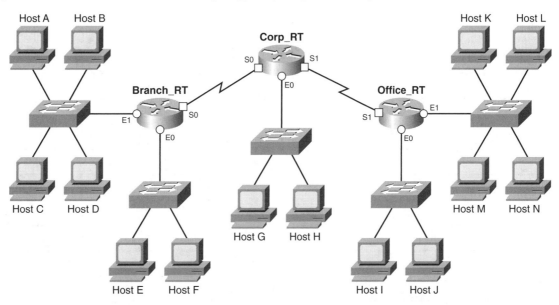

Task 1: Determine the Number of Subnets That Must Be Created

How many broadcast domains can be found in the network?

_____

Task 2: Borrow Bits to Create the Required Subnets

The network has been assigned the 204.173.55.0 Class C address. How many bits need to be borrowed to create the needed subnets?

_____

After creating subnets, what is the maximum amount of hosts that can be placed in each subnet?

_____

If the network is built as pictured, will there be a problem with the subnet solution?

_____

Task 3: Create the Subnets and Assign IP Addresses

What is the newly created subnet mask?

_____

Complete the subnet chart shown in Table 10-18.

Table 10-18   Subnet Chart

Subnet Number	Subnet Address	Usable Address Range	Subnet Broadcast Address

Determine the subnet to broadcast domain assignment and apply addresses accordingly.

What is the IP address of Branch_RT E1?

_____

What is the IP address of Branch_RT E0?

_____

What is the IP address of Branch_RT S0?

_____

What is the IP address of Corp_RT S0?

_____

What is the IP address of Corp_RT E0?

_____

What is the IP address of Corp_RT S1?

_____

What is the IP address of Office_RT S1?

_____

What is the IP address of Office_RT E0?

_____

What is the IP address of Office_RT E1?

_____

What is the IP address of host A?

_____

What is the IP address of host D's default gateway?

_____

What is the IP address of host E?

_____

What is the IP address of host G?

_____

What is the IP address of host J's default gateway?

_____

What is the IP address of host K?

_____

What is the IP address of host N?

_____

CHAPTER 11

TCP/IP Transport and Application Layers

The Study Guide portion of this chapter uses a combination of fill in the blank, compare and contrast, and open-ended question exercises to test your knowledge of the TCP/IP transport and application layers.

The Lab Exercises portion of this chapter includes a curriculum lab and a challenge lab to ensure that you have mastered the practical, hands-on skills needed to gather TCP information and access servers using client applications.

As you work through this chapter, use Module 11 in the CCNA 1 online curriculum or use the corresponding Chapter 11 in the *Networking Basics CCNA 1 Companion Guide* for assistance.

Study Guide

TCP/IP Transport Layer

The TCP/IP protocol suite contains multiple protocols. IP is a connectionless, best-effort Layer 3 protocol, and TCP is a connection-oriented Layer 4 protocol. Each protocol plays a major part in communications across information networks. UDP is another transport layer protocol that sends information to upper-layer protocols. Understanding these protocols, their functions, strengths, and deficiencies is necessary for all networking professionals.

In this section, you find exercises that focus on transport layer protocols. These exercises include identifying terminology, comparing TCP and UDP, understanding synchronization and windowing, and investigating ports and connections on local hosts.

Vocabulary Exercise: Completion

Complete the following statements by using the proper terms to fill in the blanks.

_____ ensures that a source host does not overflow the buffers in a destination host.

_____ is a connection-oriented transport layer protocol that provides reliable full-duplex data transmission.

Connection-oriented protocols require a mechanism that picks the initial sequence numbers and a _____ to exchange them.

Reliable delivery requires that a destination host _____ the receipt of segments before the source sends the next sequence.

Establishing common timing between sender and receiver is known as _____.

_____ is a simple protocol that exchanges datagrams without guaranteed delivery and relies on higher-layer protocols to handle errors and retransmit data.

_____ is a flow-control mechanism that requires the source device to receive an ACK from the destination after a certain amount of data is transmitted.

Compare and Contrast Exercise: Transport Layer Protocols

TCP and UDP are two protocols that Layer 4 uses to segment data and transport the segments end to end. Understanding the way each protocol operates and its place in today's networks is important. Complete Table 11-1 to compare and contrast these protocols.

Table 11-1   Compare and Contrast TCP and UDP

	TCP	UDP
What is the purpose of the Layer 4 protocol?		
What are the segment fields used by the protocol?		
What advantages does this protocol provide compared to the other Layer 4 protocol?		
What disadvantages does this protocol have compared to the other Layer 4 protocol?		
What are some upper-layer protocols that use the services provided by this protocol?		

Concept Questions

Completely answer the following questions:

1. The transport layer can provide both reliable and unreliable services. What are some benefits to using reliable transport services?

   _____

   _____

   _____

   _____

2. Multiple applications sharing the same transport connection in the OSI reference model is known as multiplexing. Briefly explain how this process is accomplished.

    _____

    _____

    _____

    _____

    _____

3. What are the typical causes of congestion? How is flow control implemented to minimize the effects of congestion?

    _____

    ■ _____

    ■ _____

    _____

    _____

4. Handshaking is an integral part of the synchronization process. Why does TCP use a three-way handshake?

    _____

    _____

    _____

    _____

    _____

5. TCP uses a windowing mechanism to send segments and receive acknowledgments. Explain the concept of segment windows. What is meant by sliding windows?

    _____

    _____

    _____

    _____

    _____

6. TCP and UDP port numbers keep track of multiple conversations as they simultaneously pass through the network. What are the three ranges of port numbers?

    _____

    ■ _____

    ■ _____

    ■ _____

Understanding TCP Synchronization and Windowing Exercise

TCP is a connection-oriented transport layer protocol that provides reliable communication mechanisms to upper-layer protocols. To provide reliability, TCP requires an established circuit between the communicating hosts. This is accomplished using a three-way handshake. The synchronization method involves sending an initial sequence number and receiving an acknowledgment from the destination host. Additional sequence numbers and acknowledgments are sent back and forth to finalize the synchronization process.

Figure 11-1 shows an incomplete three-way handshake process. Fill in the blanks with the information required for proper synchronization and circuit establishment.

Figure 11-1 Three-Way Handshake

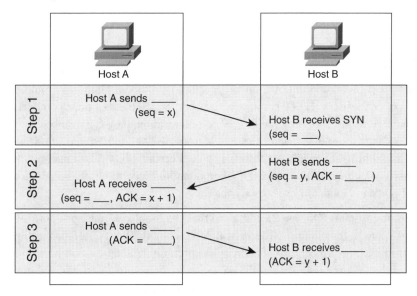

Windowing is another TCP feature that ensures reliability while maintaining flow control. Windowing is the process of determining the number of packets that will be sent before an acknowledgment is required. The destination host determines the window size and sends an acknowledgment after packets are received with the next expected packet.

Figure 11-2 shows an incomplete sliding window process. The window size for the session is five packets. Fill in the blanks with the correct information for the session.

Note: Remember that windowing is both a reliability and flow-control mechanism. Acknowledgments signify receipt and inform the source of the next expected packet. If information is lost between the source and destination, the destination requests a retransmission through the acknowledgment.

Figure 11-2 TCP Sliding Windows

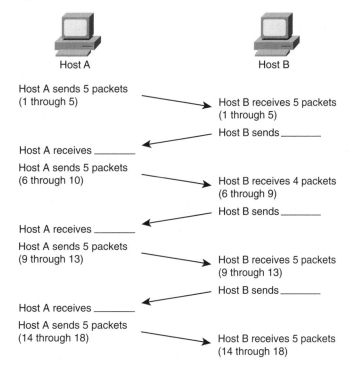

Note: Now is a good time to complete Curriculum Lab 11-1, which focuses on the analysis of TCP traffic using a frame-capture tool.

Journal Entry

TCP and UDP use ports to send information to upper-layer protocols. Unique port numbers distinguish the different types of connections. HTTP commonly uses port 80, FTP uses ports 20 and 21, and Telnet uses port 23. Although ports are necessary for TCP/IP communication, they can also be exploited by malicious code that can pose threats to information security. Viruses, worms, and Trojans often use specific ports to access and attack hosts. Firewalls are designed to keep certain ports closed and monitor others for suspicious activity, but they are not perfect. It is important for network professionals to be familiar with regularly used ports and to identify suspicious ones.

Windows operating systems (OS) have a command that lets users view the open ports on the local system and their connections to remote hosts. The **netstat** command displays TCP/IP connections. Issuing the **netstat –a** command lists the protocol, local address and port, foreign address and port, and the connection state for each current connection. Append the **–n** option to the command to show all information in numeric format and keep from resolving port names or hostnames.

Your task is to investigate the ports and connections being used by a workstation. The workstation can be a lab computer connected to a network or a home computer connected to the Internet. Use the **netstat** commands to view the status of the workstation's TCP/IP connections. Record this information in the Journal Entry. Next, define the protocols and ports that are currently being used or that are in the listening state. Use the curriculum or the Internet to determine the actual protocols associated with the ports. Finally, open additional network-enabled applications (e-mail clients, instant messengers, web browsers, and so on), and check the status of the connections again and record the differences. Can you draw any conclusions regarding information security from this information?

Application Layer

The application layer is found at the top of the TCP/IP model. This layer maps to the top three layers of the OSI model and provides session management, data representation, and network services to applications. Most application layer protocols operate using a client/server model.

This section includes exercises that reinforce your knowledge of application layer protocols. These exercises include identifying acronyms and initialisms associated with application layer protocols and investigating the services these protocols provide.

Vocabulary Exercise: Identifying Acronyms and Initialisms

An acronym is a word formed by the first letters in a multiword term. An initialism is a word made of initials pronounced separately. Identify the application layer terms associated with the following acronyms and initialisms.

DNS   _____

HTTP   _____

FTP   _____

SMTP   _____

SNMP   _____

TFTP   _____

POP   _____

IMAP   _____

NMS   _____

Concept Questions

Completely answer the following questions:

1. DNS associates domain names with IP addresses. List five top-level domain extensions and briefly describe each.

   _____
   _____
   _____
   _____

2. FTP and TFTP provide file-transfer services in a client-server environment. How are these protocols different from one another? What are the advantages of each protocol?

   _____
   _____
   _____
   _____
   _____
   _____

3. HTTP is one of the most popular services on the Internet. Briefly explain the process that occurs when a user starts a web browser and accesses a web page.

_____

_____

_____

_____

_____

_____

_____

4. E-mail services can make use of multiple protocols and server types. Why can it be difficult to troubleshoot e-mail client problems?

_____

_____

_____

_____

5. Network administrators can use SNMP to monitor network performance and manage the network if problems arise. What components are required to manage a network with SNMP?

_____

■ _____

_____

■ _____

_____

_____

_____

■ _____

_____

6. Telnet is a protocol used to remotely access network hosts and devices. What is required to telnet from one device to another?

_____

_____

_____

_____

_____

_____

_____

Journal Entry

Most application layer protocols operate using a client/server model. When configured, servers "listen" for client connections on the ports associated with the protocols. After a connection is made, a session is established to allow client/server communications. The session is terminated after the protocol's services are no longer needed. Each protocol handles this process differently.

Explore the HTTP, FTP, and Telnet application layer protocols. List the basic functions of each protocol and the ports used by the protocol, and provide an example of a protocol-specific client and server application. Finally, explain the connection and session process used by the protocol to include session establishment and termination.

Note: Explore two application layer protocols and client/server relationships with Challenge Lab 11-2.

Lab Exercises

Curriculum Lab 11-1: Protocol Inspector, TCP, and HTTP (11.2.4)

Objective

- Use Fluke Protocol Inspector (PI), Optiview Protocol Expert (OPE), or equivalent protocol-analysis software to view dynamic TCP operations and HTTP while accessing a web page.

Background/Preparation

Protocol analysis software has a feature called *capture*. This feature lets you capture all the frames through an interface. With this feature, you can see how TCP moves segments filled with user data across the network. You might find TCP a bit abstract, but with the protocol analyzer, you can see just how important TCP is to network processes (such as e-mail and web browsing).

At least one of the hosts must have the PI software installed. If you do the lab in pairs, installing the software on both machines means that each person can run the lab steps, although each host might display slightly different results.

Step 1.   Start PI and your browser.

Step 2.   Go to detail view.

Step 3.   Start a capture.

Step 4.   Request a web page.

Step 5.   Watch the monitor view while the web page is requested and delivered.

Step 6.   Stop the capture.

Step 7.   Study the TCP frames, HTTP frames, and statistics using various views, especially detail view.

Step 8.   Using detail view, explain what evidence it provides about the following:

1. TCP handshakes

_____

2. TCP acknowledgments

_____

3. TCP segmentation and segment size

_____

4. TCP sequence numbers

_____

5. TCP sliding windows

_____

6. HTTP protocol

_____

Reflection

How does this lab help you visualize TCP in action?

_____

_____

_____

_____

Challenge Lab 11-2: Accessing FTP and Telnet Servers

Figure 11-3   Workstation and Server Topology

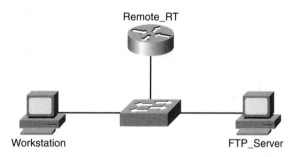

Objective

- Use typical command-line clients to access FTP and Telnet servers.

Background

Most application layer protocols follow the client/server model. FTP and Telnet are two protocols that are common in today's networks. It is important to learn how to interact with these servers using commonly available clients.

This challenge lab focuses on using command-line clients to connect to servers, establish sessions, explore protocol options, and terminate connections when complete. You need the following resources:

- A workstation running Windows 98/Me/2000/XP with an Ethernet 10/100 NIC installed

- One Ethernet switch

- A host running an FTP server that is configured by the instructor

- A router running Telnet services that is configured by the instructor

- Appropriate cables

Task 1: Ensure Basic Connectivity Between the Workstation, Server, and Router

Test the workstation's connectivity to the other devices by using the **ping** command. Table 11-2 shows the IP information for each device.

Table 11-2   Network IP Information

Computer	IP Address	Subnet Mask	Default Gateway
Workstation	192.168.10.200	255.255.255.0	192.168.10.1
FTP_Server	192.168.10.100	255.255.255.0	192.168.10.1
Remote_RT (Ethernet Interface)	192.168.10.1	255.255.255.0	Not applicable

Confirm the workstation's IP configuration and ping the server and router. Troubleshoot accordingly if the pings are unsuccessful.

Task 2: Use a Telnet Client to Access the Router

Open a command-line window on the workstation. Type **telnet** and press **Enter** to start the Telnet client. At the Telnet> prompt, type **open 192.168.10.1** and press **Enter** to initiate a Telnet session with the router. You should see a message similar to the one shown in Figure 11-4.

Figure 11-4   Telnet Access to Remote_RT

Log in the server with the username **user** and password **cisco**. Why is the password not seen when it is typed at the prompt?

_____

Once logged into the router, type **?** and press **Enter** to look at the available commands that can be initiated remotely. Figure 11-5 shows the typical output after the command is entered.

Figure 11-5   Remote_RT Command Options

Which commands can be issued to terminate the current Telnet session?

_____

_____

Leave the Telnet session connected and begin a second command-line window on the workstation. What command can be issued to see if a Telnet session exists on the workstation?

_____

_____

Terminate the Telnet session by typing **disconnect**. Check the status of open ports on the workstation. Is TCP port 23 still in use?

_____

_____

Close the Telnet client by typing **exit** and pressing **Enter**.

Task 3: Use an FTP Client to Access the Server

From the workstation's command-line window, type **ftp** and press **Enter** to initiate the FTP client. At the ftp> prompt, type **?** and press **Enter** to see a list of FTP commands. You should see a message similar to the one shown in Figure 11-6.

Figure 11-6   FTP Commands

Next, type **open 192.168.10.100** to initiate an FTP session with the FTP_Server. Log in to the server with the username **user** and password **class**. You should see a screen similar to the one shown in Figure 11-7.

Figure 11-7   FTP Commands

You are now connected to the FTP_Server and can upload and download files from the server by using FTP. What command gives a listing of the remote directory?

_____

What FTP command is used to download or retrieve files from the server?

_____

What FTP command is used to upload or place files on the server?

_____

Leave the FTP session connected and begin a second command-line window on the workstation. What command can be issued to see if an FTP session exists on the workstation?

_____

Type **disconnect** at the ftp> prompt and press **Enter** to terminate the FTP session. Type **quit** and press **Enter** to close the FTP client.

Reflection

What other tools can you use to monitor the TCP protocols used in this lab?

_____

_____